Study Guide

for

Rathus's

Psychology in the New Millennium

Eighth Edition

M. Lisa Valentino
Seminole County Community College

WADSWORTH

™

THOMSON LEARNING

Australia • Canada • Mexico • Singapore • Spain • United Kingdom • United States

For more information about our products, contact us at:
Thomson Learning Academic Resource Center
1-800-423-0563

For permission to use material from this text, contact us by:
Phone: 1-800-730-2214
Fax: 1-800-730-2215
Web: http://www.thomsonrights.com

Asia
Thomson Learning
60 Albert Complex, #15-01
Albert Complex
Singapore 189969

Australia
Nelson Thomson Learning
102 Dodds Street
South Street
South Melbourne, Victoria 3205
Australia

Canada
Nelson Thomson Learning
1120 Birchmount Road
Toronto, Ontario M1K 5G4
Canada

Europe/Middle East/South Africa
Thomson Learning
Berkshire House
168-173 High Holborn
London WC1 V7AA
United Kingdom

Latin America
Thomson Learning
Seneca, 53
Colonia Polanco
11560 Mexico D.F.
Mexico

Spain
Paraninfo Thomson Learning
Calle/Magallanes, 25
28015 Madrid, Spain

Introduction

Dear *Psychology In The New Millennium* Student,

Welcome to the study of psychology in the 21st century!

This Study Guide was prepared with you, the student, in mind. It is designed to help you understand and apply the material in Spencer Rathus's *Psychology in the New Millennium, Eighth Edition*. This book is not intended for use alone—it is for you to use alongside your *Psychology in the New Millennium* textbook. My hope is that it will help you structure your study time and efforts so that you develop a better understanding of the textbook materials.

This Study Guide was prepared using the same PQ4R study format presented by your textbook author. The chapters correspond to each chapter in the text. Each chapter is divided into five sections: Preview, Question, Reading for Understanding/Reflect, Review/Recite, and Relate/Expand/Integrate.

In the **Preview** section, you are encouraged to skim the major headings in the chapter and note anything interesting or perplexing to you. This will allow you to get an idea of the major topics in the chapter and form your basic conceptual structure for the chapter.

In the **Question** section, learning objectives for the chapter are presented in the format of the questions used in the *Psychology in the New Millennium* textbook. Space has also been provided for you to note any questions that you may develop during your preview of the chapter. Remember to return to these questions after you have completed the final review of the chapter to be sure that they have been answered. Unanswered or incompletely answered questions are great questions to pose to your study group, classmates, or instructor.

The **Reading for Understanding** and **Reflect** sections are combined and address the first two of the 4 "R's" in the PQ4R method. The Reading for Understanding section is structured as a narrative summary of the chapter with fill-in-the-blanks to encourage active reading and recitation. The narratives for each chapter are framed by the learning objective questions and parallel the text of the Recite sections of the *Psychology in the New Millennium* chapter. The Reading for Understanding section in each chapter is divided into three to four segments, which are broken up by Reflection Breaks.

The Reflection Breaks are varied in their format; some are matching exercises, others are charts and tables that you are asked to fill in, and still others are essay questions. These Reflection Breaks are presented for two purposes: First, they encourage you to review the material just covered before moving on to new material; this helps you to learn information in manageable chunks. Second, by encouraging you to take brief study breaks between each section, material just covered can be absorbed without interference from new material. Be sure to reward yourself after each of these Reflection breaks—stretch, talk to a friend on the phone, daydream, or whatever makes you feel good—but, after 5 to 10 minutes, be sure to return to your studying. By actively reading the chapter using the Reading for Understanding narrative and taking the provided Reflection Breaks, you will be studying "smarter" and have better long-term retention of chapter content.

The third "R" in the PQ4 R study method is **Review.** Upon completion of the Reading for Understanding/Reflect section, you are presented with a Final Chapter Review. In each chapter, the first part of the Review section contains a listing of important key concepts presented in the chapter. These key concepts are listed in the order in which they appear in the chapter body and contain a notation of the page number on which they first appear in the chapter. Next, you will find a reminder to be sure and visit the *Psychology in the New Millennium* Web site at www.harcourtcollege.com/psych/PNM/siteresources.html and take the chapter quizzes to test your understanding. After completing the online quizzes, you should go to the Recite section in your textbook and use the tear-off card provided at the back of the book to cover the answers of the Recite section. **Recite** is the fourth and final "R" in the PQ4R study method. Read the questions aloud, and recite aloud your answers to the questions. Then uncover the answers in your textbook to see how closely your recited answer matches the answer provided. Remember that the answers provided in your textbook are to serve as answer guidelines—your answer need not match the provided answer exactly. Reading and reciting aloud will help you cement your knowledge of key concepts. The last part of the Final Chapter Review section is a series of essay questions for you to answer.

The final section of this Study Guide is entitled **Relate/Expand/Integrate.** Here I provide you with ideas for projects, Weblinks, and other learning experiences that you can complete either individually or with your study group. It is my hope that these exercises will allow you to expand and relate chapter topics to your everyday life.

I hope that you find this study guide helpful in your journey into the study of *Psychology in the New Millennium.* Enjoy!

M. Lisa Valentino
Seminole Community College, Sanford, Florida

If you have any questions, comments, or suggestions for future updates or activities, e-mail me at lvaltino@aol.com

Contents

Chapter 1

What Is Psychology?

PREVIEW

Skim the major headings in this chapter in your textbook. Jot down anything that you are suprised or curious about. After this, write down four or five questions that you have about the material in this chapter.

Things that surprised me/I am curious about from Chapter 1:

Questions that I have about psychology, its history, and methods of study:

▲

▲

▲

▲

QUESTION

These are some questions that you should be able to answer after you finish studying this chapter:

What Is Psychology?

▲ What is the best definition for psychology in the new millennium?

▲ What are the four goals of psychology?

▲ What are theories, and how do psychologists use them?

What Do Psychologists Do?

▲ How are clinical psychologists different from counseling psychologists? How are they the same? How are psychiatrists different from either psychologist?

▲ How are school and educational psychologists different?

▲ What are the differing concerns for developmental, personality, social, and experimental psychologists?

▲ How are the interests of industrial/organizational, human factors, and consumer psychologists different?

▲ What aspects of behavior might a health psychologist examine? How is this different from the interests of a sports psychologist?

▲ What is critical thinking, and why is it important for psychologists?

Psychology's History

▲ How did the ancient Greeks influence psychology? When and where did psychology begin? Who is the founder of psychology?

▲ What is structuralism? What are its basic beliefs?

▲ What is functionalism? What are its basic beliefs? How do they differ from those of structuralism?

▲ What is behaviorism? What are its basic beliefs? How do they differ from those of structuralism and functionalism?

▲ What is Gestalt psychology? How do the beliefs of Gestalt psychology differ from those of behaviorism?

▲ Who is Sigmund Freud? What is psychoanalysis, and what are the basic beliefs of psychodynamic psychology?

Psychology Today

▲ What are the basic beliefs of the biological, evolutionary, cognitive, humanistic-existential, psychodynamic, learning, and sociocultural perspectives? How does each of these views differ? How are they the same?

Diversity in Psychology

▲ Is it true that men receive the majority of degrees in psychology? What contributions have women made to the field of psychology? Has psychology always been diverse? What contributions have been made by members of various racial and ethnic groups?

How Psychologists Study Behavior and Mental Processes

▲ Is psychology a science? What is the scientific method? How is it used in psychology?

▲ How do psychologists use samples to reach conclusions about people in general?

▲ What three methods do psychologists use to observe subjects? How are case studies, survey, and naturalistic observation different?

▲ What is a correlation? What type of question would psychologists ask in a correlational study? What are the limitations of correlation research?

▲ What is an experiment? What type of research questions would a psychologist ask in an experimental study?

▲ What are independent and dependent variables? What is a placebo? How do psychologists use blind and double-blind experiments?

Ethical Issues in Psychological Research

▲ What ethical issues are psychologists concerned with when researching on human subjects? How do psychologists assure that they are not violating any of these ethical issues in research?

▲ What ethical issues are psychologists concerned with when researching on animal subjects?

READING FOR UNDERSTANDING/REFLECT

The following section provides you with the opportunity to perform three of the R's of the PQ4R study method. In this section you are encouraged to check your understanding of your reading of the text by filling in the blanks in the brief paragraphs that relate to each of the preview questions. You will also be prompted to rehearse your understanding of the material with periodic Rehearsal/Reflection breaks. Remember, it is better to study in more frequent, short sessions than in one long "cram session." Be sure to reward yourself with short study breaks before each Rehearsal/Reflection exercise.

Reading for Understanding About "What Is Psychology?"

What is the best definition for psychology in the new millennium? Psychology is best defined as the (1) _____ study of (2) _____ and (3) _____ processes. Psychologists study all aspects of living organisms from the (4) _____ system, to learning and (5) _____, as well as personality and the behavior of people in (6) _____ settings.

What are the four goals of psychology? What are theories, and how do psychologists use them? Psychologists have four goals. They seek to (7) _____, (8) _____, (9) _____, and (10) _____ behavior and mental processes. Psychologists use (11) _____, or formulations of apparent relationships among observed events, to develop explanations and predictions.

Reading for Understanding on "What Do Psychologists Do?"

Psychologists can be found in almost any employment setting. Psychologists engage in (12) _____ and (13) _____. Research that has no immediate application is said to be (14)

_____ research, whereas (15) _____ research seeks solutions to specific problems. (16) _____ psychologists help people by applying psychological knowledge in order to help people change their behaviors.

How are clinical psychologists different from counseling psychologists? How are they the same? How are psychiatrists different from either psychologist? (17) _____ psychologists help people with psychological disorders adapt to the demands of life; they may help their clients to resolve problems that range from anxiety and (18) _____ to sexual dysfunction. (19) _____ differ from clinical psychologists in that they are medical doctors who specialize in the study and treatment of psychological disorders. The clients of (20) _____ psychologists often have less serious problems than the clients of clinical psychologists, although both types of psychologists tend to use the same methods to diagnose and treat. Although more than half of doctoral students in psychology are enrolled in counseling or (21) _____ psychology programs, there are many other specializations in psychology.

How are school and educational psychologists different? (22) _____ psychologists are employed by school systems to identify and assist students who have learning problems. They differ from (23) _____ psychologists in that the school psychologist will make decisions about the (24) _____ of students, working directly with the students. The educational psychologist, on the other hand, attempts to facilitate learning by focusing on course (25) _____ and development of instructional methods.

What are the differing concerns for developmental, personality, social, and experimental psychologists? (26) _____ psychologists study physical, (27) _____, social, and personality changes that occur throughout the lifespan. Psychologists who attempt to define human traits and determine influences on thoughts, feelings, and behavior are known as (28) _____ psychologists. Social psychologists are primarily concerned with the (29) _____ of an individual's thoughts, feelings, and behaviors in (30) _____ settings. Finally, (31) _____ psychologists specialize in conducting research into basic processes such as sensation and perception or learning and memory.

How are the interests of industrial/organizational, human factors, and consumer psychologists different? Psychologists who focus on the behavior of people in businesses and organizations are known as (32) _____ psychologists, while (33) _____ psychologists study the relationship between people and work. (34) _____ psychologists are more technically oriented in their jobs and focus on people-friendly design of equipment. Department stores and supermarkets are more likely to hire a (35) _____ psychologist to examine and predict the behaviors of shoppers.

What aspects of behavior might a health psychologist examine? How is this different from the interests of a sports psychologist? (36) _____ psychologists are likely to spend much of their time studying the effects of stress on health problems like headaches and cancer, while a professional football team would be most interested in having a (37) _____ psychologist on staff to help athletes improve their overall performance.

Reflection Break 1

Types of Psychologists

Match the description of the psychologist with the proper title.

a. Counseling
b. Clinical
c. Applied Research
d. Basic Research
e. Psychiatrist

f. School
g. Educational
h. Developmental
i. Personality
j. Consumer

k. Social
l. Industrial
m. Organizational
n. Health
o. Sports

_____ 1. Works with a young gymnast to help her use visualization to complete a flip on the balance beam.

_____ 2. Works with a new Internet startup company to target its market audience.

_____ 3. Works in an elementary school, developing programs for children with special needs and administering assessment tests.

_____ 4. Works at a university, spends most of his/her time researching processes involved in learning and designing new teaching methods.

_____ 5. Spends most of his/her time researching general questions on animal behavior.

_____ 6. A medical doctor who specializes in the study and treatment of psychological disorders.

_____ 7. This subspecialist might work to define the characteristics or traits that make up an individual's unique personality.

_____ 8. A psychologist who might work to advise clients to help them clarify their goals or overcome obstacles.

_____ 9. This psychologist would be interested in social pressures or influences that might change an individual's behavior.

_____ 10. This specialist would most likely work to help people with more severe psychological disorders adjust to the demands of life.

_____ 11. A psychologist who might be interested in examining the effects of stress on headaches or cardiovascular disease.

_____ 12. This psychologist might work with a Fortune 500 company to improve its employee relations.

_____ 13. This researcher would be interested in designing research studies to find solutions to specific real-life problems.

_____ 14. This psychologist would be interested in identifying how the thinking of a 3-year-old might differ from that of a 7-year-old.

_____ 15. This psychologist would most likely study the behavior of people in different business organizations.

Goals of Psychology

Described below are some activities of psychologists. Identify which of the four goals is being pursued.

_____ 1. A psychologist is observing a group of 4-year-olds in a playroom and counting the number of times they each talk to another child.

_____ 2. A psychologist counts the number of times people of different ages visit specific Web sites to see whether a person's age is related to his/her Internet interests.

_____ 3. A psychiatrist gives some of his depressed patients sugar pills and others a new drug to see whether the new drug will help them experience less depression.

_____ 4. Another psychologist examines the relationship between an athlete's anger and his/her win/loss record.

_____ 5. A student is interested in whether there is a gender difference in the degree of neatness of office space.

_____ 6. An industrial psychologist is interested in whether a change in temperature will increase the productivity of assembly-line workers.

_____ 7. A researcher is interested in whether too much sugar in the diet is the cause of hyperactivity in young boys.

_____ 8. An organizational psychologist is interested in why employees who work for one division of a company are more likely to quit than those who work at another division.

Reading for Understanding About "Psychology and Critical Thinking"

What is critical thinking, and why is it important for psychologists? Psychologists are (38) _____, and as such they use critical thinking when examining problems. Critical thinking means having a (39) _____ attitude. This means taking nothing for granted. Critical thinking refers to a process of thoughtfully (40) _____ and probing the arguments of others. Critical thinkers examine (41) _____ of terms, they examine the (42) _____, or premises of arguments, and they are (43) _____ in drawing conclusions. Critical thinkers consider (44) _____ interpretations of research evidence and are careful not to (45) _____ or overgeneralize.

Psychologists rely on (46)_____ before they will accept any claims or arguments about what is true. Psychologists apply critical thinking when examining the claims of (47) _____, or false sciences. (48) _____, or the claim that you are able to predict someone's personality based on the positions and movements of stars and planets, is one such area that psychologists approach with skepticism. Because psychology is an (49) _____ science, its beliefs about behavior must be supported by evidence; persuasive arguments and reference to (50) _____ figures are not considered scientific evidence.

Reflection Break 2

1. What does your textbook author mean when he says that critical thinkers are "skeptical"? Think about some questions that you might ask if you were using a skeptical approach.

2. Try critically thinking about current issues in psychology yourself. Find an article from a recent issue of *Psychology Today (Psychology Today* is available online at http://www.psychologytoday.com.) Pick a feature article and read it using the perspective of a skeptical, critical thinker. Evaluate the claim made in the article from the viewpoint of a critical thinker using the following series of questions. Present this information to your classmates in the format specified by your instructor.
   a. What is the claim being made by the author?
   b. What evidence does the author use to support the claim?
      Does the author use empirical research?
      Does the author use reference to authority opinion?
   c. Does the author oversimplify or overgeneralize in making the argument?
   d. Is there enough good evidence to support the argument's claim?
   e. Should a critical thinker "buy" the claim being made by the author?

Reading for Understanding About "Psychology's History"

How did the ancient Greeks influence psychology? When and where did psychology begin? Who is the founder of psychology? Peri Psyches, or About the Psyche, was written by (51) _____. This book began with a history of psychological thought and the nature of the (52) _____ and behavior. Aristole was a proponent of (53) _____, the view that science could rationally treat only information gathered by the senses. Aristotle argued that human behavior is subject to (54) _____ and laws.

Other Greek philosophers who contributed to psychology's early development included (55) _____, who was the first to raise the question of whether there is free will, and (56) _____, who argued that we could not attain reliable self-knowledge through our senses. He argued that we should rely on rational thought and (57) _____, a careful examination of one's own thoughts and emotions, to achieve self-knowledge.

Although the early Greeks are considered to have influenced the thinking of psychology, most historians set the modern debut of psychology as a lab science in the year (58) _____, when (59) _____ established the first psychological laboratory in Leipzig, Germany. Wundt saw the (60) _____ as a natural event that could be studied scientifically.

What is structuralism? What are its basic beliefs? Wundt and his students worked to break the conscious experience into (61) _____ sensations, (62) _____ feelings, and mental images. This approach was known as (63) _____ and argued that the mind functioned by combining objective and subjective elements of experience.

What is functionalism? What are its basic beliefs? How do they differ from those of structuralism? Toward the end of the 19th century, an American psychologist adopted a broader view of psychology. William (64) _____ argued that there was a relationship between conscious experience and behavior, that the stream of consciousness is fluid and continuous, and that (65) _____ could not be used to study this experience. (66) _____, another early school of psychology, placed more emphasis on the way in which our experience allows us to function more adaptively. Whereas (67) _____ would ask, "What pieces make up that experience?" the (68) _____ would ask, "What is the purpose of this behavior or mental process?"

What is behaviorism? What are its basic beliefs? How do they differ from those of structuralism and functionalism? Around the turn of the 20th century, functionalism was the dominant view in psychology; however, John (69) _____ believed that if psychology was to be a natural science, it must limit it self to the study of (70) _____ observable, measurable events. This belief that psychology should not study mental processes or stream of consciousness, but that it should be the scientific study of behavior, was known as (71) _____.

Although (72) _____ is considered the founder of behaviorism, he was not the only major contributor to behaviorism. Harvard University psychologist B. F. (73) _____ was also a leading behaviorist. He believed that organisms learn to behave in certain ways because they have been (74) _____, or encouraged by the positive outcomes of their behavior. Both Watson and Skinner believed that behavior occurred because it was (75) _____.

What is Gestalt psychology? How do the beliefs of Gestalt psychology differ from behaviorism? Another school of psychology developed in Germany. This school of psychology argued that we cannot hope to understand human nature by focusing on overt behavior only, and was known as (76) _____ psychology. These psychologists focused on human (77) _____ and argued that the (78) "_____ was more than the sum of the parts."

Who is Sigmund Freud? What is psychoanalysis, and what are the basic beliefs of psychodynamic psychology? Freud is the founder of the school of psychology known as (79) _____. This approach differs from all the other schools in that it places emphasis on the role of the (80) _____ in our behavior. Freud was a (81) _____, not a psychologist. He was astounded as to how little insight his patients had into their motives. He argued that most of the (82) _____ is unconscious-a seething cauldron of conflicting (83) _____, urges, and wishes. Because of this belief in the notion of underlying forces, this theory is referred to as (84) _____ psychology.

Reading for Understanding on "Psychology Today"

What are the basic beliefs of the biological, evolutionary, cognitive, humanistic-existential, psychodynamic, learning, and sociocultural perspectives? How do each of these views differ? How are they the same? Today, psychology has many perspectives. These include the biological, evolutionary, cognitive, humanistic-existential, psychodynamic, learning, and sociocultural perspectives. Each approach has its own beliefs about behavior and mental processes. Psychologists who believe that our thoughts and behavior are made possible by the nervous system and the activities in our body are known as (85) _____. This type of psychologist sees the links between events in the (86) _____ and behavior and mental processes. They are also concerned with the influence of (87) _____ and heredity. (88) _____ psychologists are psychologists who are especially interested in the role of evolution in behavior and mental processes. This type of psychologist suggests that most of human social behavior has a (89) _____ basis.

Psychologists with a (90) _____ perspective investigate the ways in which we perceive and mentally represent the world. These types of psychologists, in short, study those things we refer to as the (91) _____. The humanistic-existential perspective is similar to the cognitive perspective. However, humanism stresses the human capacity for (92) _____ and the central roles of consciousness, self-awareness, and decision making. (93) _____ psychology considers personal or subjective experience to be the most important event in psychology. (94) _____ views people as free to choose and be responsible for choosing ethical conduct. In contrast to other theories, Freud's (95) _____ theory argues that the unconscious is more important in explaining behavior and mental processes. Contemporary psychologists who follow Freud are likely to call themselves (96) _____; Karen Horney and Eric Erickson are two of these.

Many psychologists today study the effects of (97) _____ on behavior. To them, (98) _____ is the essential factor in describing, predicting, explaining, and controlling behavior. John Watson, a (99) _____, argued that people do things because of their learning histories, their situations, and the rewards, not because of their (100) _____ choice. Watson and other behaviorists emphasize environmental influences and the learning of habits through repetition and (101) _____. Learning theorists who suggest that people can modify or even create their environments are known as (102) _____ theorists. They note that people engage in intentional learning by (103) _____ others.

The psychological perspective that focuses on the many ways in which people differ from one another by studying the influences of ethnicity, gender, culture, and socioeconomic status is known as the (104) _____ perspective. This type of psychologist may examine the effects of cultural heritage, race, and language of various (105) _____ groups on their behavior.

Reading for Understanding About "Diversity in Psychology"

Is it true that men receive the majority of degrees in psychology? Has psychology always been diverse? What contributions have women and various racial and ethnic groups made to the field of psychology? Although it was true that in the 1800s and early 1900s an overwhelming majority of psychologists were European American (106) _____, women and people of ethnic minority backgrounds have made key contributions to psychology. Today, nearly (107) _____ of the undergraduate degrees in psychology are awarded to women. In the early 1900s, even though women were expected to remain at (108) _____ and were excluded from careers in science, women did play an important role in psychology's history. Christine (109) _____ formulated a theory of color vision; Margaret (110) _____ was the first woman to receive a Ph.D. in psychology; and Helen Bradford Thompson was the first psychologist to study psychological (111) _____ differences. She was ahead of her time in her beliefs that gender differences were strongly influenced by the (112) _____ environment from early infancy through adulthood. Finally, Mary Whiton Calkins became, in 1905, the first female (113) _____ of the American Psychological Association, even without the doctoral degree she was denied. Additionally, numerous early psychologists came from different (114) _____ backgrounds. Early African American psychologists include Gilbert Haven Jones, who was the first African American to receive his (115) _____ in psychology and J. Henry Alston, who was the first to be (116) _____ in a major psychological journal.

Today, psychology does belong to everyone. Two thirds of the Ph.D.s in psychology are awarded to (117) _____, and (118) _____ Americans make up about 7% of first-year doctoral students; another (119) _____ are Latino.

Reflection Break 3: Psychology Today

Identify the current perspective from the descriptions.

_____ 1. Someone who might look at the relationship between an individual's cultural heritage and the frequency of specific psychological disorders.
_____ 2. A psychologist who might argue that the reason that males may exhibit more aggressive behavior is due to their hormonal makeup.
_____ 3. A psychologist who would focus on how we mentally represent the world to explain behaviors.
_____ 4. A psychologist who would tend to attribute dreams to unconscious processes.
_____ 5. A psychologist who might argue that your behavior is the result of your freedom to make choices in life.
_____ 6. A psychologist who argues that children who are shy and withdrawn engage in this behavior because of environmental influences and reinforcement.

Key Figures in the History of Psychology

Match the person with the description of his/her significance to psychology.

a. Aristotle
b. Socrates
c. Gustav Fechner
d. Wilhelm Wundt
e. William James
f. Charles Darwin
g. John Watson
h. B. F. Skinner
i. Wertheimer, Koffka, and Kohler
j. Sigmund Freud
k. Christine Ladd Franklin
l. Margaret Floy Washburn
m. Helen Bradford Thompson
n. Mary Whiton Calkins
o. Gilbert Haven Jones
p. J. Henry Alston
q. Robert Williams
r. Kenneth B. Clark

_____ 1. Psychologist who is sometimes referred to as the "father of Ebonics."
_____ 2. Author of *Peri Psyches*.
_____ 3. First African American to receive his Ph.D. in psychology.
_____ 4. Greek philosopher who claimed that one could not attain reliable self-knowledge through one's senses.

_____ 5. Psychologist whose research was cited when the U.S. Supreme Court overturned the "separate-but-equal" schools doctrine.

_____ 6. Founder of the structuralism school of thought.

_____ 7. Published his landmark book *Elements of Psychophysics* in 1860.

_____ 8. First African American psychologist to be published in a major psychology journal.

_____ 9. First female president of the American Psychological Association.

_____ 10. Chief proponent of functionalism; author of *The Principles of Psychology*.

_____ 11. Early female psychologist, taught at Johns Hopkins and Columbia Universities and formulated a theory of color vision.

_____ 12. Considered to be one of the first behaviorists, he had an affair with a student, which led him to resign from his post at Johns Hopkins and begin a career in advertising.

_____ 13. The first psychologist to study gender differences; she authored *The Mental Traits of Sex*.

_____ 14. First woman to receive her Ph.D. in psychology; she wrote *The Animal Mind*.

_____ 15. Leading proponents of Gestalt psychology.

_____ 16. A Harvard University professor; one of the major contributors to behaviorism; believed that organisms learn to do things because they are reinforced for doing so.

_____ 17. A Viennese physician who is the founder of the psychodynamic school of psychology; believed in the importance of the unconscious.

_____ 18. Originator of the idea of evolution; argued the principle of "survival of the fittest"; was a strong influence on William James.

Reading for Understanding About "How Psychologists Study Behavior and Mental Processes"

Is psychology a science? What is the scientific method? How is it used in psychology?
Psychology is an (120) _____ science. This means that assumptions about the behavior of people must be supported by (121) _____. In science, strong (122) _____, reference to authority figures, or tightly knitted theories are not considered to be (123) _____ scientific evidence.

Psychologists are scientists because they use the (124) _____ method to solve problems. The scientific method is an organized way of using experience and (125) _____ of ideas to expand knowledge. Research psychologists begin by formulating a research (126) _____. These can come from anywhere: daily experiences, common knowledge, or psychological (127) _____. A research question is often reworded as a (128) _____, or a specific statement about behavior and mental processes that can be tested. After formulating the hypothesis, the researcher would then (129) _____ the hypothesis through controlled methodology. Once the research tests are concluded the psychologist will draw a (130) _____ on the accuracy of the hypothesis based on the findings of the test. Research psychologists are guided by the principles of (131) _____ thinking; they are (132) _____; they examine all possible explanations for a behavior. For example, they try not to confuse (133) _____ between findings with cause and effect. Once their research is completed, researchers are obligated to (134) _____, or repeat their study to see whether the findings will hold up over time. Finally, many researchers will (135) _____ their findings in professional journals to allow the whole scientific community to evaluate the methods and conclusions of their research.

How do psychologists use samples to reach conclusions about people in general? Psychologists use a (136) _____, or a segment of the targeted group, to represent the (137) _____, or targeted group, when conducting psychological research. They must be drawn so that they accurately (138) _____ the population they are intended to reflect. Only the use of a representative sample allows us to (139) _____, or extend our findings. Too often, psychologists may have problems in obtaining a (140) _____ sample. Much early research in psychology relied on samples that were exclusively (141) _____, and they underrepresented members of ethnic (142)_____ groups. This presents a problem in (143) _____ early findings to women and ethnic minorities.

One method used by researchers to try to obtain a representative sample is to use (144) _____ sampling, so that each member of the population has an equal chance of being selected to participate. Another sampling method is to use a (145) _____ sample in which identified groups in the population are represented proportionately. Often haphazardly drawn samples, like those taken by magazines, may show a (146) _____ bias, where the people who willingly participate in the study may be systematically different from those who do not. Obviously, (147) _____ is an important concern for psychologists.

What three methods do psychologists use to observe subjects? How are case studies, survey, and naturalistic observation different? Unscientific accounts of people's behavior are referred to as (148) _____. Scientists have devised controlled methods of (149) _____ others. (150) _____ studies, or information we collect about individuals and small groups, are often used to investigate rare occurrences. Although they can provide compelling portraits of individuals, case studies often have many sources of (151) _____. For example, people may (152) _____ or misrepresent their pasts, interviewers may have (153) _____ and encourage subjects to fill in gaps with information that is consistent with them.

Psychologists use questionnaires and interviews to conduct (154) _____. This method of observing subjects has the advantage of allowing psychologists to study (155) _____ of people at one time. Survey research, however, also has its problems. People may recall their behavior inaccurately or purposely (156) _____ themselves. Some people try to ingratiate themselves with their interviewer by answering in what they perceive to be a more (157) _____ desirable response; others may (158) _____ attitudes and exaggerate problems to draw attention to themselves.

When psychologists observe subjects in their natural environment, they are said to have used (159) _____. This approach has the advantage of allowing psychologists to (160) _____ behavior as it happens. Researchers conducting naturalistic observation use methods that try to avoid interfering with the behaviors they are observing; they try to be (161) _____.

What is a correlation? What type of question would psychologists ask in correlational studies? What are the limitations of correlation research? Questions that address therapeutic relationships between variables are answered using the (162) _____ method. A number called the correlation (163) _____ is used to indicate the direction and size of the correlation between the variables. The numerical value of the correlation may vary between −1.00 and (164) _____. When variables are (165) _____ correlated, one variable increases as the other variable increases; when variables are (166) _____ correlated, as one variable increases the other variable decreases. The most significant limitation of correlational research is that it does not prove cause and (167) _____.

What is an experiment? What type of research questions would a psychologist ask in an experimental study? The best research method for answering cause-and-effect questions is considered to be an (168) _____. In this method a group of subjects receives a (169) _____, such as a medication or drug. The subjects are then carefully (170) _____ to determine whether the treatment makes a difference in their behavior. Experiments are used because they allow psychologists to (171) _____ the experiences of subjects and allow experimenters to draw conclusions about (172) _____ and effect.

What are independent and dependent variables? What is a placebo? How do psychologists use blind and double-blind experiments? In an experiment, the researcher manipulates the (173) _____ variable so that its effect may be determined. The measured results, or outcomes in the experiment, are called (174) _____ variables. It is believed that the appearance of the (175) _____ variable depends on the (176) _____ variable. In most experimental studies there are at least two groups of subjects. Subjects in the (177) _____ group receive the treatment, whereas subjects in the (178) _____ group do not. In good experiments every effort is made to ensure that all other (179) _____ are kept constant for subjects in both groups. In this way researchers have confidence that the differences between the control and experimental groups are not due to (180) _____.

Sometimes in experiments it is unclear whether the results of the study are due to the subjects' (181) _____ about the effects of the independent variable. Therefore, it is sometimes important for the subjects to be (182) _____ the treatment they have received. This is accomplished through the use of a (183) _____, or a "sugar pill." Studies in which the subjects are unaware of the treatment they have obtained are known as (184) _____ studies. Studies in which both subjects and experimenters are unaware of who has obtained the treatment are called (185) _____ studies.

Reflection Break 4

Briefly list and describe the basic principles (procedures) of the scientific method followed by psychologists.

▲

▲

▲

▲

▲

Reading for Understanding on "Ethical Issues in Psychological Research and Practice"

What ethical issues are psychologists concerned with when researching on human subjects? How do psychologists assure that they are not violating any of these ethical issues in research? Psychologists adhere to a number of ethical standards that are intended to promote individual (186) _____, human welfare, and scientific (187) _____. These standards are also intended to ensure that psychologists do not undertake research methods or treatments that are (188) _____. In almost all institutional settings, (189) _____ committees help researchers consider the potential harm of their methods and review proposed studies according to (190) _____ guidelines.

To avoid harming subjects, when psychologists conduct research with human subjects, the subjects must give (191) _____ consent before they participate in research programs. Additionally, psychologists treat the records of research subjects and clients as (192) _____. Psychologists do this because they respect people's (193) _____ and because people are more likely to express their true thoughts and feelings when researchers or therapists keep their disclosures private. Ethical guidelines also limit the type of research that psychologists may conduct. Many experiments like the Milgram study cannot be run without (194) _____ subjects. Psychological ethics require that subjects who are deceived be (195) _____ afterward to help eliminate misconceptions and anxieties about the research.

What ethical issues are psychologists concerned with when researching on animal subjects? Psychologists and other scientists frequently turn to (196) _____ to conduct harmful or potentially harmful research that cannot be carried out on humans. Although the studies are carried out with animals, psychologists still face the (197) _____ dilemma of subjecting study participants to harm.. As with people, psychologists follow the principal that animals should be subjected to (198) _____ only when there is no alternative and they believe that the benefits of the research will justify the harm.

REVIEW: KEY TERMS AND CONCEPTS

psychology	3	existentialism	14	correlation coefficient	5
theory	3	social-cognitive theory	15	positive correlation	25
pure research	4	sociocultural perspective	15	negative correlation	25
applied research	4	ethnic group	15	experiment	26
critical thinking	6	gender	16	treatment	26
introspection	8	hypothesis	21	independent variable	26
structuralism	8	selection factor	21	dependent variable	26
functionalism	9	replicate	22	experimental groups	27
behaviorism	10	generalize	22	control groups	27
reinforcement	10	sample	22	placebo	28
Gestalt psychology	10	population	22	blind study	28
insight	11	random sample	23	double-blind study	28
psychoanalysis	12	stratified sample	23	ethical	30
psychodynamic	12	volunteer bias	23	ethics review committee	30
genes	14	case study	23	informed consent	30
cognitive	14	survey	24	debrief	31
humanism	14	naturalistic observation	24	lesion	32

FINAL CHAPTER REVIEW

Review

Visit the *Psychology in the New Millennium* Web site at www.harcourtcollege.com/psych/PNM/
siteresources.html and take the Chapter Quizzes to test your knowledge.

Recite

Go to the Recite section for this chapter in your textbook. Use the tear-off card provided at the
back of the book to cover the answers of the Recite section. Read the questions aloud, and recite
the answers. This will help you cement your knowledge of key concepts.

Essay Questions

1. Imagine that you are the president of a large corporation that designs and manufactures
   different cosmetic products. Describe three types of psychologists you would hire to work
   in your company. What would a typical day at work for each of them consist of, and why
   would having them on staff benefit your company?

2. Compare how each of the current perspectives of psychology would view the same
   problem. Provide an example of a question or a claim that each perspective would make
   about the problem.

3. Pretend that you are in a discussion with friends and the topic is "What is a science?" It is argued that psychology is not a true science like chemistry and physics. How would you defend the proposition that psychology is a true science?

4. You are a researcher interested in whether students enrolled in introductory college courses learn more about the subject than students enrolled a self-study course. Design an experiment that will examine this question. Be sure to identify your independent and dependent variables. Who will be your control group, and who will be your treatment group? Discuss how you will measure your dependent variable and the procedures you will use to conduct the experiment.

5. Explain the difference between correlational and experimental research studies. Be sure to explain how each type of study is conducted and what type of conclusions can be drawn from each. What are the limitations of each type of study?

RELATE/EXPAND/INTEGRATE

1. **Careers in Psychology:** Search the following Internet resources for information about an area of specialization in psychology, for example, clinical work or experimental psychology. Write a summary of the information included. Information such as degree requirements necessary, any skills necessary for that specialization, and any other important information should be provided. *(Your instructor will provide specific requirements such as length, and formatting. Be sure to include the URL or Web address of the source for your information.)*

   - American Psychological Association: http://www.apa.org
   - American Psychological Society: http://www.psychologyscience.org/about.htm
   - Frank Fullerton's Web site: http://www.wiu.edu/users/mffef
   - Marky Lloyd's Careers in Psychology: http://www.psychwww.com/careers/index.htm
   - Indiana State's Careers in psychology: http://web.indstate.edu/psych/toc.htm

2. **History of Psychology:** Visit the following Web site on the history of psychology: http://www.cwu.edu/~warren/today.html. Pick three dates, and note any import events that occurred on those dates. Share your results with three or four of your classmates, and compile a master list of dates and important events in the history of psychology. Present this information to the rest of the class in a visual format.

3. **APA and APS:** Visit the Web sites of the two professional psychological associations. Explain for the class what the acronyms APA and APS stand for. What are the goals of each association? How are they the same, and how do they differ? When were they each founded, and how many members does each association currently have?

4. **Scientific Journals in Psychology:** Visit Psychweb at http://www.psywww.com/journals and get an idea of the variety of journals available in psychology. Visit the home page for four different journals. Answer the following questions:

- What kind of articles does the journal publish?
- How often is the journal published?
- Who is the journal's target audience?
- What is the journal's goal?

Share your results with your classmates in a format specified by your instructor.

5. **Reading and Identifying Scientific Research in Psychology:** Locate one of the following published scientific research studies (or find one of your own) and read the study for an understanding of the scientific methods used.

As you read the study, answer the following questions:

a. What topical area of psychology is represented by the study?
b. What is the target population of the study?
c. What are the characteristics of the sample (for example, number of subjects, demographics, etc.)?
d. What type of research is this study (experimental, correlational, case study, survey)?
e. If the study is an experimental study, what are the independent and dependent variables? The control and treatment groups?
f. Describe the procedures used to observe the subjects.
g. What does the author conclude is the outcome of the study?

Suggested articles:

Milgram, S. (1963). Behavioral study of obedience. *Journal of Abnormal and Social Psychology, 67,* 371–378.

Milgram, S. (1964). Group pressure and action against a person. *Journal of Abnormal and Social Psychology, 69,* 137–143.

Steele, K., Bass, K., & Crook, M. (1999). The mystery of the Mozart effect: Failure to replicate. *Psychological Science, 10,* 366–369.

Vasta, R., Rosenberg, D., Knott, J.A., & Gaze, C.E. (1997). Experience and the water-level task revisited: Does experience exact a price? *Psychological Science, 8,* 336–339.

ANSWERS FOR CHAPTER 1

Answers to the Reading for Understanding on "What Is Psychology?"

1. scientific
2. behavior
3. mental
4. nervous
5. memory
6. social
7. describe
8. predict
9. explain
10. control
11. theories
12. research
13. practice
14. basic
15. applied
16. Practicing
17. Clinical
18. depression
19. Psychiatrists
20. Counseling
21. clinical
22. School
23. educational
24. placement
25. planning
26. Developmental
27. cognitive
28. personality
29. causes
30. social
31. experimental
32. organizational
33. industrial
34. Human factors
35. consumer
36. Health
37. sports

Reflection Break 1

Types of Psychologists

1. o
2. j
3. f
4. g
5. d
6. e
7. i
8. a
9. k
10. b
11. n
12. l
13. c
14. h
15. m

Goals of Psychology

1. Description
2. Prediction
3. Control
4. Prediction
5. Description
6. Control
7. Explanation
8. Explanation

Answers to the Reading for Understanding on "Critical Thinking"

38. scientists
39. skeptical
40. analyzing
41. definitions
42. assumptions
43. cautious
44. alternative
45. oversimplify
46. evidence
47. pseudosciences
48. Astrology
49. empirical
50. authority

Reflection Break 2

1. Skeptical thinkers are those who are willing to believe claims; however, they require good evidence in support of claims. They might ask: What am I being asked to believe? What type of evidence is being given? Is there empirical evidence given? Does the author attempt to oversimplify or overgeneralize? Does the evidence fully support the claim?

2. Your answers may vary depending on the article you read.

Answers to the Reading for Understanding on "History of Psychology and Psychology Today"

51. Aristotle
52. mind
53. empiricism
54. rules
55. Democritus
56. Socrates
57. introspection
58. 1879
59. Wundt
60. mind
61. objective
62. subjective
63. structuralism
64. James
65. introspection
66. Functionalism
67. structuralists
68. functionalists
69. Watson
70. behavior
71. Behaviorism
72. Watson
73. Skinner

74. reinforced
75. conditioned
76. Gestalt
77. perception
78. whole
79. psychoanalysis
80. unconscious
81. physician
82. mind
83. impulses
84. psychodynamic
85. biological
86. brain
87. hormones
88. Evolutionary
89. hereditary
90. cognitive
91. mind
92. self-fulfillment
93. Humanistic
94. Existentialism
95. psychodynamic
96. neoanalysts

97. experience
98. learning
99. behaviorist
100. conscious
101. reinforcement
102. social-cognitive
103. observing
104. socio-cultural
105. ethnic
106. males
107. *****
108. home
109. Ladd Franklin
110. Floy Washburn
111. gender
112. social
113. president
114. ethnic
115. Ph.D.
116. published
117. women
118. Africa\
119. 5 %

Reflection Break 3

Psychology Today

1. Sociocultural
2. Biological
3. Cognitive
4. Psychodynamic
5. Humanistic–Existential
6. Learning

Key Figures in the History of Psychology

1. q	7. c	13. m
2. a	8. p	14. l
3. o	9. n	15. i
4. b	10. e	16. h
5. r	11. k	17. j
6. d	12. g	18. f

Answers to the Reading for Understanding on "Psychological Methods"

120. empirical	142. minority	164. +1.00
121. vidence	143. generalizing	165. positively
122. arguments	144. random	166. negatively
123. good	145. stratified	167. effect
124. scientific	146. volunteer	168. experiment
125. testing	147. sampling	169. treatment
126. question	148. anecdotes	170. observed
127. theory	149. observing	171. control
128. hypothesis	150. Case	172. cause
129. test	151. inaccuracy	173. independent
130. conclusion	152. distort	174. dependent
131. critical	153. expectations	175. dependent
132. skeptical	154. surveys	176. independent
133. correlation	155. thousands	177. experimental
134. replicate	156. misrepresent	178. control
135. publish	157. socially	179. variables
136. sample	158. falsify	180. chance
137. population	159. naturalistic observation	181. expectations
138. represent	160. observe	182. unaware
139. generalize	161. unobtrusive	183. placebo
140. representative	162. correlational	184. blind
141. male	163. coefficient	185. double-blind

Reflection Break 4

▲ Formulate a research question and hypothesis.

▲ Test the hypothesis using controlled methods.

▲ Draw conclusions based on the outcome of the testing.

▲ Replicate the outcome of the study.

▲ Publish the results of the study in a scientific journal.

Answers to the Reading for Understanding on "Ethics in Psychology"

186. dignity
187. integrity
188. harmful
189. ethics review
190. ethical

191. informed
192. confidential
193. privacy
194. deceiving
195. debriefed

196. animals
197. ethical
198. harm

Chapter 2

Biology and Behavior

PREVIEW

Skim the major headings in this chapter in your textbook. Jot down anything that you are surprised or curious about. After this, write down four or five questions that you have about the material in this chapter.

Things that surprised me/I am curious about from Chapter 2:

Questions that I have about biology and behavior:

▲

▲

▲

▲

QUESTION

These are some questions that you should be able to answer after you finish studying this chapter:

An Introduction to the Field of Biological Psychology

▲ What is biological psychology?

Neurons: Into the Fabulous Forest

▲ What are neurons? What kind of neurons are found in the human body? What is their role in human behavior?

▲ What are neural impulses? What happens when a neuron fires?

▲ What is a synapse?

▲ Which neurotransmitters are of interest to psychologists? What do they do?

The Nervous System

▲ What is the nervous system?

▲ What are the divisions and functions of the peripheral nervous system?

▲ What are the divisions and functions of the central nervous system?

The Brain and Cerebral Cortex

▲ How do researchers learn about the functions of the brain and nervous system?

▲ What are the structures and functions of the brain?

▲ What are the parts of the cerebral cortex? What parts of the cerebral cortex are involved in thinking and language?

▲ What does it mean to be "right-brained" or "left-brained"? Does it matter whether one is left- or right-handed? Why are people right-handed or left-handed?

▲ What happens when the brain is split in two?

The Endocrine System

▲ What is the endocrine system?

▲ What functions of hormones are of interest to psychologists?

Evolution and Evolutionary Psychology and Heredity

▲ What are the basic beliefs of the theory of evolution? What is evolutionary psychology?

▲ What is meant by the concept of heredity? What are the roles of genes and chromosomes in heredity?

▲ What are kinship studies, and how do they help psychologists study the role of heredity in behavior?

READING FOR UNDERSTANDING/REFLECT

The following section provides you with the opportunity to perform three of the R's of the PQ4R study method. In this section you are encouraged to check your understanding of your reading of the text by filling in the blanks in the brief paragraphs that relate to each of the preview questions. You will also be prompted to rehearse your understanding of the material with periodic Rehearsal/Reflection breaks. Remember, it is better to study in more frequent, short sessions than in one long "cram session." Be sure to reward yourself with short study breaks before each Rehearsal/Reflection exercise.

What is biological psychology? Biological psychologists work at the interface between psychology and (1) _____. They study the ways in which (2) _____ processes and behavior are linked to (3) _____ structures and processes. Biological psychologists explore the links between biology and behavior by examining numerous areas of interest, including: neurons, the (4) _____ system, the (5) _____ cortex, the endocrine system, evolution, and (6) _____.

Reading for Understanding on "Neurons"

What are neurons? What kinds of neurons are found in the human body? What is their role in human behavior? Neurons are (7) _____ that have branches, trunks, and roots. Neurons lie end to end and (8) _____ messages from a number of sources such as light, other (9) _____, and pressure on the skin. They can also pass along messages. Neurons communicate by releasing chemicals called (10) _____, which are taken up by other neurons, muscles, and glands. Neurotransmitters cause (11) _____ changes in the receiving neuron so that the messages, or neural (12) _____, can travel along the "trunk" of the neuron.

The nervous system also contains (13) _____ cells that remove dead neurons and waste products from the nervous system. Glial cells also (14) _____ and (15) _____ neurons and direct their growth. (16) _____, however, are the most important cells in the nervous system. They vary as to their function and location, but all contain (17) _____, or short fibers that extend like roots from the cell body to receive incoming messages, and an (18) _____, the trunk that extends from the cell body. Neuronal axons end in small bulblike structures named (19) _____.

Neurons carry messages in (20) _____ direction. Within a neuron, the information flows from the (21) _____, through the (22) _____, to the (23) _____. Neuronal axons are wrapped tightly with a white, fatty substance called (24) _____ that insulates the axon from the electrically charged atoms found in the fluids that surround the nervous system. Myelin is part of the maturation process and minimizes the leakage of the (25) _____ current being carried along the axon, thus allowing the messages to be carried more (26) _____. Neurons that transmit the sensory information from the body to the nervous system are known as (27) _____ neurons, and (28) _____ neurons send messages back to the muscles and sensory organs.

What are neural impulses? What happens when a neuron fires? Luigi Galvani demonstrated that neural messages are (29) _____ in nature. This process involves (30) _____ changes that cause an electrical charge to be transmitted along the lengths of neuronal axons. This electrical charge results from a process that allows positively charged (31) _____ to enter the cell. The entry of these (32) _____ charged ions into the cell causes the cell to become (33) _____ with respect to the outside. Once the cell is depolarized, the positively charged ions are (34) _____ out of the cell, and the cell returns to its negative (35) _____ potential. Most neurons have a (36) _____ potential of –70 millivolts and an (37) _____ potential of +40 millivolts; thus, it takes approximately 110 millivolts of charge to create an all-or-none neural message that will travel the length of the axon. This explains the (38) "_____" portion of neural communication, but this is not the whole story. Neural messages also travel via chemical messengers called (39) _____.

The conduction of the electrical neural messages is what is being referred to when biological psychologists say a neuron has "(40) _____." Once a neuron fires and its electrical impulse travels to the end of the axon, it releases (41) _____. In accordance with the (42) _____ principle, each time a neuron fires it transmits an impulse of the same strength. Thus neurons will fire more frequently when they have been stimulated by a (43) _____ number of neurons. Also, for a brief period of time, a few (44) _____ of a second after the neuron fires, it is insensitive to messages from other neurons. This is known as the (45) _____ period.

What is a synapse? Neurons relay their messages across junctions known as (46) _____. They consist of an axon terminal from the (47) _____ neuron; a (48) _____ from the receiving neuron, and a fluid-filled gap called the (49) _____. Although the neuronal impulse is (50) _____, it does not jump the synaptic cleft; instead, the axon terminals release (51) _____ into it.

Which neurotransmitters are of interest to psychologists? What do they do? Neurotransmitters are the chemical keys to neural communication; they are released from the (52) _____ into the synaptic cleft, and from there they influence the receiving neuron. Dozens of neurotransmitters have been identified; each has it own (53) _____ structure and can fit into a specific (54) _____ on the receiving cell. Unused neurotransmitters are either broken down or reabsorbed by the axon terminal in a process known as (55) _____.

Some neurotransmitters act to (56) _____, or cause other neurons to fire; others act to (57) _____, or keep other receiving neurons from firing. Neurotransmitters have been shown to be involved in all kinds of processes from muscle (58) _____ to thoughts and (59) _____. Excesses or (60) _____ of neurotransmitters have also been linked to psychological disorders such as (61) _____ and schizophrenia. Some neurotransmitters of interest to psychologists include: (62) _____, which controls muscle contractions; dopamine, which has been shown to be involved in voluntary movements, (63) _____ and memory, and (64) _____ arousal and has been linked to schizophrenia and (65) _____ disease; (66) _____, produced largely in the brain stem, acts as both a neurotransmitter and a hormone, and is believed to be involved in general arousal, learning, memory, and eating; serotonin, primarily an (67) _____ neurotransmitter, deficiencies of which have been linked to (68) _____ disorders, alcoholism, (69) _____, aggression, and insomnia; and the (70) _____, which occur naturally in the brain and may increase our sense of competence, enhance the functioning of the immune system, and have been linked to the pleasurable "runners high" reported by long-distance runners.

Reflection Break 1

Neurons: Label the neuronal diagram:

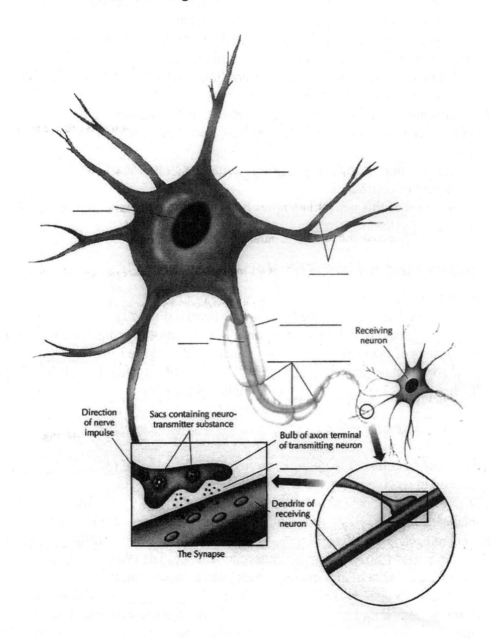

Direction of nerve impulse

Sacs containing neuro-transmitter substance

Receiving neuron

Bulb of axon terminal of transmitting neuron

Dendrite of receiving neuron

The Synapse

Neurotransmitters and Their Actions

Name the neurotransmitter from a description of its actions.

_____ 1. Neurotransmitter that causes muscle contractions and is involved in the formation of memories.

_____ 2. These neurotransmitters work to inhibit pain by blocking pain, causing chemicals out of their receptor sites.

_____ 3. Neurotransmitter involved in muscle contraction, learning and memory, and emotional response.

_____ 4. Neurotransmitter that accelerates the heart rate, affects eating, and has been linked with activity levels, learning, and remembering.

_____ 5. Neurotransmitter involved in psychological problems, including obesity, depression and insomnia, alcoholism, and aggression.

_____ 6. Imbalances of this neurotransmitter are linked with mood disorders such as depression and bipolar disorder.

_____ 7. Neurotransmitter found at synapses between motor neurons and muscles; deficiencies of this neurotransmitter have been linked with Alzheimer's disease.

_____ 8. Drugs that block the reuptake of this neurotransmitter are helpful in the treatment of depression.

_____ 9. Low levels of this neurotransmitter have been linked to the tremors of Parkinson's disease.

Reading for Understanding on "The Nervous System"

What is the nervous system? The nervous system is a bundle of (71) _____ and (72) _____; it is the system that regulates the body and is involved in (73) _____ processes, (74) _____ responses, heartbeat control, visual-motor coordination, and so on. The nervous system consists of the (75) _____, spinal cord, and the (76) _____ linking them to the sensory organs, muscles, and glands. The nervous system is divided into two major divisions. The brain and (77) _____ cord make up the (78) _____ nervous system, while the (79) _____ (afferent) and motor (80) _____ neurons make up the (81) _____ nervous system.

What are the divisions and functions of the peripheral nervous system? The (82) _____ nervous system allows us to receive information from the outside world. The peripheral nervous system consists of two main divisions: (83) _____ and (84) _____. The somatic nervous system contains (85) _____ (afferent) and (86) _____ (efferent) neurons and transmits messages about skeletal muscles, (87) _____, and joints to the (88) _____ nervous system. It also controls (89) _____ muscular activity. The (90) _____ nervous system (ANS) regulates the glands and activities such as heartbeat, (91) _____, and dilation of the pupils. The ANS also has two branches. The (92) _____ division helps the body expend its resources from stored reserves during a fight-or-flight response to a predator. The (93) _____ branch or division of the autonomic nervous system has the opposite effect from that of the (94) _____; it helps the body (95) _____ the body's reserves of energy.

What are the divisions and functions of the central nervous system? Your (96) _____ nervous system (CNS) enables you to use symbols and language and to adapt to and create new environments. The CNS consists of the (97) _____ cord and the (98) _____. The spinal cord is a true "information superhighway." It consists of a column of (99) _____ that transmit messages from sensory (100) _____ to the brain and from the brain to muscles and (101) _____ throughout the body. Spinal (102) _____ are unlearned responses to stimuli that involve only two neurons. Spinal reflexes do not involve the (103) _____ .

The brain and spinal cord both contain (104) _____ matter, which is composed of short, nonmyelinated neurons, and (105) _____ matter, which contains bundles of longer, myelinated axons.

Reflection Break 2

The Organization of the Nervous System

Fill in the blanks in the nervous system organizational chart.

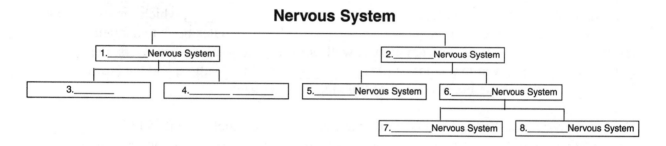

Nervous System

1. _____ Nervous System

2. _____ Nervous System

3. _____

4. _____ _____

5. _____ Nervous System

6. _____ Nervous System

7. _____ Nervous System

8. _____ Nervous System

Reading for Understanding on "The Brain and Cerebral Cortex"

How do researchers learn about the functions of the brain and nervous system? Historically, researchers have learned about the brain by studying the effects of (106) _____ , but they provide uncontrolled opportunities. The case of Phineas (107) _____ is one example of how scientists have learned about the functions of the brain as a result of an accident.

Scientists have also used experimental methods like purposeful (108) _____ to the brain, electrical (109) _____ of certain brain structures and brain (110) _____ . When scientists purposely damage a specific section of the brain, they are said to create a (111) _____ . Studies have shown that lesions of a monkey's (112) _____ create a rage response, while lesions of a rat's hypothalamus leads it to stop (113) _____ . Surgeon Wilder (114) _____ used electrical stimulation rather than lesions to study the brain. Researchers have also used the (115) _____ (EEG) to record the natural electrical activity of the brain. The EEG has been used to locate the areas of the (116) _____ that respond to certain stimuli and to diagnose types of abnormal behavior and to help locate (117) _____ .

In recent years, new technology has allowed scientists to use the (118) _____ to generate images of the brain from different sources of radiation; these methods include the (119) _____ , or CAT, the (120) _____ , or PET, and the (121) _____ , or MRI. The CAT scan passes a narrow (122) _____ beam through the head and measures the structure that reflects the x-rays from various angles, generating a (123) _____ -dimensional image of the brain. The PET scan forms computer-based images of parts of the brain by tracing the amount of (124) _____ used and has been used by researchers to see which parts of the brain are most (125) _____ during various activities. The MRI uses a powerful (126) _____ field and (127) _____ waves that cause parts of the brain to emit signals that are measured from various angles.

What are the structures and functions of the brain? The (128) _____, where the spinal cord rises to meet the brain, consists of three major structures: the (129) _____, which regulates the heart rate, blood pressure, and respiration; the (130) _____, which is involved in movement, attention, and respiration; and the (131) _____, which is involved in balance and coordination. Also beginning in the hindbrain and ascending through the midbrain into the lower portion of the forebrain is the (132) _____ system that is vital to the functions of attention, sleep, and arousal.

The important structures of the forebrain include: the (133) _____, which serves as a relay station for sensory stimulation; the (134) _____, which regulates body temperature and various aspects of motivation and emotion as well as eating and drinking behaviors; the limbic system, which is involved in memory, (135) _____, and motivation; and the (136) _____, which is the brain's center of thinking and language.

The limbic system of the brain is made up of several structures, including the (137) _____, which studies have shown is involved in aggressive behavior, vigilance, and learning and memory; and the (138) _____, which has been shown to be involved in memory.

What are the parts of the cerebral cortex? What parts of the cerebral cortex are involved in thinking and language? The (139) _____, or cerebral cortex, is the crowning glory of the brain; it is responsible for the (140) _____ abilities of thinking and language. Its surface is wrinkled, or (141) _____, with ridges and valleys that allow a great deal of surface to be packed into the brain. The valleys in the cortex are called (142) _____, and a key one divides the cerebrum into two halves, or (143) _____, which are connected by the (144) _____, a bundle of some 200 million nerve fibers.

Each of the cerebral hemispheres is divided into four (145) _____: the (146) _____ lobe is located in front of the central fissure, while the (147) _____ lobe lies behind it. The (148) _____ lobe lies on the side of the brain, below the lateral fissure; and the (149) _____ lobe lies in the back of the brain, behind and below the parietal lobe. The (150) _____ cortex is found in the occipital lobe, and the (151) _____ cortex is found in the temporal lobe. The (152) _____ cortex is found in the parietal lobe, and the (153) _____ cortex, the executive center of the brain, is found in the frontal lobe, along with the (154) _____ cortex.

In some ways, the left and right (155) _____ of the brain are alike; however, when it comes to speech and language, the two hemispheres (156) _____. For nearly all right-handed people and most left-handed people, the (157) _____ hemisphere controls language function. Two key language centers lie within this "language" hemisphere, they are (158)

_____ area, an egg-sized area located in the left frontal lobe near the section of the motor cortex that controls the muscles of the tongue, throat, and other areas of the face; and (159) _____ area, an area in the temporal lobe near the auditory cortex that responds mainly to auditory information. Damage to either area results in (160) _____, or a disruption of the ability to understand or produce language. In Broca's aphasia, the individual would be unable to (161) _____ speech, whereas an individual with Wernicke's aphasia would have difficulty in (162) _____ speech.

What does it mean to be "right-brained" or "left-brained"? Does it matter whether one is left- or right-handed? Why are people right-handed or left-handed? When we refer to a person as either "left- or right-brained," we are referring to the notion that the (163) _____ of the brain are involved in very different kinds of functions. According to this view, (164) _____-brained people would be primarily logical and intellectual since the left hemisphere has been shown to be more involved in cognitive functions involving (165) _____ analysis and (166) _____ solving. "(167) _____-brained" individuals would, on the other hand, tend to be more intuitive, creative, and emotional due to the right hemisphere's superiority in visual-spatial functions and (168) _____, emotional, and creative mathematical (169) _____. However, this notion is (170) _____; research does not support it, and it is erroneous to think that the hemispheres of the brain act (171) _____.

We usually label individuals as right- or left-handed on the basis of their (172) _____ preferences, yet some people write with one hand and throw with another. About 1 person in 10 is (173) _____. Being left-handed appears to be connected with (174) _____ problems such as dyslexia and (175) _____. Learning disabilities and some health problems, like (176) _____ headaches and allergies, are also somewhat more common in left-handers, but so is (177) _____. Handedness appears to have a (178) _____ component, but Daniel Geschwind of UCLA suggests that it is not likely to be a single (179) _____ characteristic.

What happens when the brain is split in two? For the most part, the behavior of people who have had split-brain operations, where their (180) _____ is severed, is perfectly (181) _____. However, they may be able to (182) _____ describe an unseen object such as a pencil held in the hand connected to the hemisphere that contains (183) _____ functions, yet they (184) _____ describe it when the object is held in the other hand.

Reflection Break 3

The Brain and Cerebral Cortex

Match the brain structure to its function.

Brain Structures:

a. Electroencephalograph
b. Computerized axial tomograph
c. Magnetic resonance imaging
d. Medulla
e. Pons
f. Cerebellum
g. Reticular activating system
h. Thalamus
i. Hypothalamus
j. Limbic system
k. Amygdala
l. Cerebrume
m. Corpus callosum
n. cerebral cortex
o. frontal lobe

p. parietal lobe
q. temporal lobe
r. occipital lobe
s. somstosensory cortex
t. motor cortex
u. association cortex
v. prefrontal region
w. Broca's area
x. Wernicke's area
y. Angular gyrus
z. Aphasia
aa. Positron emission tomography
bb. Fissur
cc. hippocampus

Functions

_____ 1. Its name comes from the Latin word meaning "bark"; it is involved in almost every bodily activity; the surface of the cerebrum.

_____ 2. Language center that is essential to understanding relationships between words and meanings.

_____ 3. When this structure is damaged people usually understand language well enough but speak slowly and laboriously.

_____ 4. Brain imaging technique that can reveal deformities in shape or structure by passing a narrow x-ray beam through the head and measures the structures that reflect the x-rays.

_____ 5. A disruption of the ability to understand or produce language.

_____ 6. Lies in the frontal lobe just across the valley of the central fissure from the somatosensory cortex; activity in this area causes parts of the body to move.

_____ 7. Located in the frontal lobe, near the forehead; is known as the brain's executive center.

_____ 8. Lies between the visual cortex and Wernicke's area; translates visual information into auditory information.

_____ 9. Areas of the cortex not primarily involved in sensation or motor activity.

_____ 10. Lies just behind the central fissure from the parietal lobe and receives messages from the skin senses all over the body.

_____ 11. Used by neuroscientists to record the natural electrical activity of the brain.

_____ 12. Brain imaging technique where a computer image of the activity of the parts of the brain is produced by tracing the amount of glucose used.

_____ 13. The cortical lobe that lies in front of the central fissure and contains the motor cortex.

_____ 14. The cortical lobe that lies below the side, or lateral, fissure and contains the auditory cortex.

_____ 15. The cortical lobe that lies in the back of the brain and contains the visual cortex.

_____ 16. The cortical lobe that lies behind the central fissure and contains the somatosensory cortex.

_____ 17. Brain imaging technique in which the patient lies in a powerful magnetic field and is exposed to radio waves that cause parts of the brain to emit signals.

_____ 18. The crowning glory of the brain, it is responsible for the cognitive abilities of thinking and language.

_____ 19. A valley in the cortex.

_____ 20. Hindbrain structure that regulates vital functions like heart rate, blood pressure, and respiration.

_____ 21. The thick bundle of nerve fibers that connects the two hemispheres of the cortex.

_____ 22. A bulge in the hindbrain that contains bundles of nerves that transmit information about body movement and is involved in functions related to attention, sleep, alertness, and respiration.

_____ 23. Limbic structure that is connected with aggressive behavior, fear, and vigilance.

_____ 24. Made up of several structures including the amygdala, hippocampus, and parts of the hypothalamus; it is involved in memory and emotion and in the drives of hunger, sex, and aggression.

_____ 25. Damage to this limbic structure leads to an inability to store new memories.

_____ 26. Begins in the hindbrain and ascends through the midbrain into the lower part of the forebrain and is vital to the functions of attention, sleep, and arousal; injury may result in coma.

_____ 27. Lies below the thalamus and above the pituitary gland and is vital in the regulation of body temperature, concentration of fluids, storage of nutrients, and aspects of motivation and emotion.

_____ 28. Located near the center of the brain and serves as a relay station for sensory stimulation.

_____ 29. Means "little brain" in Latin; has two hemispheres that are involved in maintaining balance and in controlling motor behavior.

Reading for Understanding on "The Endocrine System"

What is the endocrine system? The body contains two types of (185) _____, ducted, or those glands with (186) _____ that carry substances to specific locations, and (187) _____. The (188) _____ system consists of the ductless glands that secrete (189) _____, chemicals that are released into the bloodstream. Like (190) _____, hormones have specific receptor sites, and they act only in certain locations. The (191) _____ releases a number of releasing hormones that influence only the pituitary gland; other hormones are released by the (192) _____ gland and influence other areas of the body.

What functions of hormones are of interest to psychologists? Much (193) _____ action helps the body maintain steady states, such as fluid and blood sugar levels. The pituitary gland is so central to the body's functioning that it is known as the (194) "_____ gland;" it lies below the (195) _____ and is connected to it by a dense network of blood vessels. The pituitary gland secrets (196) _____ hormone, which regulates the growth of muscles, bones, and glands; (197) _____, which regulates maternal behavior in lower mammals and stimulates milk production in women; (198) _____, which inhibits production of urine when body fluid levels are low; and (199) _____, which stimulates labor in pregnant women and is connected with maternal behavior.

The (200) _____ gland secretes the hormone melatonin, which helps regulate the (201) _____ cycle and may affect the onset of (202) _____. The thyroid gland produces (203) _____, a hormone that affects the body's metabolism. Deficiencies in thyroxin, or (204) _____, can result in obesity and sluggishness in adults, or (205) _____, characterized by stunted growth and mental retardation, if it occurs in children. Too much thyroid hormone, (206) _____, is characterized by excitability and weight loss.

The adrenal (207) _____ of the adrenal gland produces corticosteriods, which help increase resistance to (208) _____, promote muscle development, and encourage the liver to release stored (209) _____. The adrenal (210) _____ of the adrenal gland produces the hormones adrenaline and noradrenaline. (211) _____, or epinephrine, is produced solely by the adrenal medulla and has been shown to intensify most (212) _____ and to be critical to the experience of fear and (213) _____. (214) _____ helps (along with adrenaline) the body cope with threats and stress; it also raises blood pressure and acts as a neurotransmitter.

The male sex hormone, (215) _____, is responsible for prenatal sexual differentiation. During puberty it also encourages the growth of (216) _____ and bone and the development of primary and secondary (217) _____ characteristics. The (218) _____ sex hormones, estrogen and progesterone, are produced in the (219) _____ and together regulate the female menstrual cycle. (220) _____ fosters female reproductive capacity and secondary sex characteristics, while (221) _____ stimulates the growth of the female reproductive organs and prepares the uterus to maintain pregnancy. The female sex hormones have also been connected with (222) _____ functioning and psychological (223) _____ in women.

Reflection Break 4

Review on "Hormones and the Endocrine System"

Match the hormone with the description of its action.

Hormones:

a. Prolactin
b. Corticosteroids
c. Oxytocin
d. Noradrenaline
e. Growth hormone
f. Testosterone

g. Melatonin
h. Thyroxin
i. Adrenaline
j. Progesterone
k. Antidiuretic hormone
l. Estrogen

Actions:

_____ 1. Hormone released by the pituitary gland, responsible for regulation of the growth of muscles, bones, and glands.

_____ 2. Hormone that stimulates the growth of female reproductive organs and prepares the uterus to maintain pregnancy.

_____ 3. Pituitary hormone that regulates maternal behavior and stimulates production of milk in women.

_____ 4. Released by the pituitary gland and inhibits the production of urine when body fluids are low.

_____ 5. The male sex hormone. Is responsible for the development of both primary and secondary sex characteristics.

_____ 6. When released by the pituitary gland, this hormone stimulates labor in pregnant women.

_____ 7. These hormones are released by the adrenal glands and have been shown to increase resistance to stress, promote muscle development, and cause the liver to release stored sugar.

_____ 8. Produced by the adrenal medulla, this hormone is exclusively produced by the adrenal gland. It is of interest to psychologists since it intensifies most emotions and is crucial to the experience of fear and anxiety.

_____ 9. Hormone secreted by the adrenal medulla but also produced elsewhere in the body. Also acts as a neurotransmitter.

_____ 10. Female sex hormone produced by both the ovaries and the testes. This hormone fosters reproductive capacity and development of secondary sex characteristics.

_____ 11. This hormone affects the body's metabolism. Too little of it leads to obesity and sluggishness; too much is characterized by insomnia, excitability, and weight loss.

_____ 12. Produced by the pineal gland, this hormone helps to regulate the sleep–wake cycle.

Reading for Understanding on "Evolution and Evolutionary Psychology and Heredity"

What are the basic beliefs of the theory of evolution? What is evolutionary psychology? According to Darwin's theory of (224) _____, there is a struggle for survival as various species and individuals compete for the same territories. Species that are (225) _____ manage to survive, or are naturally selected; their numbers (226) _____ and they transmit their traits to future generations. Species that do not adapt dwindle in numbers and may eventually become (227) _____. Evolutionary psychology is the field of psychology that studies ways in which (228) _____ and (229) _____ are connected with mental processes and behavior.

What is meant by the concept of heredity? What are the roles of genes and chromosomes in heredity? Heredity is the transmission of traits from generation to generation by means of (230) _____ and chromosomes. (231) _____ is involved in almost all human traits and behavior. Behavioral genetics bridges the science of (232) _____ and biology and is concerned with the genetic transmission of traits that give rise to patterns of (233) _____.

(234) _____, which consist of DNA, are the building blocks of heredity. A thousand or more genes make up each (235) _____. Each cell in the body contains (236) _____ chromosomes, arranged in 23 (237) _____. The sequence of the (238) _____ in the DNA molecule is the genetic code that will cause the organism to develop. Behavioral geneticists are attempting to sort out the relative importance of (239) _____, or heredity, and (240) _____, or environmental influences on the origins of behavior.

What are kinship studies, and how do they help psychologists study the role of heredity in behavior? The more closely people are related, the more (241) _____ they have in common. If genes are involved in a trait or behavior, then people who are closely related are (242) _____ likely to show similar traits or behavior. (243) _____ studies are studies of the distribution of traits, or behavior patterns, among related people. Examples of kinship studies are (244) _____ studies and (245) _____ studies. In twin studies, the presence of traits and behavior patterns are compared in monozygotic, or (246) _____, and dizygotic, or (247) _____, twins. When certain behaviors are shared by identical twins or close blood relatives, it is suggested that the behavior may have a (248) _____ component. This is especially true when the behavior is shared by close blood relatives reared in different (249) _____ from an early age.

Reflection Break 5

Evolution and Evolutionary Psychology and Heredity

1. Briefly explain what is meant by heredity and how genetics can play a role in behavior.

2. Explain how kinship studies like twin and family studies can help researchers answer questions on the role of biological versus environmental influences on behavior. Be sure to discuss both the advantages and disadvantages of this type of research.

REVIEW: KEY TERMS AND CONCEPTS

FINAL CHAPTER REVIEW

Review

Visit the *Psychology in the New Millennium* Web site at www.harcourtcollege.com/psych/PNM/siteresources.html and take the Chapter Quizzes to test your knowledge.

Recite

Go to the Recite section for this chapter in your textbook. Use the tear-off card provided at the back of the book to cover the answers of the Recite section. Read the questions aloud, and recite the answers. This will help you cement your knowledge of key concepts.

Essay Questions

1. Imagine meeting four different people who have each sustained injury to different sections of their brain. Person A has irreversible damage to her frontal lobe. Person B has irreversible damage to his parietal lobe. Person C has irreversible damage to her temporal lobe, and person D has irreversible damage to his occipital lobe. In general what would be the effects of each of these injuries?

2. Imagine taking a bite of a juicy apple. Briefly discuss the role that each part of the brain plays in this simple act.

3. What is the advantage of knowing that a mental illness is caused by a neurochemical problem? How might a better understanding of brain chemistry help psychologists develop a better definition of mental illness?

4. Design experiments using each of the following methods to learn something about the brain:
   a. MRI
   b. PET
   c. CAT

   In each case think about what your research question would be and how you would go about answering it. Specify your subject population, your research question, and the design of your experiment. How would the information gained from the different studies be different?

5. Design an experiment in which you test whether language is only localized in the left hemisphere by using split-brain subjects. Explain how you would resolve the controversy concerning the localization of language with your experimental design.

RELATE/EXPAND/INTEGRATE

1. **Neurons:**
   a. Visit John Krantz's Internet page at http://psych.hanover.edu/Krantz/tutor.html and complete the Neuron and Synapse Tutorials.
   b. Visit http://faculty.washington.edu/chudler.color/pic1.html to color a neuron online, or http://faculty.washington.edu/chudler/colorbook.html and print out the pages.

2. **Neuroscience:** Visit http://faculty.washington.edu/chudler/hunt3.html and participate in the Neuroscience Treasure Hunt. See whether you can be the first in your class to win the Golden Neuron Award.

3. **Spinal cord and nervous system:** Draw a diagram demonstrating the sensory (afferent) and motor nerve pathways involved when you touch a hot stove. Share your pictures with your study mates and note any differences. Together with your study mates review each of the pictures with the material in your textbook to correct any inaccuracies.

4. **Cerebral cortex:**
   A. Revisit http://faculty.washington.edu/chudler.color/pic1.html to color the different lobes of the cortical tissue.
   B. Visit http://www.pbs.org/wgbh/aso/tryit/brain. Probe the motor cortex and observe the movements that arise as a result of the probing.

5. **Neurotransmitters and hormones:** With your study group, play "Neurochemical Bingo."

   Preparation:
   • Game can be played by up to four players: three players and a caller.
   • Each person should be given a different game board.
   • Cut the descriptions into single strips of paper that can be drawn randomly.
   • Use coins (pennies) or candy (M & Ms) or slips of paper as place markers. Each player will need 16 place markers.

   To play:
   1. The caller reads the descriptions of the neurochemical. As soon as a player knows which neurochemical is being described, the player should place his/her marker on that square.
   2. The first player to have a "Bingo," or four answers in a row, either horizontally, vertically, or diagonally, wins.
   3. The game can be repeated until each member of the group has had a turn at being the caller.

6. **Drugs and their actions:** Pick a popular drug, medication, or herb and research its neurochemical actions. What neurotransmitters or hormone does it affect? What are its actions? How does the information that you find fit with the information presented in your textbook? Present your findings to your classmates in a format specified by your instructor.

ANSWERS FOR CHAPTER 2

Reading for Understanding on
"An Introduction to the Field of Biological Psychology"

1. biology
2. mental
3. biological
4. nervous
5. cerebral
6. heredity
7. cells
8. receive
9. neurons
10. neurotransmitters
11. chemical
12. impulse
13. glial
14. nourish
15. insulate
16. Neurons
17. Dendrites
18. Axon
19. Terminals
20. One
21. dendrite
22. axon
23. terminals
24. myelin
25. electrical
26. efficiently
27. afferent
28. efferent
29. electro-chemical
30. chemical
31. ions
32. positively
33. depolarized
34. pumped
35. resting
36. resting
37. action
38. electro
39. neurotransmitters
40. Fired
41. Neurotransmitters
42. All-or-none
43. large
44. Thousandths
45. Refractory
46. Synapses
47. Transmitting
48. Dendrite
49. Synaptic cleft
50. Electrical
51. Neurotransmitters
52. Axon terminal
53. Chemical
54. Receptor site
55. Reuptake
56. Excite
57. Inhibit
58. Contraction
59. Emotions
60. Deficiencies
61. Depression
62. Acetylcholine
63. Learning
64. Emotional
65. Parkinson's
66. Noradrenaline
67. Inhibitory
68. Eating
69. Depression
70. Endorphin

Reflection Break 1

Neurons

Check the drawing on page 40 of your textbook to see whether you correctly named the parts of the neuron.

Neurotransmitters and Their Actions

1. Acetylcholine
2. Endorphins
3. Dopamine
4. Noradrenaline
5. Serotonin
6. Noradrenaline
7. Acetylcholine
8. Serotonin
9. Dopamine

Reading for Understanding on "The Nervous System"

71. axons
72. dendrites
73. thought
74. emotional
75. brain
76. nerves
77. spinal
78. central
79. sensory
80. efferent
81. peripheral
82. peripheral
83. somatic
84. autonomic
85. sensory
86. motor
87. skin
88. central
89. skeletal
90. autonomic
91. digestion
92. sympathetic
93. parasympathetic
94. sympathetic
95. build
96. central
97. spinal
98. brain
99. nerves
100. receptors
101. glands
102. reflexes
103. brain
104. gray
105. white

Reflection Break 2

1. Central
2. Peripheral
3. Brain
4. Spinal cord
5. Somatic
6. Autonomic
7. Parasympathetic
8. Sympathetic

Reading for Understanding on "The Brain and Cerebral Cortex"

106. accidents
107. Gage
108. damage
109. stimulation
110. scans
111. lesion
112. limbic system
113. eating
114. Penfield
115. Electroencephalogram
116. Brain
117. Tumors
118. Computer
119. computerized axial tomograph
120. positron emission tomography
121. magnetic resonance imaging
122. x-ray
123. three
124. glucose
125. active
126. magnetic
127. radio
128. hindbrain
129. medulla
130. pons
131. cerebellum
132. reticular activating
133. thalamus
134. hypothalamus
135. emotion
136. cerebrum
137. amygdala
138. hippocampus
139. cerebrum
140. cognitive
141. convoluted
142. fissure
143. hemispheres
144. corpus callosum
145. lobes
146. frontal
147. parietal
148. temporal
149. occipital
150. visual
151. auditory
152. somatosensory
153. prefrontal

154. motor
155. hemisphere's
156. differ
157. left
158. Broca's
159. Wernicke's
160. Aphasia
161. Producing
162. understanding
163. hemispheres

164. left
165. logical
166. problem
167. Right
168. Aesthetic
169. Reasoning
170. Exaggerated
171. Independently
172. Handwriting
173. left-handed

174. language
175. stuttering
176. migrane
177. creativity
178. genetic
179. gene
180. corpus callosum
181. normal
182. verbally
183. language

Reflection Break 3
Review on "The Brain and Cerebral Cortex"

1. n
2. x
3. w
4. aa
5. z
6. t
7. v
8. y
9. u
10. s

11. a
12. b
13. o
14. q
15. r
16. p
17. c
18. l
19. bb
20. d

21. m
22. e
23. k
24. j
25. cc
26. g
27. i
28. h
29. f

Reading for Understanding on "The Endocrine System"

184. cannot
185. glands
186. passageways
187. ductless
188. Endocrine
189. Hormones
190. Neurotransmitters
191. Hypothalamus
192. Pituitary
193. Hormonal
194. Master
195. Hypothalamus
196. Growth
197. Prolactin

198. antidiuretic hormone
199. oxytocin
200. pineal
201. sleep wake
202. puberty
203. thyroxin
204. hypothyroidism
205. cretinism
206. hyperthyroidism
207. cortex
208. stress
209. glucose
210. medulla
211. Adrenaline

212. Emotions
213. Anxiety
214. Noreadrenaline
215. Testosterone
216. Muscle
217. Sex
218. Female
219. ovaries
220. Estrogen
221. Progesterone
222. Cognitive
223. well-being

Reflection Break 4
Review on "Hormones and the Endocrine System"

1. e	5. f	9. d
2. j	6. c	10. l
3. a	7. b	11. h
4. k	8. i	12. g

Reading for Understanding on "Evolution and Evolutionary Psychology and Heredity"

224. evolution	233. Behaviors	242. more
225. adaptive	234. Genes	243. Kinship
226. increase	235. Chromosome	244. Twin
227. extinct	236. 46	245. Adoption
228. adaptation	237. pairs	246. Identical
229. natural selection	238. rungs	247. Fraternal
230. genes	239. nature	248. Genetic
231. Heredity	240. nurture	249. environments
232. Psychology	241. genes	

Reflection Break 5
Review on "Evolution, Evolutionary Psychology, and Heredity"

1. Heredity refers to the biological transmission of traits from generation to generation by means of chromosomes and genes. Behavioral geneticists study the genetic transmission of traits that give rise to patterns of behavior.

2. Kinship studies like those that compare identical (monozygotic) twins allow scientists to hold the biological makeup of the individual constant and compare the effects of different environments. Disadvantages include the inability to totally control differences in environment and the fact that family members will have both similar genetics and similar environments, thus making it difficult to separate the effects of one over the other.

Neurochemical Bingo

ACETYLCHOLINE	TESTOSTERONE	PROLACTIN	ADRENALINE
CORTICO-STEROIDS	SEROTONIN	NORADRENALINE	MELATONIN
ANTIDIURETIC HORMONE	ESTROGEN	OXYTOCIN	DOPAMINE
ENDORPHINS	THYROXIN	PROGESTERONE	GROWTH HORMONE

ACETYLCHOLIN	SEROTONIN	PROLACTIN	ADRENALINE
CORTICO-STEROIDS	ENDORPHINS	GROWTH HORMONE	MELATONIN
ANTIDIURETIC HORMONE	ESTROGEN	PROGESTERONE	DOPAMINE
TESTOSTERONE	THYROXIN	OXYTOCIN	NORADRENALINE

DOPAMINE	TESTOSTERONE	PROLACTIN	SEROTONIN
CORTICO-STEROIDS	ADRENALINE	ANTIDIURETIC HORMONE	MELATONIN
NORADRENALINE	ESTROGEN	OXYTOCIN	ACETYLCHOLINE
ENDORPHINS	THYROXIN	PROGESTERONE	GROWTH HORMONE

Descriptions to be read by the caller:

▲ Neurotransmitter that causes muscle contractions and is involved in the formation of memories.   **Acetylcholine**

▲ These neurotransmitters are suggested to inhibit pain by locking pain-causing chemicals out of their receptor sites.   **Endorphins**

▲ Neurotransmitter involved in muscle contraction, learning and memory, and emotional response.   **Dopamine**

▲ Neurotransmitter that accelerates the heart rate, affects eating, and has been linked with activity levels, learning, and remembering.   **Noradrenaline**

▲ Neurotransmitter involved in psychological problems, including obesity, depression, insomnia, alcoholism, and aggression.   **Serotonin**

▲ Imbalances of this neurotransmitter are linked with mood disorders such as depression and bipolar disorder.   **Noradrenaline**

▲ Neurotransmitter found at synapses between motor neurons and muscles; deficiencies of this neurotransmitter have been linked with Alzheimer's disease.   **Acetylcholine**

▲ Drugs that block the reuptake of this neurotransmitter are helpful in the treatment of depression.   **Serotonin**

▲ Low levels of this neurotransmitter have been linked to the tremors of Parkinsons's disease.   **Dopamine**

▲ Hormone released by the pituitary gland responsible for regulation of the growth of muscles, bones, and glands.   **Growth hormone**

▲ Hormone that stimulates the growth of female reproductive organs and prepares the uterus to maintain pregnancy.   **Progesterone**

▲ Pituitary hormone that regulates maternal behavior and stimulates production of milk in women.   **Prolactin**

▲ Released by the pituitary gland and inhibits the production of urine when body fluids are low.   **Antidiuretic hormone**

▲ The male sex hormone. Is responsible for the development of both primary and secondary sex characteristics.   **Testosterone**

▲ When released by the pituitary gland, this hormone stimulates labor in pregnant women.   **Oxytocin**

▲ These hormones are released by the adrenal glands and have been shown to increase resistance to stress, promote muscle development, and cause the liver to release stored sugar.   **Corticosteroids**

▲ Produced by the adrenal medulla, this hormone is exclusively produced by the adrenal glands. It is of interest to psychologists since it intensifies most emotions and is crucial to the experience of fear and anxiety.   **Adrenaline**

▲ Hormone secreted by the adrenal medulla, but also produced elsewhere in the body. Also acts as a neurotransmitter.   **Noreadrenaline**

▲ Female sex hormone produced by both the ovaries and the testes. This hormone fosters reproductive capacity and development of secondary sex characteristics.   **Estrogen**

▲ This hormone affects the body's metabolism. Too little of it leads to obesity and sluggishness; too much is characterized by insomnia, excitability, and weight loss. **Thyroxin**

▲ Produced by the pineal gland, this hormone helps to regulate the sleep-wake cycle. **Melatonin**

Chapter 3

Sensation and Perception

PREVIEW

Skim the major headings in this chapter in your textbook. Jot down anything that you are surprised or curious about. After this write down four or five questions that you have about the material in this chapter.

Things that surprised me/I am curious about from Chapter 3:

Questions that I have about sensation and perception:

▲

▲

▲

▲

QUESTION

These are some questions that you should be able to answer after you finish studying this chapter.

Sensation and Perception: Your Tickets of Admission to the World Outside

▲ *What are sensation and perception?*

▲ *How do we know when something is there? How do we know when it has changed?*

▲ *What is signal-detection theory?*

▲ *What are feature detectors?*

▲ *How do our sensory systems adapt to a changing environment?*

Vision: Letting the Sun Shine In

▲ *Just what is this stuff called light?*

▲ *How does the eye work?*

▲ *How do we perceive color?*

▲ *What is color-blindness? Why are some people color-blind?*

Visual Perception: How Perceptive!

▲ *How do we organize bits of information like perceptions into meaningful wholes?*

▲ *How do we perceive movement?*

▲ *How do we perceive depth?*

▲ *What are perceptual constancies? Why do we perceive a door to be a rectangle even when it is ajar?*

▲ *How can the principles of visual perception be used to trick the eye?*

Hearing: Making Sense of Sound

▲ *What is sound?*

▲ *How does the ear work? How do we locate sounds?*

▲ *How do we perceive loudness and pitch?*

▲ *What is deafness? What can we do about it?*

The Chemical Senses: Smell and Taste

▲ *How does the sense of smell work?*

▲ *How does the sense of taste work?*

The Skin Senses (Yes, It Does)

▲ *What are the skin senses? How do they work?*

▲ *What is pain? What can we do about it?*

Kinesthesis and the Vestibular Sense

▲ *What is kinesthesis?*

▲ *How does the vestibular sense work?*

Sensation and Perception on the Edge: Virtual Reality and ESP

▲ *Is there really such as thing as extrasensory perception? (ESP)*

READING FOR UNDERSTANDING/REFLECT

The following section provides you with the opportunity to perform three of the R's of the PQ4R study method. In this section you are encouraged to check your understanding of your reading of the text by filling in the blanks in the brief paragraphs that relate to each of the preview questions. You will also be prompted to rehearse your understanding of the material with periodic Rehearsal/Reflection breaks. Remember, it is better to study in more frequent, short sessions than in one long "cram session." Be sure to reward yourself with short study breaks before each Rehearsal/Reflection exercise.

Reading for Understanding About "Sensation and Perception: Your Tickets of Admission to the World Outside"

What are sensation and perception? (1) _____ is a mechanical process that involves the stimulation of sensory receptors (neuron) and the transmission of sensory information to the (2) _____ nervous system. Sensory receptors are located in (3) _____ organs such as eyes and ears. Stimulation of the senses results from sources of (4) _____ like light and sound or from the presence of chemicals. (5) _____ is the active organization of sensations into a representation of the outside world, and it reflects (6) _____ and expectations.

How do we know when something is there? How do we know when it has changed? We know something is there when the (7) _____ of the stimulus, such as light, exceeds the (8) _____ threshold for the stimulus. The absolute threshold is the term used by Gustav (9) _____ to refer to the (10) _____ intensity at which the stimulus can be detected. (11) _____ determine the absolute threshold of the senses by exposing subjects to progressively stronger stimuli. The method of (12) _____ stimuli presents subjects with sets of stimuli with magnitudes close to the expected threshold; subjects note whether they detect a stimulus or not.

We know that something has changed when the change in intensity exceeds the (13) _____ threshold. The difference threshold is the (14) _____ difference in intensity that can be discriminated. Difference thresholds are expressed in (15) _____ constants Closely related to difference thresholds is the concept of (16) _____ (17) _____ difference, or the minimal amount by which a source of energy must be increased or decreased so that a difference in intensity will be perceived.

What is signal-detection theory? According to signal- (18) _____ theory, the intensity of the signal is just one factor that determines whether people will perceive sensory stimuli. The theory explains the ways in which stimuli (19) _____, background noise and (20) _____ factors like motivation, familiarity with a stimulus, and attention interact to influence whether a stimulus will be detected.

What are feature detectors? Feature detectors were first discovered by David (21) _____ and Torsten (22) _____ and are neurons that fire in response to specific (23) _____ of sensed stimuli. Feature detectors in the visual cortex respond to particular features of visual input such as lines sensed at various (24) _____, or specific colors, and (25) _____ feature detectors respond to the pitch and loudness of sound stimuli.

How do our sensory systems adapt to a changing environment? We become more (26) _____ to stimuli of low magnitude and less sensitive to stimuli that remain the same. Sensory (27) _____ refers to these processes of adjustment. Growing more sensitive to stimulation is referred to as (28) _____, or positive adaptation. Growing less sensitive to continuous stimulation is called (29) _____, or negative adaptation.

Reflection Break 1

1. Without using the terms *sense* or *perceive,* clearly differentiate between the processes of sensation and perception.

2. Using the principles of signal-detection theory, explain why for the first few nights after moving from the country to the city you might first notice all of the street noise, but your roommate, who has lived the city all his life, would not. What might happen if you took your "city slicker" roommate to the country?

Reading for Understanding About "Vision: Letting the Sun Shine In"

Just what is this stuff called light? Visible light triggers visual sensations and is part of the spectrum of (30) _____ energy. Light is made up of (31) _____ of energy; different colors have different (32) _____. The wavelength of light determines its color, or (33) _____. The color violet has the (34) _____ wavelength, and red has the (35) _____. White sunlight can be broken down into the colors of the rainbow by the means of a (36) _____.

How does the eye work? The eye senses and transmits visual stimulation to the (37) _____ lobe of the cerebral cortex. Light first passes through the (38) _____, or the transparent covering of the eye's surface. The size of the (39) _____ determines the amount that can pass through the cornea. The pupil is an opening of the (40) _____, or the colored part of the eye. Once light passes through the pupil, it encounters the (41) _____. The lens focuses light into the (42) _____ by changing its thickness. The retina is composed of (43) _____, or neurons that are sensitive to light, called rods and cones. (44) _____ permit perception of color. (45) _____ transmit sensations of light and dark only.

Light is transmitted from the retina to the brain via the (46) _____ nerve, which is made up of the axons of retinal (47) _____ cells. In the (48) _____, or most sensitive area of the retina, the photoreceptor cells are densely packed. The (49) _____ spot, or the area of the retina where the axons of the ganglion cells collect to form the optic nerve, is insensitive to visual stimulation. Visual (50) _____, or sharpness of vision, is connected with the (51) _____ of the eye and age. As we age, our lenses grow brittle, making it difficult to focus; this condition is called (52) _____.

The fovea of the retina is made up almost exclusively of (53) _____. Rods are nearly absent from the (54) _____ and are more sensitive than cones to lowered lighting. The process of adjusting to lower lighting conditions is called (55) _____ adaptation;

adaptation to bright lighting conditions takes place more rapidly than dark adaptation. Dark adaptation takes longer because (56) _____ continue to adapt to darkness once cones have reached their peak adaptation.

How do we perceive color? There are three psychological dimensions of color; they are hue, (57) _____, and warmth. The (58) _____ of light determines its hue. The (59) _____ of a color is its degree of lightness or darkness. Yellow is the (60) _____, violet blue the (61) _____. Colors on the green-blue side of a color wheel are considered to be (62) _____ in temperature; those on the red-orange side are considered (63) _____. Colors across from one another on the color wheel are labeled (64) _____ colors. Red-(65) _____ and blue-(66) _____ are the major complementary color pairs. When lights of complementary colors are mixed, they dissolve to (67) _____. (68) _____ result when there has been a persistent sensation of one color of a complementary pair; you perceive the complementary color when the first color is removed.

There are two theories as to how we perceive color. According to the (69) _____ theory, there are three types of cones-some are sensitive to (70) _____, others to (71) _____, and still others to (72) _____. Research shows that there are indeed (73) _____ that are sensitive to blue, green, and red. The (74) _____ theory proposes three types of color receptors: (75) _____-green, (76) _____-yellow, and light-(77) _____. Opponent-process theory is supported by the appearance of (78) _____.

What is color-blindness? Why are some people color-blind? People with normal color vision are called (79) _____. (80) _____ see no color, and (81) _____ are blind to some parts of the spectrum. (82) _____ color-blindness is rare. (83) _____ color-blindness is more common and is a sex-linked trait that affects mostly (84) _____.

Reflection Break 2

a. red light
b. violet light
c. cornea
d. iris
e. pupil
f. sclera
g. lens
h. retina
i. rods
j. cones

k. dark adaptation
l. acuity
m. optic nerve
n. fovea
o. blind spot
p. nearsightedness
q. farsightedness
r. complementary colors
s. afterimage
t. trichromatic theory

u. opponent process theory
v. trichromat
w. monochromat
x. dichromat
y. hue
z. brightness
aa. warm colors

_____ 1. Individuals able to discriminate among all color of the visible spectrum.
_____ 2. The colored part of the eye.
_____ 3. Colors that are located directly across from each other on the color wheel.
_____ 4. Individuals who are sensitive to only lightness and darkness; fully color-blind.
_____ 5. Photoreceptors that provide color vision.

_____   6. An image that is the result of persistent sensation of colors; contains the complementary colors of the original image.

_____   7. The part of the eye that focuses the light by adjusting its thickness.

_____   8. Colors on the yellow-orange-red side of the color wheel.

_____   9. The opening in the eye that allows light to pass through.

_____   10. Individuals that can discriminate among red and green, or blue and yellow, but not all.

_____   11. Inability to see things in a distance clearly; must be unusually close to an object to discriminate its details.

_____   12. Light with the longest wavelength.

_____   13. The hard, protective "white" of the eye.

_____   14. The degree of lightness or darkness of a color.

_____   15. Made up of the axons of the ganglion cells; travels from the eye to the occipital lobe of the brain.

_____   16. States that color vision results from action of blue-yellow, red-green and brightness cells.

_____   17. Cells that are sensitive only to the intensity of light.

_____   18. The photoreceptive part of the eye.

_____   19. Inability to see objects close up; can discriminate distant objects clearly.

_____   20. The transparent surface that covers the front of the eye's surface.

_____   21. Proposes that there are three types of color receptors, red, green, and blue-violet.

_____   22. Term used to refer to the sharpness of vision.

_____   23. The portion of the retina that is insensitive to visual stimulation.

_____   24. The wavelength of light.

_____   25. The process of adjusting to lower light conditions.

_____   26. The most sensitive area of the retina; contains densely packed cones.

_____   27. Light with the shortest wavelength.

Reading for Understanding About "Visual Perception: How Perceptive!"

How do we organize bits of information like perceptions into meaningful wholes? Perceptual organization involves (85) _____ patterns and processing information about (86) _____ between parts and the whole. (87) _____ rules of perceptual organization involve figure-ground relationships, proximity, similarity, continuity, common fate, and closure. The principle of (88) _____ refers to our tendency to perceive a complete, or whole, figure, even when there are gaps in the sensory input. (89) _____ refers to the fact that when you look out your window and see many things, these objects tend to be perceived as figures against backgrounds. If the figure-ground relationship is (90) _____, our perceptions tend to be unstable. The (91) _____ vase and the (92) _____ cue are two of psychologists' favorite examples of perceptual shifts that result from an ambiguous figure-ground.

The perceptual law of (93) _____ refers to our tendency to group objects that are close together or near one another as a perceptual unit. (94) _____ refers to our tendency to perceive objects that are like one another as belonging together. The rule of (95) _____ refers to our tendency to perceive a series of points or broken lines as having unity. According to the law of (96) _____, elements seen moving together are perceived as belonging together. Perception of a whole followed by perception of parts is termed (97) _____ processing, whereas perception of the parts that leads to perception of a whole is termed (98) _____ processing.

How do we perceive movement? We visually perceive movement when the light reflected by moving objects moves across the (99) _____, and also when objects shift in relation to one another. Distant objects appear to move more (100) _____ than nearby objects, and objects in the middle ground may give the illusion of moving (101) _____. In addition to studying real movement, psychologists also study three types of (102) _____ movement: the autokinetic effect, stroboscopic motion, and the phi phenomenon. The (103) _____ effect refers to the tendency to perceive a stationary point of light in a dark room as moving. (104) _____ motion, responsible for the illusion of motion pictures, occurs through the presentation of a rapid progression of images of stationary objects, or (105) _____. The (106) _____ refers to the apparent motion of a series of lights turned on and off.

How do we perceive depth? (107) _____ perception involves monocular and binocular cues. (108) _____ cues rely on the use of one eye and include the (109) _____ cues of perspective, relative size, clearness, interposition, shadows, and texture gradient, and the (110) _____ cues of motion parallax and accommodation. Distant objects stimulate (111) _____ areas on the retina, then those nearby; as a result, (112) _____ occurs, that is, parallel lines appear to come closer together as they recede from us. (113) _____ refers to the fact that distant objects look smaller then nearby objects; (114) _____ refers to the fact that closer objects provide more detail than distant objects. The monocular cue of (115) _____ refers to the fact that nearby objects will overlap and block our view of distant objects. (116) _____ refers to the fact that we learn that an opaque object blocks light and produces shadows, and this gives us information about the dimensionality of objects. Another monocular cue is the use of (117) _____; in this cue, we learn that closer objects are perceived as having rougher textures. Motion cues are also (118) _____ cues; the tendency of objects to seem to move backward or forward as a function of their distance is known as (119) _____.

(120) _____ cues, or cues that involve the use of both eyes to judge depth, include retinal disparity and convergence. (121) _____ refers to the fact that the retina of each eye receives a different image of an object. The degree of (122) _____ in these images is the retinal disparity. (123) _____ objects have greater retinal disparity. (124) _____ refers to the tension in the eye muscles that occurs when we attempt to maintain a single image of a nearby object by turning our eyes inward.

What are perceptual constancies? Why do we perceive a door to be a rectangle even when it is ajar? How can the principles of visual perception be used to trick the eye? Perceptual (125) _____ are acquired through experience and make the world a stable place. There are a number of perceptual constancies including size, color, brightness, and shape. We (126)

_____ to assume that objects retain their size, shape, brightness, and color despite their (127) _____ from us, their position, or changes in (128) _____ conditions. Visual (129) _____ such as the Hering-Helmholtz and Müller-Lyer tend to trick the eye because they play with perceptual constancies.

Reflection Break 3

Gestalt Laws of Perceptual Organization

Label each of the following examples as to which Gestalt law of perceptual organization it illustrates.

_____ 1.   XXXXXXXXX
            OOOOOOOOO
            XXXXXXXXX
            OOOOOOOOO

_____ 2.   X   O   X   O
            X   O   X   O
            X   O   X   O
            X   O   X   O

_____ 3.   ——————————|————————-|————————

_____ 4.   XXXXXXXXXXX
                OOOOOOOOOOOOO
                    YYYYYYYYYYYYYY
                        QQQQQQQQQQQQQQQQQ

Perceptual Organization, Movement, Depth, Constancies, and Illusions

a. top-down processing
b. bottom-up processing
c. autokinetic effect
d. stroboscopic motion
e. phi phenomenon
f. monocular cues
g. binocular cues
h. perspective
i. relative size
j. interposition
k. shadowing

l. texture gradient
m. motion parallax
n. retinal disparity
o. convergence
p. clearness
q. pictorial cues
r. color constancy
s. brightness constancy
t. shape constancy
u. visual illusions
v. size constancy

_____ 1. Images that trick the eye because of our tendency to use perceptual rules that do not apply.

_____ 2. The tendency for us to perceive objects as retaining their color even if lighting conditions alter their appearance.

_____ 3. An example of apparent motion in which movement is provided by the presentation of a rapid progression of images of stationary objects.

_____ 4. The perception of larger objects as being closer to us.

_____ 5. The tendency to perceive a stationary point of light in a dark room as moving.

_____ 6. The perception of objects with greater detail as being closer to us.

_____ 7. Perception of shadows and highlights as giving depth to two-dimensional objects.

_____ 8. Perception of objects with rougher texture as being closer to the observer.

_____ 9. Perceptual processes that rely on knowledge of the "big" picture to organize a perception.

_____ 10. Perception of objects that seem to move forward with us as distant and those that move backward as nearby.

_____ 11. The tendency to perceive objects as maintaining their shape even if they look different.

_____ 12. An example of apparent motion in which an on/off process is perceived as movement.

_____ 13. The tendency to perceive one color as brighter or darker due to our expectations of that color.

_____ 14. Perceptual processing that begins with smaller units and works toward the whole.

_____ 15. Perceiving objects that cast large differences in retinal images on the retina as being closer.

_____ 16. Perception of objects that require greater inward movement of the eyes as being closer.

_____ 17. The perception of overlapping objects as being dimensional.

_____ 18. Perceptual cues commonly used by artists to create an impression of a third dimension in two-dimensional works.

_____ 19. The tendency to perceive objects as the same size even though the size of the image on the retina varies.

_____ 20. Perceptual cues that involve both eyes.

_____ 21. Perceptual cues that rely on the input from one eye.

_____ 22. The perception of parallel lines coming closer together, or converging, as they recede from us.

Reading for Understanding About "Hearing: Making Sense of Sound"

What is sound? Sound waves, also called (130) _____ stimulation, require a medium such as air or water in order to be transmitted. Sound (131) _____ alternately compress and expand molecules of the medium, creating (132) _____. The human ear can hear sounds varying in (133) _____ from 20 to 20,000 cycles per second (Hz). Pitch and (134) _____ are two psychological dimensions of sound. The (135) _____ of a sound is determined by its (136) _____, or the number of cycles per second, and is expressed in the unit Hertz. One cycle per second is (137) _____ Hz. The greater the frequency, the (138) _____ the sound's pitch. The loudness of a sound corresponds to the (139) _____, or height, of sound waves as measured in (140) _____(dB). (141) _____ dB is equivalent to the threshold of hearing, the lowest sound that the typical person can hear. We can experience hearing (142) _____ if we are exposed to protracted sounds of 85 to 90 dB or more.

How does the ear work? How do we locate sounds? The (143) _____ is shaped and structured to capture sound waves and has three parts, the (144) _____ ear, the (145) _____ ear, and the (146) _____ ear. The outer ear is shaped to funnel sound waves to the (147) _____, a thin membrane that vibrates in response to sound waves. The middle ear functions as an (148) _____ and contains the eardrum and three small (149) _____, the hammer, the anvil, and the stirrup, which also transmit sound by (150) _____. The stirrup is attached to another vibrating membrane, the (151) _____ window. The oval window transmits vibrations into the inner ear, which is composed of the bony tube known as the (152) _____. The cochlea is divided into three fluid-filled (153) _____ by membranes. One of the membranes is the (154) _____ membrane, and vibrations in the fluid of the cochlea press against this membrane. Attached to the basilar membrane is the organ of (155) _____. The organ of Corti contains some 16,000 receptors, or (156) _____ cells that dance in response to vibrations of the (157) _____ membrane. The up and down movements of these hair cells generate neural impulses that are carried via the (158) _____ nerve to the temporal lobes of the brain.

When sounds come from the right or left we locate sounds by determining in which ear they are (159) _____. It is more difficult for us to locate sounds that come from directly in (160) _____ or behind us; in this case, we might (161) _____ our heads to pin down the directional information.

How do we perceive loudness and pitch? The (162) _____ of sounds appear to be related to the number of and how often the receptor neurons in the organ of (163) _____ fire. Sounds are perceived as (164) _____ when more sensory neurons fire. Explaining (165) _____ perception appears to be more difficult and takes at least two processes. The (166) _____ theory of pitch perception holds that the pitch of a sound is sensed according to the place along the basilar membrane that vibrates in response to it; it accounts for sounds whose frequencies exceed 4,000 Hz. (167) _____ theory states that pitch perception depends on the stimulation of neural impulses that match the frequency of the sound waves and accounts for frequencies of 20 to 1,000 Hz. The (168) _____ principle states that groups of neurons take turns firing and accounts for pitch discrimination between a few hundred and 4,000 cycles per second.

What is deafness? What can we do about it? There are two major types of (169) _____. (170) _____ deafness-common among older people-is caused by damage to the middle ear and is often ameliorated by (171) _____, which amplify sounds. (172) _____ deafness is usually caused by damage to neurons in the inner ear and can sometimes be corrected by (173) _____ implants.

Reflection Break 4

1. Summarize the processes involved in the transduction of sound waves by the ear.

2. Describe the claims of the place, frequency, and volley theories of pitch perception. Explain why all three theories are needed to account for pitch discrimination.

Reading for Understanding About "The Chemical Senses: Smell and Taste"

How does the sense of smell work? The sense of smell is a (174) _____ sense. It samples molecules of substances called (175) _____ through the olfactory membrane in each nostril. Receptor neurons fire when a few drops of a substance in a (176) _____ form come in contact with them. The firing of the receptor neurons is then transmitted to the brain via the (177) _____ nerve. Smell makes a key contribution to the (178) _____ of foods.

How does the sense of taste work? (179) _____ is the other chemical sense. There are four primary taste qualities: sweet, (180) _____, salty, and (181) _____. Flavor involves the odor, (182) _____, and temperature of food, as well as its taste. Taste is sensed through taste cells, which are located in taste buds on the (183) _____. Taste buds appear to specialize; some appear to be more responsive to (184) _____, whereas others react to several tastes. People live in different taste worlds; those of us with low sensitivity for sweet taste may require (185) _____ the sugar to sweeten our food, and people who enjoy bitter food may actually be taste (186) _____ to them. These types of taste sensitivities appear to have a strong (187) _____ component. Although older people often complain that their food has no (188) _____, it is more likely to be a result of a decline in the sense of (189) _____, and thus the flavor of food, and then a decline in taste.

Reading for Understanding About "The Skin Senses (Yes, It Does)"

What are the skin senses? How do they work? The (190) _____ senses include touch, pressure, warmth, cold, and pain. We have distinct sensory receptors for pressure, (191) _____, and pain, but some nerve endings may receive more than one type of sensory input. (192) _____ and (193) _____ are sensed by receptors located around the roots of hair cells below the surface of the skin. Psychophysicists use methods like the (194) _____ threshold, where the subject is touched at two different points until he/she reports that there are two rods, to determine sensitivity to pressure. This type of research has shown that the fingertips, lips, nose, and cheeks are (195) _____ sensitive than other areas of the body. The receptors for temperature are located just beneath the (196) _____. We have (197) _____ receptors for warmth and cold.

What is pain? What can we do about it? (198) _____ means there is something wrong in the body. We can sense pain throughout most of the body, but it is usually (199) _____ where nerve endings are densely packed. Pain (200) _____ at the point of contact and is transmitted to the brain by various (201) _____, including prostaglandins, and bradykinin and subtance P. (202) _____ facilitate transmission of the pain message to the brain and heighten circulation to the injured area, causing the redness and swelling we know as (203) _____. Analgesic drugs like (204) _____ and ibuprofen alleviate pain by inhibiting the production of prostaglandins.

Melzack's theory of the "(205) _____" suggests that perception of pain also involves other aspects of our physiology and psychology and reflects our cognitive interpretation of the situation, our emotional response, and the ways in which we respond to stress. This theory fits well with the (206) _____ theory. Melzack also proposes a (207) "_____" theory of pain. Amputees often experience pain in (208) "_____" limbs. Rubbing or scratching painful areas can (209) _____ perception of pain by transmitting additional messages that have the effect of shutting down a "gate" in the (210) _____. Traditional (211) _____ believe that the practice balances the body's flow of energy, but research reveals that it stimulates nerves that reach the (212) _____ and may decrease pain by causing release of (213) _____.

Coping with pain has traditionally been a (214) _____ issue; however, more recently, psychology has provided expanded methods of fighting pain. Psychological research has shown that giving people accurate (215) _____ about their condition often helps them manage pain. Distraction and fantasy, hypnosis, and relaxation and biofeedback training have also proved (216) _____ in pain management.

Reading for Understanding About "Kinesthesis and the Vestibular Sense" and "Virtual Reality and ESP"

What is kinesthesis? How does the vestibular sense work? (217) _____ is the sensation of body position and movement. It relies on information from sensory organs in the joints, (218) _____, and muscles that is fed back to the brain. The (219) _____ sense is housed primarily in the semicircular canals of the ears and tells us whether we are in an upright position.

Is there really such as thing as extrasensory perception (ESP)? (220) _____ uses electronic media to feed false information about the world outside through the senses. Psychologists are using virtual reality to help individuals overcome (221) _____. Virtual rooms and (222) _____ are new areas of psychological research that have arisen due to the increase in the availability of virtual reality.

ESP, or (223) _____ communication, refers to the perception of objects or events through means other than sensory organs. Many psychologists do not believe that (224) _____ is an appropriate area for scientific inquiry. The ganzfeld procedure studies (225) _____ by having one person (the sender) try to mentally transmit visual information to a receiver in another room. Because of the (226) _____ problem and lack of replication of positive results, there is no reliable evidence for the existence of ESP.

Reflection Break 5

1. Using the material presented in this section, explain why food often "tastes" funny when you have a stuffy nose or cold.

2. Explain why some parts of the body are more sensitive to touch and pressure than others.

3. What is the general opinion of the psychological community as to whether ESP exists? Why?

REVIEW: KEY TERMS AND CONCEPTS

FINAL CHAPTER REVIEW

Review

Visit the *Psychology in the New Millennium* Web site at www.harcourtcollege.com/psych/PNM/ siteresources.html and take the Chapter Quizzes to test your knowledge.

Recite

Go to the Recite section for this chapter in your textbook. Use the tear-off card provided at the back of the book to cover the answers of the Recite section. Read the questions aloud, and recite the answers. This will help you cement your knowledge of key concepts.

Essay Questions

1. You have been hired by an appliance company to develop a print advertising campaign for a washing machine. Your consumer research tells you that the public perceives the machine as "big" and "clunky," and the dials "cheap" looking. Describe how you would use your knowledge of perceptual organizing principles to create the illusion of a smaller, less cheap looking machine that would sell better.

2. Explain why it would be more difficult for a one-eyed golfer to judge the distance to the pin than it would be for a two-eyed golfer.

3. Compare and contrast conductive and sensorineural deafness. How do people with each type cope with the impairment?

4. When some people have limbs amputated due to accidents or disease, they often feel pain from their "phantom" limb. Based on your knowledge of pain sensation and brain functions, how would you account for this phenomenon?

5. Sports require great sensory and perceptual skill. Think about your favorite sport, and identify the sensory input needed to perform that sport. Describe the actions of the various sense organs during play. How does the brain help coordinate the activities of all the sensory systems?

RELATE/EXPAND/INTEGRATE

1. **Sensations:** With a partner, blindfold yourself and walk around a familiar room. Note the sensory experiences that you have. How are they different then those you normally experience? Now visit an unfamiliar room. How is your sensory experience different? What sensory information did you rely on to avoid tripping and bumping into things? How is this different from the information that you use all the time? Now cover your ears and repeat the experiences. How is your sensory experience different without auditory versus visual experience?

2. **Laws of Perceptual Organization:**

   Similarity, proximity, and common fate: Examine magazines, newspapers, or children's books for illustrations that depict the above Gestalt organizational principles.

   Closure and continuity: Make line drawings of familiar objects by tracing pictures from children's coloring books, leaving out sections of the drawing. Ask your study partners or friends to identify the objects in the pictures. See how incomplete the drawings can be and still be identified.

   Present your illustrations of each of the laws on a poster board. Do not label them. Share your board with your classmates and see whether they can identify the principles.

3. **Perceptual Illusions:** Visit http://www.illusionworks.com. Examine some of the illusions. Try to describe which of the perceptual organizing principles and constancies are being used to create these illusions. Present your findings to your classmates.

4. **Taste Versus Flavor:** Do this with a partner.

   - Prepare slices of apple and other fruits of different textures, an onion, and different varieties of potato chips (sour cream and onion, salt and vinegar, and plain).
   - Blindfold your partner.
   - Begin with the potato chips. Have your partner pinch his/her nose closed. Place a potato chip inside his/her mouth. Can your partner tell you which flavor it is? Once he/she has guessed, allow your partner to unplug his/her nose. What happens to his/her experience of taste?
   - Repeat the same procedure with the rest of the chips, the fruit, and the onion.
   - When the objects were placed in your mouth with your nose closed, was it more difficult to identify what you tasted? Why?
   - What where you able to tell about the objects with your nose plugged? Does the texture of some of the food tell you anything?

5. **ESP:** Do you think that you might have psychic abilities? For one week, keep track of the times when you have special feelings about something that is about to happen or when you try to make something happen. At the end of the week, examine your report. Do the events that you predict actually happen like you predict they will? Were you able to successfully wish things into being? Does the week's data support the fact that you have psychic ability?

ANSWERS FOR CHAPTER 3

Reading for Understanding About "Sensation and Perception: Your Tickets of Admission to the World Outside"

1. Sensation
2. Central
3. Sense
4. Energy
5. Perception
6. Learning
7. Intensity
8. Absolute
9. Fechner
10. Lowest
11. Psychophysicists
12. constant
13. Difference
14. Minimum
15. Weber's
16. Just
17. Noticeable
18. Detection
19. Characteristics
20. Psychological
21. Hubel
22. Wiesel
23. Features
24. Angles
25. Auditory
26. Sensitive
27. Adaptation
28. Sensitization
29. Desensitization

Reflection Break 1

1. Sensation is a mechanical process that involves the stimulation of sensory receptors and transmission of the sensory information to the brain. Perception is an active process in which sensations are organized and interpreted to form a representation of the world.

2. According to signal-detection theory, the intensity of a stimuli is one factor in determining whether people will perceive sensory stimuli; another is the degree to which the signal can be distinguished from background noise; and still another is the attention that you pay to the stimulus. Your city slicker friend will be more apt to hear the quiet sounds of nature due to the lack of the normal noise he or she is used to hearing. The intensity and novelty of the of the new city sounds will cause you to hear them until you learn to block them out.

Reading for Understanding About "Vision: Letting the Sun Shine In"

30. Electromagnetic
31. Waves
32. Wavelengths
33. Hue
34. Shortest
35. Longest
36. Prism
37. Occipital
38. Cornea
39. Pupil
40. Iris
41. Lens
42. Retina
43. Photoreceptors
44. Cones
45. Rods
46. Optic
47. Ganglion
48. Fovea

49. Blind
50. Acuity
51. Shape
52. Presbyopia
53. Cones
54. Fovea
55. Dark
56. Rods
57. Brightness
58. Wavelength
59. Brightness
60. Lightest
61. Darkest
62. Cool
63. Warm
64. Complementary
65. Green
66. Yellow
67. Gray

68. Afterimages
69. Trichromatic
70. Red
71. Green
72. blue-violet
73. cones
74. opponent process
75. red
76. blue
77. dark
78. afterimages
79. trichromats
80. Monochromats
81. Dichromats
82. Total
83. Partial
84. Males

Reflection Break 2

1. v
2. d
3. r
4. w
5. j
6. s
7. g
8. aa
9. e

10. x
11. p
12. a
13. f
14. z
15. m
16. u
17. i
18. h

19. q
20. c
21. t
22. l
23. o
24. y
25. k
26. n
27. b

Reading for Understanding about "Visual Perception: How Perceptive!"

85. Recognizing
86. Relationships
87. Gestalt
88. Closure
89. Figure-ground
90. Ambiguous
91. Rubin
92. Necker
93. Proximity
94. Similarity
95. Continuity
96. common fate
97. top-down
98. bottom-up
99. retina
100. slowly
101. backward
102. apparent
103. autokinetic
104. Stroboscopic
105. Frames
106. Phi phenomenon
107. Depth
108. Monocular
109. Pictorial
110. Motion
111. Smaller
112. Perspective
113. Relative size
114. Clearness
115. Interposition
116. Shadowing
117. texture gradients
118. monocular
119. motion parallax
120. Binocular
121. Retinal disparity
122. Difference
123. Closer
124. Convergence
125. Constancies
126. Learn
127. Distance
128. Lighting
129. Illusions

Reflection Break 3

Gestalt Laws of Perceptual Organization

1. Similarity
2. Proximity
3. Continuity
4. Common fate

Perceptual Organization, Movement, Depth, Constancies, and Illusions

1. u
2. r
3. d
4. i
5. c
6. p
7. k
8. l
9. a
10. m
11. t
12. e
13. s
14. b
15. n
16. o
17. j
18. q
19. v
20. g
21. f
22. h

Reading for Understanding About "Hearing: Making Sense of Sound"

130. Auditory
131. Waves
132. Vibrations
133. Frequency
134. Loudness
135. Pitch
136. Frequency
137. One
138. Higher
139. Amplitude
140. Decibels
141. Zero
142. Loss
143. Ear
144. Outer

145. Middle
146. Inner
147. Eardrum
148. Amplifier
149. Bones
150. Vibrating
151. Oval
152. Cochlea
153. Chambers
154. Basilar
155. Corti
156. Hair
157. Basilar
158. Auditory
159. Louder

160. Front
161. turn
162. loudness
163. Corti
164. louder
165. pitch
166. place
167. Frequency
168. volley
169. deafness
170. Conductive
171. hearing aids
172. Sensorineural
173. cochlear

Reflection Break 4

1. Vibrating air molecules are funneled via the outer ear to the eardrum, which in turn vibrates and transmits the sounds to the middle and inner ears. The three bones in the middle ear (the hammer, anvil, and stirrup) vibrate, which amplifies the sound by increasing the pressure of the air in the ear. Attached to the stirrup is another vibrating membrane, the oval window. The round window of the inner ear pushes outward when the oval window pushes in and is pulled inward when the oval window vibrates outward. The vibrations are then transmitted to the cochlea, which is a bony tube that is divided into three fluid-filled chambers. The basilar membrane is one of these membranes. The organ of Corti is attached to the basilar membrane. It contains 16,000 receptor hair cells that dance in response to the vibrations of the basilar membrane. The movements of these cells generate the neural impulses that travel via the auditory nerve to the temporal lobe of the brain.

2. Place theory claims that the pitch of a sound is sensed according to the place along the basilar membrane that vibrates in response to it. This accounts for pitches greater than 4,000 Hz. Frequency theory claims that pitch perception depends on the stimulation of neural impulses that match the frequency of the sound waves. This appears to account only for perception of pitch between 20 and a few hundred cycles per second. Volley theory argues that groups of neurons take turns firing in response to sound waves of certain frequencies. This principle appears to account for pitch discrimination between a few hundred and 4,000 cycles per second.

Reading for Understanding About "The Chemical Senses: Smell and Taste"

174. chemical
175. odors
176. gaseous
177. olfactory
178. flavor
179. Taste

180. sour
181. bitter
182. texture
183. tongue
184. sweetness
185. twice

186. blind
187. genetic
188. taste
189. smell

Reading for Understanding About "The Skin Senses (Yes, It Does)"

190. skin
191. temperature
192. Touches
193. pressure
194. two-point
195. more
196. skin
197. separate
198. Pain

199. sharpest
200. originates
201. chemicals
202. Prostaglandins
203. inflammation
204. aspirin
205. neuromatrix
206. signal d etection
207. gate

208. phantom
209. decrease
210. spinal cord
211. acupuncturists
212. hypothalamus
213. endorphins
214. medical
215. information
216. successful

Reading for Understanding About "Kinesthesis and the Vestibular Sense" and "Virtual Reality and ESP"

217. Kinesthesis
218. tendons
219. vestibular
220. virtual reality

221. phobias
222. cybersex
223. psi
224. ESP

225. telepathy
226. file-drawer

Reflection Break 5

1. The flavor of food involves its taste but is more complex The flavor of food depends on its odor, texture, and temperature as well as its taste. It is our sense of smell that detects odors, and since when we have a cold our sense of smell is disrupted, so will our sense of the flavor of food be distorted.

2. Some parts of the body have nerve endings that are more densely packed. Additionally, more sensory cortex is devoted to the perception of sensations in these same areas.

3. Due to the difficulties in investigating "psychic" phenomenon using scientific methods and the inability in replicating those studies that have been conducted, psychologists remain skeptical about ESP and psychic phenomena.

Chapter 4

Consciousness

PREVIEW

Skim the major headings in this chapter in your textbook. Jot down anything that you are surprised or curious about. After this, write down four or five questions that you have about the material in this chapter.

Things that surprised me/I am curious about from Chapter 4:

Questions that I have about consciousness:

▲

▲

▲

▲

QUESTION

These are some questions that you should be able to answer after you finish studying this chapter.

Just What Is Consciousness?

▲ *What is consciousness?*

▲ *What is a circadian rhythm?*

Sleep and Dreams

▲ *What occurs during sleep?*

▲ *Why do we sleep?*

▲ *What are dreams, and why do we dream what we dream?*

▲ *What types of problems or sleep disorders can we encounter as we sleep?*

Hypnosis: On Being Entranced

▲ *What is hypnosis?*

▲ *What changes in consciousness are induced by hypnosis?*

▲ *How do modern psychologists explain the effects of hypnosis?*

Meditation: Letting Your World Fade Away

▲ *What is meditation? What are the effects of meditation?*

BioFeedback: Getting in Touch with the Untouchable

▲ *What is biofeedback training? How is biofeedback training used?*

Altering Consciousness Through Drugs

▲ *What are substance abuse and dependence? What are the causes of substance abuse and dependence?*

Depressants

▲ *What are the effects of alcohol?*

▲ *What are the effects of opiates?*

▲ *What are the effects of barbiturates and methaqualone?*

Stimulants

▲ *What are the effects of amphetamines?*

▲ *What are the effects of cocaine?*

▲ *What are the effects of nicotine?*

Hallucinogenics

▲ *What are the effects of marijuana?*

▲ *What are the effects of LSD and other kinds of hallucinogenic drugs?*

READING FOR UNDERSTANDING/REFLECT

The following section provides you with the opportunity to perform 2 of the R's of the PQ4R study method. In this section you are encouraged to check your understanding of your reading of the text by filling in the blanks in the brief paragraphs that relate to each of the preview questions. You will also be prompted to rehearse your understanding of the material with periodic Reflection breaks. Remember, it is better to study in more frequent, short sessions than in one long "cram session." Be sure to reward yourself with short study breaks before each Reflection exercise.

Reading for Understanding About "What Is Consciousness?"

What is consciousness? The term *consciousness* is a psychological (1) _____, or a concept that has been devised to help understand our observations of behavior, that has several meanings, including sensory (2) _____; the selective aspect of (3) _____; direct inner awareness; personal unity, or the sense of (4) _____; and the (5) _____ state.

(6) _____ as sensory awareness refers to our ability to be (7) _____, or conscious of the environment around us. Sometimes, however, we are (8) _____ of sensory stimulation, that is, unless we pay attention. Focusing on a particular stimulus is referred to as (9) _____, a concept important to self-control. To adapt to our environment we must (10) _____ which stimuli to pay attention to and which to ignore. Our ability to pick out what one person is saying in a noisy room is selective attention, also adeptly termed the (11) _____ effect.

We can also be conscious, or have direct (12) _____, of thoughts, images, emotions, and memories without sensory stimulation. This aspect of consciousness is difficult to measure (13) _____. Freud, the founder of (14) _____, differentiated between thoughts that are conscious and those that are (15) _____. Material that is not currently in awareness but is readily available is said to be (16) _____ material. According to (17) _____ some painful memories and unacceptable sexual and aggressive impulses are automatically ejected from our conscious awareness. (18) _____ of these memories and impulses allows us to avoid feelings of anxiety, shame, and guilt. When we choose to stop thinking about unacceptable ideas, Freud argued that we are engaging in (19) _____.

Controversy in Psychology: Is consciousness a proper area of psychological study? (20) _____ has not always been an acceptable topic of study in psychology. Early psychologists like William (21) _____ and John (22) _____ felt that consciousness was not a proper area of study because it could not be directly observed or measured. Today, however, many psychologists believe that consciousness lies within the (23) _____ and that we cannot capture the richness of human experience without referring to consciousness.

Reflection Break 1

1. What is a psychological construct?

2. Contrast the five different meanings for the psychological construct of consciousness presented in your textbook.

3. Is consciousness an appropriate area of study for psychologists? What do you think? Explain.

Reading for Understanding About "Sleep and Dreams"

What is a circadian rhythm? A (24) _____ is a cycle that is connected with the 24-hour period of the earth's rotation, such as the sleep–wake cycle. A cycle of wakefulness and sleep is normally 24 (25) _____ long.

What occurs during sleep? We undergo several (26) _____ of sleep during a normal sleep period. According to (27) _____ (EEG) records, the brain emits waves of different frequencies and amplitudes during each stage of sleep. Waves high in frequency are associated with (28) _____. There are (29) _____ stages of non-rapid-eye-movement (NREM) sleep and one stage of (30) _____ sleep. Stage 1 sleep is the (31) _____, and stage 4 is the (32) _____ phase of sleep.

As we begin to relax before going to sleep, our brains emit (33) _____ waves. As we enter stage 1 sleep, our brain waves slow down to a pattern of (34) _____ waves that are accompanied by slow rolling (35) _____ movements. During the transition from an alpha wave state to a theta wave state, individuals may also experience a (36) _____ state in which they experience brief dreamlike images that resemble vivid photographs. After approximately 30 to 40 minutes in stage (37) _____, the sleeper undergoes a steep decline into stages 2, 3, and 4. In stage 2, brain waves are medium in (38) _____, 4 to 7 cycles in (39) _____, and are punctuated by sleep (40) _____. During stages 3 and 4 our brains produce (41) _____ waves, with stage 4 being the (42) _____ stage of sleep. After about a half hour of stage 4 sleep we begin a relatively rapid journey back up through stages 3 and 2 into a (43) _____ movement (REM) state characterized by rapid, low-amplitude brain waves resembling those of stage 1 and the rapid movement of eyes beneath the closed lids. REM sleep has also been called (44) _____ sleep because the EEG patterns resemble those of the waking state; however, it is extremely difficult to awaken a person during REM. Each 8-hour period of sleep is characterized by approximately (45) _____ trips through the stages of sleep.

Why do we sleep? Sleep apparently serves a (46) _____ function, but we do not know exactly how sleep restores us or how much sleep we need. When we are (47) _____ of sleep for several nights, research has shown that several aspects of psychological functioning deteriorate, most notably (48) _____, learning, and (49) _____. The National Sleep Foundation estimates that sleep (50) _____ is connected with 10,000 crashes and 1,500 vehicular deaths each year. Animals and people who have been deprived of (51) _____ sleep learn more slowly and forget what they have learned more rapidly. It has been suggested that REM sleep may foster the (52) _____ of the brain before birth and may also help maintain (53) _____ in adults by exercising them at night. Additionally, individuals who have been deprived of REM sleep show (54) _____; they spend more time in REM during subsequent sleep periods.

What are dreams, and why do we dream what we dream? (55) _____ are a form of cognitive activity that occurs mostly while we are sleeping. Most dreaming occurs during (56) _____ sleep. Freud believed that dreams reflected (57) _____ wishes and "protected sleep" by keeping unacceptable ideas out of (58) _____. This theory has been challenged by the observation that our dream behavior is generally (59) _____ with our waking behavior. The (60) _____ hypothesis, a more biological view on the meaning of dreams, suggests that dreams largely reflect automatic biological activity by the pons and the synthesis of subsequent sensory stimulation by the frontal part of the brain. Another view of dreams is that with the brain cut off from the outside world, (61) _____ are replayed and consolidated during sleep. Still another suggestion is that REM is a way of testing whether the individual has benefited from the (62) _____ functions of sleep. When restoration is adequate, the brain (63) _____. The content of most dreams is an extension of the events of the (64) _____ day. (65) _____ are also dreams that occur during REM sleep.

What types of problems or sleep disorders can we encounter as we sleep? A common sleep disorder is (66) _____, which is most often encountered by people who are anxious and tense. Deep sleep disorders also include narcolepsy, (67) _____, sleep terrors, bed-wetting, and (68) _____.

According to the National Sleep Foundation, more than (69) _____ of American adults are affected by insomnia in any given year, with it more prevalent in (70) _____ than (71) _____. Factors contributing to insomnia include (72) _____, pain, children, (73) _____, bedding, nasal congestion, and (74) _____. The most common method of fighting insomnia in the United States is with sleeping (75) _____. Sleeping pills generally work by (76) _____ arousal, but this is often a short lasting effect and gradually the individual will develop a (77) _____ for many types of sleeping pills, meaning they will require higher doses to achieve the same effects. (78) _____ methods for coping with insomnia include relaxation exercises, biofeedback training, challenging exaggerated fears, establishing a regular routine, and fantasizing.

A person with (79) _____ falls asleep suddenly and irresistibly. The "attack" generally lasts approximately 15 (80) _____ after which the person awakens feeling refreshed, and may be accompanied by sleep (81) _____ in which the individual experiences a sudden collapse of muscle groups or even the entire body. Narcolepsy afflicts as many as 100,000 people in the United States and is considered to be a disorder of (82) _____ sleep functioning. (83) _____ and (84) _____ drugs have proved useful in treating narcolepsy.

(85) _____ is a dangerous sleep disorder in which the air passages are obstructed and the individual stops breathing periodically. The (86) _____ may cause the individual to suddenly sit up, gasping for air before falling back to sleep. Apnea is associated with (87) _____ and chronic loud (88) _____ and can lead to high blood pressure, heart attacks, and (89) _____. Causes of apnea include anatomical (90) _____ such as thick palate and problems in the breathing centers in the brain. Treatments include (91) _____, surgery, and continuous positive airway pressure.

The deep-sleep disorders, including (92) _____, bed-wetting, and sleepwalking, all occur during stage 3 or 4 and are more common in (93) _____. Sleep terrors are similar to (94) _____, but more severe. In them the dreamer (95) _____ fully wakes up and may recall a vague image of someone pressing on his or her chest. (96) _____ is often seen as a stigma that reflects parental harshness but may result from an immaturity of the nervous system. In most cases it resolves itself before (97) _____. Finally, (98) _____ affects about 15% of children. Sleepwalkers may roam about but typically do not (99) _____ their excursions.

Reflection Break 2

Stages of Sleep

Fill in the following chart describing the stages of sleep.

Stage One	Stage Two	Stage Three	Stage Four	REM Stage
• Type of Sleep?:	• Type of Sleep?:	• Type of Sleep?:	• Type of Sleep?:	• Type of Sleep?:
• Brain Waves?:	• Brain Waves?:	• Brain Waves?:	• Brain Waves?:	• Brain Waves?:
• Eye Movements?:	• Eye Movements?:	• Eye Movements?:	• Eye Movements?:	• Eye Movements?:
• Dreams?:	• Dreams?:	• Dreams?:	• Dreams?:	• Dreams?:
				• Other?

Sleep Disorders

Match the sleep disorder with its description.

a. insomnia
b. narcolepsy

c. apnea
d. sleep terrors

e. bed-wetting
f. sleepwalking

_____ 1. Often seen as a stigma that reflects parental harshness or the child's attempt to punish parents, but may result from immaturity of the nervous system.

_____ 2. Person falls asleep suddenly and irresistibly; attack may last 15 minutes, after which person awakens refreshed.

_____ 3. Often occurs in deep sleep; similar to, but less severe than, nightmares.

_____ 4. Disorder in which individual may stop breathing periodically; has been linked to obesity, anatomical deformities like thick palate, and chronic loud snoring.

_____ 5. People with this disorder show greater restlessness and muscle tension and are more likely to worry and report racing thoughts.

_____ 6. Contrary to myth, there is no evidence that waking individuals with this sleep disturbance leads them to become violent, although they may be confused.

Reading for Understanding About "Hypnosis: On Being Entranced"

What is hypnosis? (100) _____ is an altered state of consciousness in which people are suggestible and behave as though they are in a trance. Modern hypnosis seems to have begun in the 18th century with the ideas of Joseph (101) _____ but has only recently become a respectable subject of psychological study. Hypnosis has been used as an (102) _____ in dentistry, childbirth, and even surgery, and has also been used to teach clients how to reduce (103) _____ or overcome fears, lose weight, and prompt the memory of witnesses.

What changes in consciousness are induced by hypnosis? The hypnotic trance is not sleep as is demonstrated by differences between the (104) _____ recordings between the two. People who are hypnotized may show (105) _____, narrowed attention, (106) _____ (false memories), (107) _____ (heightened memory), suggestibility, assumption of unusual roles, perceptual distortions including (108) _____ and delusions, posthypnotic (109) _____, and posthypnotic suggestion.

How do modern psychologists explain the effects of hypnosis? Current theories of hypnosis deny the existence of a special trance (110) _____. Rather, they emphasize people's ability to (111) _____ the "trance" (role theory), to do what is expected of them (112) (_____ theory), and to divide their consciousness (113) (_____ theory) as directed by the hypnotist.

Reading for Understanding About "Meditation: Letting Your World Fade Away"

What is meditation? What are the effects of meditation? In meditation, one focuses "passively" on an object or a (114) _____ in order to alter the normal relationship between oneself and the environment. In this way, (115) _____ (that is, the normal focus of attention) is altered. (116) _____ meditation is a simplified form of Far Eastern meditation that was brought to the United States by the Maharishi Mahesh Yogi and often has the effect of inducing (117) _____. TM is practiced by repeating and concentrating on mantras, (118) _____ or (119) _____ that are claimed to help the person achieve an altered state of consciousness. TM appears to reduce the respiration and blood pressure of (120) _____ individuals. Meditation produces more frequent (121) _____ waves and increases the nighttime concentrations of the hormone (122) _____.

Reading for Understanding About "BioFeedback: Getting in Touch With the Untouchable"

What is biofeedback training? How is biofeedback training used? Biofeedback is a method for increasing consciousness of (123) _____ functions. In (124) _____, the organism is continuously provided with information about a targeted biological response such as heart rate or emission of alpha waves. People and lower animals can learn to control (125) _____ functions such as heart rate, blood pressure, and even the emission of certain brain (126) _____ through biofeedback training.

Reflection Break 3

1. Briefly describe the changes in consciousness induced by hypnosis discussed in your textbook.

2. How are meditation, biofeedback, and hypnosis different?

Reading for Understanding About "Altering Consciousness Through Drugs"

What are substance abuse and dependence? What are the causes of substance abuse and dependence? Substance (127) _____ is repeated use that persists even though it impairs one's social, occupational, or physical functioning. (128) _____ is more severe and has both behavioral and physiological aspects. Dependence may be characterized by (129) _____ one's life around getting and using the substance and by the development of (130) _____, or the body's habituation to the substance so that higher amounts are needed to obtain similar effects, (131) _____ symptoms, or both. An (132) _____ syndrome often results when level of usage suddenly drops off and may include anxiety, tremor, restlessness, weakness, rapid pulse, and high blood pressure.

People usually try drugs out of (133) _____, peer pressure, (134) _____, escape from boredom or pressure, and the seeking of (135) _____. Social-cognitive theorists suggest that usage can be (136) _____ by anxiety reduction, feelings of euphoria, and other positive sensations. People are also motivated to avoid (137) _____ symptoms once they become physiologically dependent on a drug. Biological views on drug use suggest that people may have (138) _____ predispositions to become physiologically dependent on certain substances.

Reading for Understanding About "Depressants"

What are the effects of alcohol? Depressant drugs generally act by (139) _____ the activity of the CNS. Alcohol, the most widely used drug, is a (140) _____. The effects of (141) _____ vary with the dose and duration of use. Low doses of alcohol may be (142) _____, while higher doses have a (143) _____ effect. Alcohol is also (144) _____ and can lead to physiological (145) _____. It provides an (146) _____ for failure or for antisocial behavior, but it has not been shown to induce such behavior directly. Some research has shown that drinking lightly may actually be (147) _____, reducing the risk of cardiovascular and Alzheimer's disease; however, health professionals are (148) _____ to advise that people drink regularly. Negative aspects of alcohol usage include (149) _____, due to its interference in the body's absorption of vitamins, and disorders like (150) _____ of the liver and Wernicke-Korsakoff syndrome. (151) _____ treatment has shown effective in teaching problem drinkers how to cope with temptations, but (152) _____ is the most widely used program to treat alcoholism.

What are the effects of opiates? Opiates are (153) _____ that are derived from the opium poppy; (154) _____ are synthesized in the laboratory and have a similar chemical structure. The opiates morphine and heroin are (155) _____ that reduce pain, but they are also bought on the street because of the (156) _____ "rush" they provide. (157) _____ use can lead to physiological dependence. It was originally thought that the use of (158) _____ would help those addicted to morphine overcome their physiological dependence; today, (159) _____, a synthetic opioid, helps heroin addicts avert the symptoms caused by withdrawal. (160) _____ withdrawal syndromes often begin with flulike symptoms and progress through tremor, cramps, chills alternating with sweating, rapid pulse, high blood pressure, insomnia, vomiting, and diarrhea.

What are the effects of barbiturates and methaqualone? Barbiturates and a similar drug, (161) _____, are also depressants. Barbiturates have medical uses, including relaxation, (162) _____, and treatment of epilepsy, high blood pressure, and insomnia. (163) _____ are popular street drugs because they are relaxing and produce a mild euphoria; however, they lead rapidly to physiological and psychological dependence.

Reading for Understanding About "Stimulants"

What are the effects of amphetamines? (164) _____ are substances that act by increasing the activity of the nervous system. (165) _____, called speed, are stimulants that produce feelings of euphoria when taken in high doses. But high doses may also cause (166) _____, insomnia, psychotic symptoms, and a "crash" upon (167) _____.

Amphetamines and a related stimulant, (168) _____, are commonly used to treat hyperactive children.

What are the effects of cocaine? Psychologically speaking, the stimulant (169) _____ provides feelings of euphoria and bolsters self-confidence. Physically, it causes sudden rises in (170) _____ and constricts blood vessels. (171) _____ can lead to restlessness, insomnia, psychotic reactions, and cardiorespiratory collapse.

What are the effects of nicotine? (172) _____ is an addictive stimulant that can paradoxically help people relax. Nicotine stimulates discharge of the hormone (173) _____ and release of many (174) _____, including dopamine and acetylcholine. Nicotine is the drug found in (175) _____ smoke, but cigarette smoke also contains carbon monoxide and (176) _____. Cigarette smoking has been linked to death from (177) _____ disease and cancer and to other health problems. Even (178) _____ smoking has also been connected with respiratory illness, asthma, and other health problems.

Reading for Understanding About "Hallucinogenics"

What are the effects of marijuana? (179) _____ substances produce distorted sensations and perceptions. Marijuana is a (180) _____, or hallucinogenic, substance whose active ingredients, including THC, often produce relaxation, heightened and distorted perceptions, feelings of empathy, and reports of new insights. (181) _____ may occur. (182) _____ elevates the heart rate, and the smoke is likely to be harmful. Although it has some (183) _____ uses, it impairs learning and memory and may affect the growth of adolescents.

What are the effects of LSD and other kinds of hallucinogenic drugs? (184) _____ is a hallucinogenic drug that produces vivid hallucinations. Some LSD users have (185) "_____," or distorted perceptions or hallucinations that mimic the LSD "trip" but occur days or weeks later. Other hallucinogenic drugs include (186) _____ and (187) _____ (PCP). Regular use of hallucinogenic drugs may lead to tolerance and psychological (188) _____.

Reflection Break 4

Altering Consciousness Through Drugs

Match the description with the drug name.

a. LSD	f. amphetamines	k. substance abuse
b. marijuana	g. barbiturates	l. tolerance
c. nicotine	h. opiod	m. abstinence syndrome
d. mescaline	i. opiates	n. substance dependence
e. cocaine	j. alcohol	

Descriptions:

_____ 1. A stimulant that produces euphoria, reduces hunger, deadens pain, and bolsters self-confidence; is derived from the coca plant and gave *Coca-Cola* its name.

_____ 2. A hallucinogenic drug, often smoked by mouth; produces relaxation, perceptual distortions, and enhancement of experiences; major psychedelic substance is THC.

_____ 3. Synthetic substance similar in chemical structure to opiates; most well known is methadone.

_____ 4. A depressant often taken via the mouth; produces relaxation, euphoria, and lower inhibitions; has been connected with aggressive behavior, poor grades, and sexual promiscuity.

_____ 5. Repeated use of a substance despite the fact that it is causing the individual to experience social, occupational, psychological, or physical problems.

_____ 6. The body's habituation to a substance such that with regular use the individual requires higher doses to achieve similar effects.

_____ 7. Depressants with several medical uses, including relief of pain, anxiety, and tension; treatment of epilepsy; high blood pressure; and insomnia.

_____ 8. Group of narcotics including morphine, heroin, codeine, and Demerol, derived from the opium poppy; often injected or smoked by mouth; produces relaxation, euphoria, and relief from anxiety and pain.

_____ 9. A hallucinogenic drug derived from the peyote cactus often taken by mouth that may lead to tolerance and psychological dependence.

_____ 10. Characteristic withdrawal symptoms that occur when the level of usage of a substance suddenly drops off.

_____ 11. A stimulant found in tobacco; stimulates the discharge of the hormone adrenaline and the release of dopamine and acetylcholine.

_____ 12. A group of stimulants first used by soldiers in World War II to help them stay alert; called speed, uppers, bennies, and dexies; side-effects include restlessness, loss of appetite, and psychotic symptoms.

_____ 13. A powerful synthetic hallucinogenic that produces vivid and colorful hallucinations; some users have flashbacks or distorted perceptions that mimic the original "trip" but occur days or weeks later.

_____ 14. Most severe of the substance use disorders; has both behavioral and biological aspects and is behaviorally characterized by loss of control over one's use of the substance.

REVIEW: KEY TERMS AND CONCEPTS

construct	122	bed-wetting	131	abstinence syndrome	137
selective attention	122	sleepwalker	131	delirium tremens	137
cocktail party effect	122	hypnosis	131	cirrhosis of the liver	141
direct inner awareness	122	Franz Mesmer	132	Wernicke-Korsakoff	141
preconscious	123	hypnotic trance	132	syndrome	
unconscious	123	hypnotic suggestibility	132	opiates	141
repression	123	hypermnesia	132	narcotics	141
suppression	123	age regression	133	opioids	141
nonconscious	123	hallucinations	133	methaqualone	142
circadian rhythm	124	posthypnotic amnesia	133	amphetamines	143
non-rapid-eye movement	124	role theory	133	cocaine	143
rapid-eye movement	124	response set theory	133	nicotine	144
alpha waves	124	neodissociation theory	134	hydrocarbons	145
theta waves	124	meditation	134	passive smoking	146
hypnagogic state	124	Transcendental	135	hallucinogenic	146
delta waves	125	meditation		marijuana	146
paradoxical sleep	125	mantras	135	psychedelic	146
REM rebound	126	biofeedback training	136	hashish	146
activation-synthesis	128	electromyograph	136	LSD	148
depressants	137	psychoactive substances	136	insomnia	128
narcolepsy	129	flashbacks	148	mescaline	148
sleep paralysis	129	stimulants	137	phencyclidine	148
apnea	130	substance abuse	137		
sleep terrors	131	tolerance	137		

FINAL CHAPTER REVIEW

Review

Visit the *Psychology in the New Millennium* Web site at www.harcourtcollege.com/psych/PNM/siteresources.html and take the Chapter Quizzes to test your knowledge.

Recite

Go to the Recite section for this chapter in your textbook. Use the tear-off card provided at the back of the book to cover the answers of the Recite section. Read the questions aloud, and recite the answers. This will help you cement your knowledge of key concepts.

Essay Questions

1. What are circadian rhythms? Why is it important for businesses and industry to have a good understanding of circadian rhythms?

2. You come home from school and want to take a real nap (not a "power nap") in which you get the most out of your sleep. If you are going to go into a deep sleep, based on your knowledge of the sleep cycle, what is the best length of time for you to nap? What would be the worst amount of time for you to sleep?

3. What evidence does your textbook give to support the argument that sleep is a restorative process? What are some of the arguments presented in the text used to explain why we sleep?

4. Compare Freud's view and that of the activation-synthesis model on why we dream.

5. Briefly describe the actions of the psychoactive drugs discussed in your textbook. Should our society place more control on the availability of alcohol and nicotine? Should marijuana be legalized? Explain your position.

RELATE/EXPAND/INTEGRATE

1. **Circadian Rhythms:** Monitor your circadian rhythm by mapping the times that you are awake and the times that you sleep for 2 weeks on the enclosed chart.

   Take your body temperature at 7 a.m., 11 a.m., 3 p.m., 7 p.m., and 11 p.m. and graph this data as well. Be sure to record your temperature to the nearest tenth of a degree.

   Do your sleep/waking times show a cyclic nature? How long does your cycle appear to be? Twenty-four hours? Twenty-five hours?

2. **Sleep Disorders:** Take the Sleep test at http://www.sleepnet.com/sleeptest.html.
   • Do your results suggest that you maybe at risk for any of the sleep disorders? If so, research them and their treatments.
   • Share your findings with your study group.

3. **Dreams:** Describe a recent dream of yours to your study partner, and have your study partner describe a recent dream to you.
   • What would a Freudian psychologist say about the content of this dream? How would the psychologist interpret the content?
   • Compare your analysis of your partner's dream to his or her analysis of your dream. Did you both interpret the "symbolism" in the dream in the same way?
   • Now, contrast the Freudian interpretation of the meaning of the dreams with the view presented by those biological theorists who ascribe to the activation-synthesis model. How would these theorists interpret the content of the dream?

4. **Hypnosis:** Read the information on hypnosis and its use presented at http://www.hypnosis.com/faq/faq0.html#contens.

Prepare an oral report for your class on hypnosis.
- What is it?
- How accurate are memories recalled under hypnosis?
- Does the evidence suggest that hypnosis can enhance the testimony of eyewitnesses?
- How effective has hypnosis been shown to be as a pain control method?

5. **Altering Consciousness Through the Use of Drugs:** Visit http://faculty.washington.edu/chudler/introb.html and research the effects of five psychoactive drugs. Prepare a poster comparing the actions and side-effects.

ANSWERS FOR CHAPTER 4

Reading for Understanding About "What Is Consciousness?"

1. construct
2. awareness
3. attention
4. self
5. waking
6. Consciousness
7. Aware
8. Unaware
9. selective attention
10. learn
11. cocktail party
12. inner awareness
13. scientifically
14. psychoanalysis
15. unconscious
16. preconscious
17. Freud
18. Repression
19. Suppression
20. Consciousness
21. James
22. Watson
23. Brain

Reflection Break 1

1. A psychological construct is a concept or a theory that is developed to help make sense or integrate the observations made of phenomena.

2. The construct of consciousness is defined as:
- Sensory awareness, or our ability to sense the environment.
- Selective attention, or our ability to choose what sensory stimuli in our environment to pay attention to and what to ignore.
- Direct inner awareness refers to consciousness as our awareness of our own internal thoughts, emotions, images, and memories.
- Personal unity refers to consciousness as our sense of self as a different, independent person.
- Waking state refers to consciousness as the aroused, alert state of a person.

3. Most contemporary psychologists would agree that consciousness is a proper area of study. However, a student could present a view similar to John Watson's and argue that it is not. Good answers would cite support from the text.

Reading for Understanding About "Sleep and Dreams"

24. circadian rhythm
25. hours
26. stages
27. electroencephalograph
28. wakefulness
29. four
30. REM
31. Lightest
32. Deepest
33. Alpha
34. Theta
35. Eye
36. Hypnagogic
37. One
38. Amplitude
39. Frequency
40. Spindles
41. Delta
42. Deepest
43. rapid eye
44. paradoxical
45. five
46. restorative
47. deprived
48. attention
49. memory
50. deprivation
51. REM
52. Development
53. Neurons
54. REM rebound
55. Dreams
56. REM
57. Unconscious
58. Awareness
59. Consistent
60. activation-synthesis
61. memories
62. restorative
63. awakens
64. previous
65. Nightmares
66. Insomnia
67. Apnea
68. Sleepwalking
69. Half
70. Women
71. Men
72. Stress
73. Noise
74. Allergies
75. Pills
76. Reducing
77. tolerance
78. Psychological
79. Narcolepsy
80. Minutes
81. Paralysis
82. REM
83. Stimulants
84. Antidepressant
85. Apnea
86. Obstruction
87. Obesity
88. Snoring
89. Stroke
90. Deformities
91. weight-loss
92. sleep terrors
93. children
94. nightmares
95. never
96. Bed-wetting
97. Adolescence
98. sleep walking
99. remember

Reflection Break 2

Stage One	Stage Two	Stage Three	Stage Four	REM Stage
• **Type of Sleep?:** *Non Rapit eye movement sleep* • **Brain Waves?:** *Low-amplitude brain waves of 8 to 13 cycles (alpha waves) shift to waves of 6 to 8 cycles per second (theta)* • **Eye Movements?:** *Slow rolling eye movements* • **Dreams?:** *Hypnagogic state in which we experience brief dreamlike images*	• **Type of Sleep?:** *Non-rapid-eye-movement sleep* • **Brain Waves?:** *Brain waves shift from theta waves to waves medium in amplitude with a frequency of about 4 to 7 cycle per second* • *Waves are punctuated with sleep spindles, waves with a frequency of 12–16 cycles per second* • **Eye Movements?:** *None to speak of* • **Dreams?:** *No report of dreaming*	• **Type of Sleep?:** *Non-rapid-eye-movement sleep* • **Brain Waves?:** *Brain waves shift to a delta wave with a frequency of 1 to 3 cycles per second* • **Eye Movements?:** *None to speak of* • **Dreams?:** *No reports of dreaming*	• **Type of Sleep?:** *Non-rapid-eye-movement sleep* • **Brain Waves?:** *Brain waves shift to a delta wave with a frequency of .5 to 2 cycles per second* • *Is the deepest stage of sleep, most difficult to be awakened from* • **Eye Movements?:** *None to speak of* • **Dreams?:** *No reports of dreaming*	• **Type of Sleep?:** *Rapid-eye-movement sleep* • **Brain Waves?:** *Brain waves are rapid, low-amplitude brain waves that resemble those of stage one* • **Eye Movements?:** *Rapid movement of eyes under closed eyelids* • **Dreams?:** *Most sleepers' report that they have been dreaming* • **Other?** *Also known as paradoxical sleep* • *When deprived of this we experience REM rebound*

Sleep Disorders:

1. e	3. d	5. a
2. b	4. c	6. f

Reading for Understanding About "Hypnosis: On Being Entranced"

100. Hypnosis
101. Mesmer
102. Anesthetic
103. Anxiety
104. EEG

105. Passivity
106. Pseudomemories
107. Hypermnesia
108. Hallucinations
109. Amnesia

110. State
111. role-play
112. response set
113. neodissociation

Reading for Understanding About "Meditation: Letting Your World Fade Away"

114. mantra
115. consciousness
116. Transcendental

117. Relaxation
118. Words
119. Sounds

120. Hypertensive
121. Alpha
122. Melatonin

Reading for Understanding About "BioFeedback: Getting in Touch With the Untouchable"

123. Bodily
124. Biofeedback
125. Involuntary
126. Waves

Reflection Break 3

1. The state of consciousness is referred to as the hypnotic trance. Traditionally, subjects are asked to narrow their attention to a small light or an object held by the hypnotist. The hypnotist usually suggests that the person's limbs are becoming warm, heavy, and relaxed. Subjects may also be told that they are becoming sleepy. Hypnosis is, however, different from sleep as shown on EEG recordings. Hypnotized people are said to have hypnotic suggestibility and are prone to fantasy, can compartmentalize unwanted memories, and want to cooperate with the hypnotist. Subjects are passive; have narrowed attention, pseudomemories, and hypermnesia; are suggestible; play unusual roles and experience perceptual distortions; apparently do not remember events that took place in the trance state; and are prone to posthypnotic suggestions.

2. In meditation the individual purposely (actively) thinks of a mantra, a word or sound that is designed to allow the person to achieve an altered state of consciousness. In meditation the individual demonstrates a relaxation response and the blood pressure of the individual may decrease; in hypnosis there does not appear to any change in blood pressure. In biofeedback, again, the individual purposely learns to change his or her body functions voluntarily.

Reading for Understanding About "Altering Consciousness Through Drugs"

127. Abuse
128. Dependence
129. Organizing
130. Tolerance

131. Withdrawal
132. Abstinence
133. Curiosity
134. Rebellion

135. Excitement
136. Reinforced
137. Withdrawal
138. Genetic

Reading for Understanding About "Depressants"

139. Slowing
140. Depressant
141. Alcohol
142. Stimulating
143. Sedative
144. Intoxicating
145. Dependence
146. Excuse
147. Healthy

148. Reluctant
149. Malnutrition
150. Cirrhosis
151. Cognitive-behavior
152. Alcoholics Anonymous
153. Narcotics
154. Opioids
155. Depressants
156. Euphoric

157. Opiate
158. Heroin
159. Methadone
160. Narcotic
161. methaqualone
162. pain management
163. Barbiturates

Reading for Understanding About "Stimulants"

164. Stimulants
165. Amphetamines
166. Restlessness
167. Withdrawal
168. Ritalin

169. Cocaine
170. blood pressure
171. Overdoses
172. Nicotine
173. Adrenaline

174. Neurotransmitters
175. Cigarette
176. Hydrocarbons
177. Heart
178. Passive

Reading for Understanding About "Hallucinogenics"

179. Hallucinogenic
180. Psychedelic
181. Hallucinations
182. Marijuana

183. Medical
184. LSD
185. Flashbacks
186. Mescaline

187. Phencyclidine
188. Dependence

Reflection Break 4

1. e
2. b
3. h
4. j
5. k

6. l
7. g
8. i
9. d
10. m

11. c
12. f
13. a
14. n

Time	Day 1	temp	Day 2	temp	Day 3	temp	Day 4	temp
11 pm								
10 pm		█		█		█		█
9 pm		█		█		█		
8 pm		█		█		█		█
7 pm								
6 pm		█		█				█
5 pm		█		█		█		█
4 pm		█		█		█		█
3 pm								
2 pm		█		█		█		█
1 pm		█		█		█		█
12		█		█		█		█
11 am								
10 am		█		█		█		█
9 am		█		█		█		█
8 am		█		█		█		█
7 am								
6 am		█		█		█		█
5 am		█		█		█		█
4 am		█		█		█		█
3 am		█		█		█		█
2 am		█		█		█		█
1 am		█		█		█		█
0 am		█		█		█		█

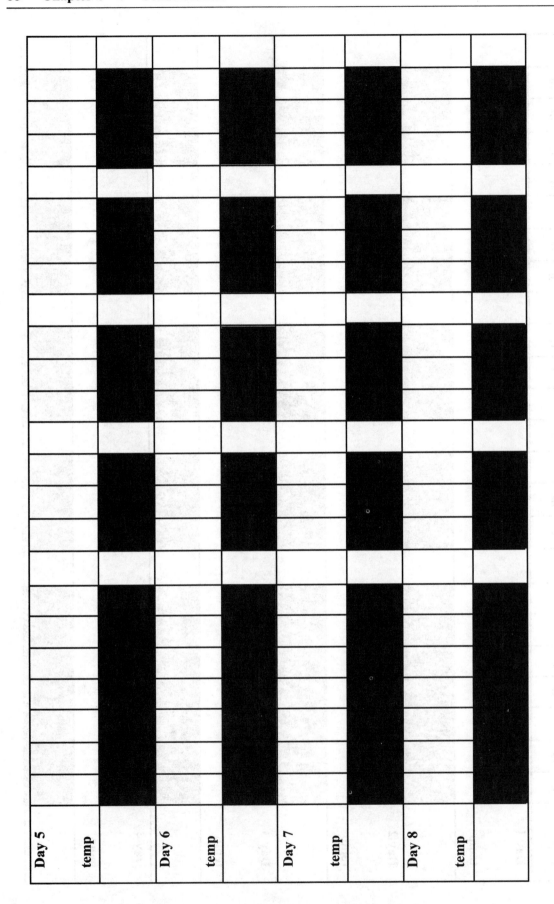

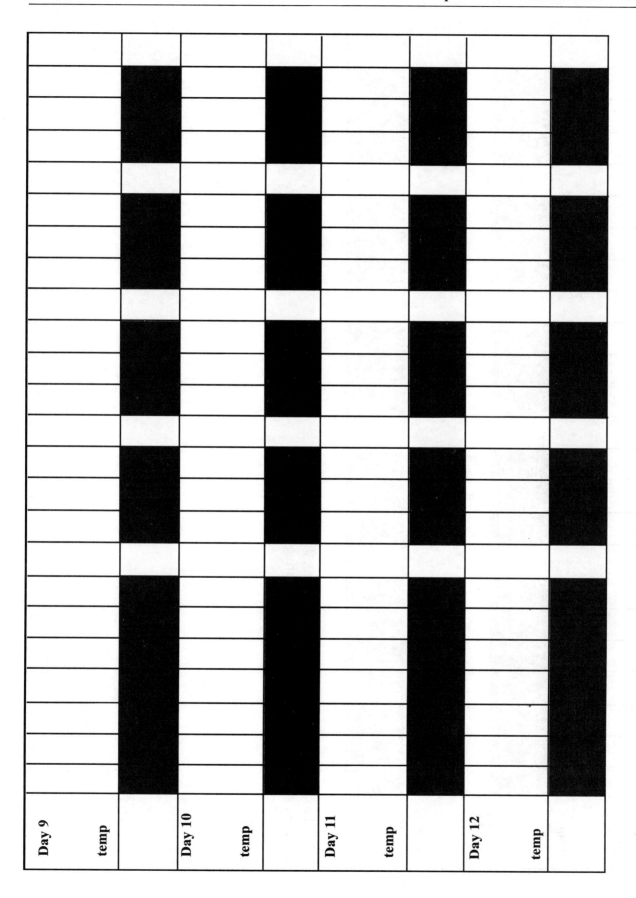

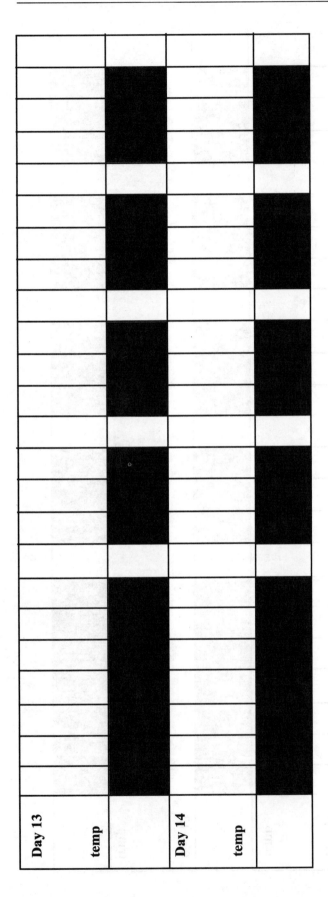

Color the squares red if you were asleep during those hours.
Color the squares green if you were awake during those hours.

Chapter 5

Learning

PREVIEW

Skim the major headings in this chapter in your textbook. Jot down anything that you are surprised or curious about. After this, write down four or five questions that you have about the material in this chapter.

Things that surprised me/I am curious about from Chapter 5:

Questions that I have about learning:

▲

▲

▲

▲

QUESTION

These are some questions that you should be able to answer after you finish studying this chapter:

Learning and Classical Conditioning

▲ *What is learning?*

▲ *What is classical conditioning?*

▲ *What is the contribution of Ivan Pavlov to the psychology of learning?*

▲ *What are the various types of classical conditioning?*

▲ *What are taste aversions? Why are they of special interest to psychologists?*

▲ *What are the roles of extinction and spontaneous recovery in classical conditioning?*

▲ *What are the roles of generalization and discrimination in classical conditioning?*

▲ *What is higher-order conditioning?*

▲ *What are some applications of classical conditioning?*

Operant Conditioning

▲ *What is the contribution of B. F. Skinner to the psychology of learning?*

▲ *What is operant conditioning?*

▲ *What are the various kinds of reinforcers?*

Factors in Operant Conditioning

▲ *What are the roles of extinction and spontaneous recovery in operant conditioning?*

▲ *Why did Skinner make a point of distinguishing between reinforcers on the one hand and rewards and punishments on the other?*

▲ *Why do many psychologists disapprove of punishment?*

▲ *What are discriminative stimuli?*

▲ *What are the various schedules of reinforcement? How do they affect behavior?*

▲ *How can we use shaping to teach complex behavior patterns?*

▲ *What are some applications of operant conditioning?*

Cognitive Factors in Learning

▲ *How do we explain what happens during classical conditioning from a cognitive perspective?*

▲ *What is the evidence that people and lower organisms form cognitive maps of their environments?*

▲ *How do people learn by observing others?*

▲ *What do we know about the effects of media violence?*

READING FOR UNDERSTANDING/REFLECT

The following section provides you with the opportunity to perform 2 of the R's of the PQ4R study method. In this section you are encouraged you to check your understanding of your reading of the text by filling in the blanks in the brief paragraphs that relate to each of the Preview questions. You will also be prompted to rehearse your understanding of the material with periodic Reflection breaks. Remember, it is better to study in more frequent, short sessions than in one long "cram session." Be sure to reward yourself with short study breaks before each Reflection exercise.

Reading for Understanding About
"Learning" and "Classical Conditioning"

What is learning? (1) _____ is the process by which experience leads to modified representations of the environment (the (2) _____ perspective) and relatively permanent changes in behavior (the (3) _____ perspective).

What is classical conditioning? What is the contribution of Ivan Pavlov to the psychology of learning? Classical conditioning is a simple form of (4) _____ learning that enables organisms to (5) _____ events. The Russian physiologist Ivan (6) _____ happened upon conditioning by chance, as he was studying (7) _____ in laboratory dogs. The salivation in response to meat powder is a (8) _____, or an unlearned response to a stimuli. Pavlov discovered that reflexes can be learned, or(9) _____, through association. Pavlov called his trained salivary responses (10) "_____ reflexes" because they were "conditional" upon the repeated pairing of a previously neutral stimulus and a (11) _____ that predictably elicited the target response. Today Pavlov's conditional reflexes are referred to as (12) _____ responses.

Thus, in (13) _____ conditioning, a previously neutral stimulus (the conditioned stimulus, or (14) _____) comes to elicit the response evoked by a second stimulus (the (15) _____ stimulus, or US) as a result of repeatedly being paired with the second stimulus. Behavioral psychologists explain the outcome of this process in terms of the publicly (16) _____ conditions of learning. The organism forms associations between stimuli because the stimuli are (17) _____, that is, they occur at the same time. Cognitive psychologists, on the other hand, view classical conditioning as the learning of (18) _____ among events-in other words, the focus is on the information gained by the organism.

What are the various types of classical conditioning? There are (19) _____ different types of classical conditioning. In (20) _____ conditioning, the CS is presented before the US. In the most efficient delayed conditioning procedure, the CS is presented about 0.5 second (21) _____ the US. Other classical conditioning procedures include (22) _____ conditioning, where the conditioned stimulus is presented and then removed prior to the presentation of the unconditioned stimulus; (23) _____ conditioning, in which the conditioned stimulus is presented at the same time as the unconditioned stimulus; and backward conditioning, in which the (24) _____ is presented first.

What are taste aversions? Why are they of special interest to psychologists? (25) _____ are examples of classical conditioning in which organisms learn that a food is noxious on the basis of a nauseating experience. Taste aversions are of special interest because they differ from other kinds of (26) _____ conditioning in two ways. First, learning may occur on the basis of a (27) _____ association, and second, the unconditioned stimulus (in this case, nausea) can occur (28) _____ after the conditioned stimulus (in this case, the flavor of food). Psychologists believe that taste aversions may provide organisms with an (29) _____ advantage because they motivate organisms to avoid potentially harmful foods.

Reading for Understanding About "Factors in Classical Conditioning" and "Psychology and Modern Life: Applications of Classical Conditioning"

What are the roles of extinction and spontaneous recovery in classical conditioning? Extinction and spontaneous (30) _____ help organisms adapt to environmental changes by updating their (31) _____ or revising their representations of the changing environment. (32) _____ is the process by which conditioned stimuli (CSs) lose their ability to elicit conditioned responses (CRs) because the CS is no longer associated with the US. According to the cognitive perspective, extinction teaches the organism to change its (33) _____ of the environment because the learned, or conditioned, stimulus (CS) no longer allows it to make (34) _____. Extinguished responses may show (35) _____ as a function of the time that has elapsed since extinction occurred. Thus, it appears that extinction of a conditioned response is not a permanent eradication but an (36) _____ of the response. (37) _____ psychologists argue that both spontaneous recovery and extinction are adaptive processes that allow organisms to successfully handle situations that recur from time to time.

What are the roles of generalization and discrimination in classical conditioning? What is higher-order conditioning? Generalization and discrimination are also (38) _____. (39) _____ helps organisms adapt to new events by responding to a range of stimuli similar to the CS. In (40) _____, organisms learn to show a CR in response to a more limited range of stimuli by pairing only the limited stimulus with the US. In (41) _____ conditioning, a previously neutral stimulus comes to serve as a CS after being paired repeatedly with a stimulus that has already become a CS.

What are some applications of classical conditioning? Some applications of classical conditioning include the bell-and-pad method for treating (42) _____, the conditioning of (43) _____ responses (as in the case of "Little Albert"), extinction of fears through methods such as (44) _____, where the client is exposed to the fear-evoking stimulus until the fear response is extinguished, (45) _____, in which the client is gradually exposed to fear-evoking stimuli while remaining relaxed, and (46) _____ in which a pleasant stimulus is repeatedly paired with a fear-evoking object, thereby counteracting the fear response.

Reflection Break 1

1. Briefly define learning from the perspective of a behavioral psychologist. How would the definition of a cognitive psychologist be different?

2. Identify the unconditioned stimulus (US), unconditioned response (UR), conditioned stimulus (CS), and conditioned response (CR) in the following scenario:

> Christy is a 1-year-old child. Since she was born, every time her parents go out they leave her with Aleshia, a babysitter. On every occasion as soon as Aleshia arrives, Christy's parents leave. Every time Christy's parents leave, she cries. At her birthday party, as soon as Christy sees Aleshia arrive, she begins to cry.

(US)_____   (UR)_____

(CS)_____   (CR)_____

Matching

a. counterconditioning
b. backward conditioning
c. delayed conditioning
d. spontaneous recovery
e. discrimination
f. higher-order conditioning
g. simultaneous conditioning

h. trace conditioning
i. taste aversions
j. extinction
k. generalization
l. flooding
m. systematic desensitization

_____ 1. The tendency for a conditioned response to be evoked by stimuli that are similar to the original CS.

_____ 2. Conditioning in which the US is presented before the CS.

_____ 3. A behavior therapy method used to reduce specific fears in which the individual is gradually exposed to the fear-producing stimulus under circumstances in which he or she remains relaxed.

_____ 4. Conditioning in which the CS is presented before the US and left on until the CR.

_____ 5. Adaptive conditioned responses in which an organism will avoid a potentially harmful food after a single exposure.

_____ 6. The tendency for an organism to elicit a CR to only a narrow range of stimuli.

_____ 7. A process by which CSs lose the ability to elicit CRs because the CSs are no longer associated with a US.

_____ 8. Conditioning in which a previously neutral stimulus comes to serve as a CS after being paired with another CS.

_____ 9. Conditioning in which the CS is presented and removed before the US is presented.

_____ 10. A behavior therapy method used to reduce specific fears in which the individual is exposed to the fear-evoking stimulus until the fear response is extinguished.

_____ 11. Conditioning in which the CS and US are presented together, alongside each other.

_____ 12. A behavior therapy method used to reduce specific fears in which a pleasant stimulus is repeatedly paired with the fear-evoking object.

_____ 13. The return of a previously extinguished CR as a function of the passage of time.

Reading for Understanding About
"Operant Conditioning" and "Factors in Operant Conditioning"

Pavlov's classical conditioning focused on how organisms form (47) _____ about their environments. (48) _____ conditioning, as you will see in this section, focuses on what they do about them.

The historic work of Edward (49) _____ at Columbia University was psychology's first formal study of the effects of rewards and punishments on learning. Thorndike studied cats in puzzle boxes and found that with (50) _____ it took progressively less time for the cat to solve the puzzle. Thorndike explained the cats learning in terms of the Law of (51) _____, which stated that a response is "stamped in" or strengthened in a particular situation by a reward. (52) _____, on the other hand, "stamp out" stimulus response connections.

What is the contribution of B. F. Skinner to the psychology of learning? B. F. Skinner developed the concept of (53) _____, encouraged the study of discrete behaviors such as lever pressing by rats, and innovated many techniques for studying (54) _____ conditioning such as the "Skinner box" and the (55) _____ recorder. He was also involved in the development of behavior (56) _____ and programmed learning. During World War II, Skinner was responsible for "Project Pigeon," in which he proposed that pigeons be trained to guide (57) _____ to their targets. Unfortunately for Skinner, and fortunately for the pigeon population, the Defense Department scrapped the project.

What is operant conditioning? Operant conditioning is a simple form of learning in which organisms learn to engage in behavior because of the (58) _____ of that behavior. Organisms learn to engage in voluntary behavior, or (59) _____, that result in desirable consequences. Operant behaviors that are (60) _____ occur with greater frequency.

To study operant behavior efficiently, Skinner devised an animal cage, or operant (61) _____. The operant chamber, or "(62) _____," allows for careful experimentation because experimental conditions can be carefully introduced and removed. In the box, an animal (usually a rat or pigeon) is reinforced for (63) _____ a lever.

What are the various kinds of reinforcers? Any stimulus that increases the (64) _____ that responses preceding it will be repeated serves as a reinforcer. (65) _____ include positive, negative, immediate, delayed, primary, and secondary reinforcers. Positive reinforcers (66) _____ the probability that an operant will occur when they are applied. Negative reinforcers also (67) _____ the probability that operants will occur, but by their removal. (68) _____ reinforcers are more effective than delayed reinforcers. Primary reinforcers have their value because of the organism's (69) _____ makeup. (70) _____ reinforcers such as money and approval acquire their value through association with established reinforcers.

What are the roles of extinction and spontaneous recovery in operant conditioning? (71) _____ and spontaneous recovery are also adaptive in operant conditioning. In operant conditioning, learned responses are extinguished as a result of repeated performance in the absence of (72) _____. (Why continue to engage in a response that goes unreinforced?) And, as in classical conditioning, (73) _____ occurs as a function of the passage of time, which is adaptive because things may return to the way they were.

Why did Skinner make a point of distinguishing between reinforcers on the one hand and rewards and punishments on the other? Reinforcers are defined as stimuli that (74) _____ the frequency of behavior. Rewards and punishments are defined, respectively, as pleasant and aversive (75) _____ that affect behavior. (76) _____, like reinforcers, tend to increase the frequency of behavior. Skinner preferred the concept of (77) _____ because its definition does not rely on getting inside the head of the organism. Instead, lists of reinforcers are obtained empirically, by observing their (78) _____ on behavior. (79) _____ are defined as aversive events that decrease or suppress the frequency of the behavior they follow.

Why do many psychologists disapprove of punishment? Many psychologists recommend not using punishment because it (80) _____, it does not suggest (81) _____ behavior, it may create feelings of (82) _____, it may only suppress behavior in the (83) _____ situation in which it is used, it may (84) _____ to the suppression of wide varieties of behavior, and it may suggest that recipients punish others as a way of coping with (85) _____. Psychologists suggest that it is preferable to focus on (86) _____ desirable behavior, or by using (87) _____ from positive reinforcement for unwanted behavior by ignoring the unwanted behavior.

What are discriminative stimuli? (88) _____ stimuli (such as a colored light) indicate when operants (such as pecking a button) will be reinforced (as with food). Discriminative stimuli act as (89) _____; they provide information about when an operant will be reinforced.

What are the various schedules of reinforcement? How do they affect behavior? (90) _____ reinforcement, in which every response is reinforced, leads to the most rapid (91) _____ of new responses; but operants are maintained most economically through (92) _____, or intermittent reinforcement. Responses acquired or maintained via partial reinforcement are said to be (93) _____ to extinction. A cognitive theorist would argue that this occurs because the organism does not (94) _____ reinforcement every time, therefore it persists in the absence of reinforcement.

There are (95) _____ basic schedules of partial reinforcement. In a (96) _____ schedule, a specific amount of time must elapse after a previous correct response before reinforcement again becomes available. In a (97) _____ schedule, the amount of time between reinforcements is allowed to vary. In a (98) _____ schedule, a fixed number of correct responses must be performed before one is reinforced. In a (99) _____ schedule, this number is allowed to vary. (100) _____ schedules maintain high response rates and fixed-interval schedules result in characteristic upward moving waves on a cumulative recorder known as a "fixed-interval (101) _____."

How can we use shaping to teach complex behavior patterns? In (102) _____, successive approximations of the target response are reinforced, leading to the performance of a complex sequence of behaviors.

Reading for Understanding on "Psychology in Modern Life: Applications of Operant Conditioning"

What are some applications of operant conditioning? We use applications of operant conditioning every day in our attempts to (103) _____ other people. Applications of operant conditioning include socialization, (104) _____ training, the token (105) _____, avoidance learning, behavior modification, and (106) _____ learning.

In (107) _____ children learn to be generous because their peers are more likely to play with them when they are. In (108) _____ organisms can gain control over functions that can be manipulated voluntarily, like muscle tension, by being provided with information. The (109) _____ apply operant conditioning by the use of tokens, such as poker chips, as a reinforcement for desired behavior when the tokens can be exchanged for other desirable things. (110) _____ learning uses both classical and operant conditioning to suppress behavior, and behavior modification uses reinforcers to increase desirable behavior and its absence decrease undesirable ones. Finally, programmed learning uses (111) _____ techniques to encourage the correct sequence of behavioral responses.

Reflection Break 2

1. How are classical and operant conditioning different? How are they the same?

2. Fill in this summary chart on reinforcement and punishment.

	Stimulus is desired (wanted, pleasant)	Stimulus is undesired (not wanted, unpleasant)
Stimulus is applied	**Example:** *Dog is given a treat when he obeys a command.* Does behavior increase or decrease? _____ Is this reinforcement or punishment? _____ If it is reinforcement, is it positive or negative? _____	**Example:** *You cursed, so you must do extra chores.* Does behavior increase or decrease? _____ Is this reinforcement or punishment? _____ If it is reinforcement, is it positive or negative? _____
Stimulus is removed	**Example:** *A student gets an F on a test, so he cannot go to Friday night's party.* Does behavior increase or decrease? _____ Is this reinforcement or punishment? _____ If it is reinforcement, is it positive or negative? _____	**Example:** *Your headache goes away when you take aspirin.* Does behavior increase or decrease? _____ Is this reinforcement or punishment? _____ If it is reinforcement, is it positive or negative? _____

Matching

a. programmed learning
b. shaping
c. punishments
d. variable-interval schedule
e. discriminative stimuli
f. token economy

g. fixed-ratio schedule
h. continuous reinforcement
i. biofeedback training
j. partial reinforcement
k. fixed-interval schedule
l. variable-ratio schedule

_____ 1. Application of operant conditioning techniques in which learners are presented with poker chips as reinforcement for desired behavior.

_____ 2. Schedule of reinforcement that a piecemeal worker is on when he or she is told that he or she will be paid for every five items produced.

_____ 3. Aversive events that suppress or decrease the frequency of the behavior they follow.

_____ 4. A method of learning that assumes that any complex task can broken down into a number of smaller steps.

_____ 5. A light or sound that acts as a cue in operant conditioning.

_____ 6. Behavioral training method in which successive approximations of the goal response are reinforced to encourage the acquisition of the response.

_____ 7. Schedule of reinforcement used by a car dealer offering cash rebates for car buying only in the months of January, April, July, and October.

_____ 8. Conditioning in which every response is followed by reinforcement.

_____ 9. Schedule of reinforcement used by a professor who gives unpredictable pop quizzes.

_____ 10. Conditioning in which only some responses are followed by reinforcements.

_____ 11. Schedule of reinforcement often used by casinos in their slot machines-payoff can come at anytime; the more responses you make, the more rewards; but you never know when the rewards will come.

_____ 12. Based on the principles of operant conditioning, this method trains individuals to gain control of autonomic functions such as blood pressure or control over a muscle.

Reading for Understanding on "Cognitive Factors in Learning"

How do we explain what happens during classical conditioning from a cognitive perspective?
Cognitive psychologists see people as searching for (112) _____, weighing evidence and making (113) _____; they use concepts such as mental structures, (114) _____, templates, and information processing to explain learning. According to (115) _____ theory, in classical conditioning organisms learn associations between stimuli only when stimuli provide new information about each other. From this perspective, classical conditioning does not occur mechanically but because it provides (116) _____.

What is the evidence that people and lower organisms form cognitive maps of their environments? Some evidence is derived from Tolman's research on (117) _____ learning. He demonstrated that rats can modify their cognitive map of the environment in the absence of (118) _____. Tolman differentiated between learning and (119) _____. He argued that organisms "learn," or acquire information about the environment, without being (120) _____ for doing so. This learning remains hidden, or latent, until the reinforcement provides the (121) _____ for the organism to perform what it has learned.

How do people learn by observing others? Albert (122) _____ has shown that people can learn to do things simply by observing others; it is not necessary that they emit responses that are reinforced in order to learn. Learners may then choose to perform the behaviors they have (123) _____ "when the time is ripe," that is, when they believe that the learned behavior is appropriate or is likely to be (124) _____. (125) _____ learning may actually account for most human learning.

What do we know about the effects of media violence?
Media violence can contribute to violent behavior by providing violent (126) _____, disinhibiting (127) _____ impulses, increasing the viewer's level of (128) _____, priming aggressive thoughts and memories, and (129) _____ the viewer to violence. Since the emphasis of observational learning is on (130) _____ processes, it appears that the effects of exposure to violent behavior can be toned down in children by (131) _____ them that the behavior does not represent the behavior of most people; that the behavior is not real; and that the real-life (132) _____ for violent behavior are harmful to both the victim and aggressor.

Reflection Break 3

1. In the first Reflection Break of this chapter you were asked to identify the unconditioned stimulus (US), unconditioned response (UR), conditioned stimulus (CS), and conditioned response (CR) in the following scenario:

   Christy is a 1-year-old child. Since she was born, every time her parents go out they leave her with Aleshia, a babysitter. On every occasion as soon as Aleshia arrives, Christy's parents leave. Every time Christy's parents leave, she cries. At her birthday party, as soon as Christy sees Aleshia arrive, she begins to cry.

   Now, that you have finished this last section on the cognitive factors in learning, explain why Christy cried when Aleshia arrived at the birthday party in terms of Rescorla's contiguity theory.

2. How do the results of research into cognitive factors in learning challenge behaviorist principles? In your answer be sure to discuss the impact of contingency theory and latent and observational learning.

REVIEW: KEY TERMS AND CONCEPTS

FINAL CHAPTER REVIEW

Review

Visit the *Psychology in the New Millennium* Web site at www.harcourtcollege.com/psych/PNM/siteresources.html and take the Chapter Quizzes to test your knowledge.

Recite

Go to the Recite section for this chapter in your textbook. Use the tear-off card provided at the back of the book to cover the answers of the Recite section. Read the questions aloud and recite the answers. This will help you cement your knowledge of key concepts.

Essay Questions

1. What are taste aversions? Think of a taste aversion that you have acquired. In a brief essay to your instructor and using your own experience as an example, explain the concept of taste aversion and how you acquired the aversion you have. Be sure to use the proper terms

to describe the learned behavior and its acquisition. Finally, in your essay answer the question "Do you agree with the notion that the existence of taste aversions provides support for the evolutionary perspective in psychology? Why or Why not?"

2. Briefly explain the difference between extinction and forgetting. Use concrete examples to illustrate each concept, and be sure to use clear operational definitions for all terms.

3. Your textbook author provides four examples of applications of classical conditioning (bell-and-pad training, flooding, systematic desensitization training, and counterconditioning). Briefly explain how each of these applications is an example of classical conditioning.

4. You have decided to run for public office in your town.. The local landfill is close to its capacity, and the major issue in this year's election has to do with trash. You feel that the solution to the town's problem is to encourage more recycling among the town's citizens. How would you encourage (shape) the town citizens to recycle? What type of incentives (rewards) might you offer?

5. Should children be punished for misbehavior? What are the effects of punishment? Does the research indicate that it works? If so, when is it most effective? Why do most psychologists disapprove of punishment?

RELATE/EXPAND/INTEGRATE

1. **Advertising and Conditioning:** You and your study partners are an advertising team, and you have been asked to develop an advertising strategy for a new brand of carbonated beverage (soda). With your study group, watch some current TV commercials for various brands of soda. What associations are the advertisers conditioning? How does this relate to the way the soda companies want you to see their product?

   With your study group, develop an advertisement for this new brand of soda. Present your advertisement to the class, and explain the conditioning principles that you used. What associations do you want to make with your brand? What rewards will you give consumers after they buy your product?

2. **Positive Reinforcement Tutorial:** Do you understand the concept of positive reinforcement? Take this tutorial and be sure you do!
   URL: http://server.bmod.athabascau.ca/html/prtut/reinpair.htm

3. **Negative Reinforcement U.:** Understanding negative reinforcement is often one of the most difficult concepts for students to grasp. A visit to Negative Reinforcement University will assure that you have clear understanding of this difficult concept.
   URL: http://www.mcli.dist.maricopa.edu/proj/nru

4. **Train Fuzz:** Have you ever tried to train an animal using conditioning techniques? Here's an opportunity for you to train a virtual animal. While you are training Fuzz, pay attention

to the various factors that influence whether Fuzz "learns" the desired behavior. Do you think that you also had to "learn" how to train Fuzz at the same time Fuzz had to learn what you wanted him to do? Do you think you could train Fuzz faster a second time? Why? URL: http://epsych.msstate.edu/adaptive/Fuzz/index.html

5. **Psychology in Modern Life: Applications of Classical and Operant Conditioning:** Think of the last time you learned something new; for example, a dance step, how to play a new song on an instrument, or how to play a new game. How did you learn this new skill? Did you learn it through associative learning? What form of conditioning was used?

ANSWERS FOR CHAPTER 5

Reading for Understanding About "Learning" and "Classical Conditioning"

1. Learning
2. cognitive
3. behavioral
4. associative
5. anticipate
6. Pavlov
7. salivation
8. reflex
9. conditioned
10. conditional
11. stimulus
12. conditioned
13. classical
14. CS
15. unconditioned
16. observable
17. contiguous
18. relationships
19. four
20. delayed
21. before
22. trace
23. simultaneous
24. US
25. Taste aversions
26. classical
27. single
28. hours
29. evolutionary

Reading for Understanding About "Factors in Classical Conditioning" and "Psychology and Modern Life: Applications of Classical Conditioning"

30. recovery
31. expectations
32. Extinction
33. representation
34. predictions
35. spontaneous recovery
36. inhibition
37. Evolutionary
38. adaptive
39. Generalization
40. discrimination
41. higher-order
42. bed-wetting
43. emotional
44. flooding
45. systematic desensitization
46. counterconditioning

Reflection Break 1

1. Behavioral psychologists define learning in terms of a change in observable behavior. Cognitive psychologists define learning in terms of mental changes that may or may not be observable. To the cognitive psychologist, learning is demonstrated by changes in behavior; to the behaviorist, the change in behavior is the learning.

2. Fill in the blanks:

(US) Christy's parents leaving   **(UR)** Christy crying when her parents leave

(CS) Aleshia the babysitter   **(CR)** Christy crying at the party

3. Matching:

1. k   6. e   11. g
2. b   7. j   12. a
3. m   8. f   13. d
4. c   9. h
5. i   10. 1

Reading for Understanding About "Operant Conditioning" and "Factors in Operant Conditioning"

47. anticipations
48. Operant
49. Thorndike
50. repetition
51. Effect
52. Punishments
53. reinforcement
54. operant
55. cumulative
56. modification
57. missiles
58. effects
59. operants
60. reinforced
61. chamber
62. Skinner box
63. pressing
64. probability
65. Reinforcers
66. increase
67. increase
68. Immediate
69. biological
70. Secondary
71. Extinction
72. reinforcement
73. spontaneous recovery
74. increase
75. events
76. Rewards
77. reinforcement
78. effects
79. Punishments
80. hurts
81. acceptable
82. hostility
83. specific
84. generalize
85. stress
86. rewarding
87. time out
88. Discriminative
89. cues
90. Continuous
91. acquisition
92. partial
93. resistent
94. expect
95. four
96. fixed-interval
97. variable-interval
98. fixed-ratio
99. variable-ratio
100. Ratio
101. scallops
102. shaping

Reading for Understanding on "Psychology and Modern Life: Applications of Operant Conditioning"

103. influence
104. biofeedback
105. economy
106. programmed
107. socialization
108. biofeedback
109. token economies
110. Avoidance
111. Shaping

Reflection Break 2

1. In classical conditioning we learn to associate stimuli so that a simple passive response that is made to one stimulus can also be made to another. In operant conditioning organisms learn to do or not to do things based on the consequences of their behavior. In both types of conditioning associations are formed; classical conditioning focuses on how organisms form anticipations about their environments, and operant conditioning focuses on what they do about them.

2.

	Stimulus is desired (wanted, pleasant)	Stimulus is undesired (not wanted, unpleasant)
Stimulus is applied	**Example:** *Dog is given a treat when he obeys a command.* Does behavior increase or decrease? **Increase** Is this reinforcement or punishment? **Reinforcement** If it is reinforcement, is it positive or negative? **Positive**	**Example:** *You cursed, so you must do extra chores.* Does behavior increase or decrease? **Decrease** Is this reinforcement or punishment? **Punishment** If it is reinforcement, is it positive or negative? **N/A**
Stimulus is removed	**Example:** *A student gets an F on a test, so he cannot go to Friday night's party.* Does behavior increase or decrease? **Decrease** Is this reinforcement or punishment? **Punishment** If it is reinforcement, is it positive or negative? **N/A**	**Example:** *Your headache goes away when you take aspirin.* Does behavior increase or decrease? **Increase** Is this reinforcement or punishment? **Reinforcement** If it is reinforcement, is it positive or negative? **Negative**

3. Matching:

1. f	5. e	9. d
2. g	6. b	10. j
3. c	7. k	11. l
4. a	8. h	12. i

Reading for Understanding on "Cognitive Factors in Learning"

112. information	119. performance	126. models
113. decisions	120. rewarded	127. aggressive
114. schemas	121. motivation	128. arousal
115. contingency	122. Bandura	129. habituating
116. information	123. observed	130. cognitive
117. latent	124. rewarded	131. informing
118. reinforcement	125. Observational	132. consequences

Reflection Break 3

1. According to Rescorla's contiguity theory, Christy cried when Aleshia arrived at the party because Aleshia's arrival (CS) provided information that the US, her parents leaving, was likely to happen.

2. Research into cognitive factors in learning challenges the traditional behaviorist idea that you must engage in behavior to learn. Both latent learning and observational learning suggest that organisms learn by watching; suggesting that an organism's mental representations of the environment may be important areas of study for psychologists.

Chapter 6

Memory

PREVIEW

Skim the major headings in this chapter in your textbook. Jot down anything that you are surprised or curious about. After this, write down four or five questions that you have about the material in this chapter.

Things that surprised me/I am curious about from Chapter 6:

Questions that I have about memory:

▲

▲

▲

▲

QUESTION

These are some questions that you should be able to answer after you finish studying this chapter:

Kinds of Memory: Looking Back, Looking Ahead

▲ *What is meant by explicit memory?*

▲ *What is meant by episodic memory?*

▲ *What is meant by semantic memory?*

▲ *What is meant by implicit memory?*

▲ *What is the difference between retrospective memory and prospective memory?*

Processes of Memory: Processing Information in our Most Personal Computer

▲ *What is the role of encoding in memory?*

▲ *What is the role of storage in memory?*

▲ *What is the role of retrieval in memory?*

Stages of Memory: Making Sense of the Short and Long of It

▲ *What is the Atkinson-Shiffrin model of memory?*

▲ *How does sensory memory function?*

▲ *How does short-term memory function?*

▲ *Why are we most likely to remember the first and last items in a list?*

▲ *Is seven a magic number, or did the phone company get lucky?*

▲ *How does long-term memory function?*

▲ *What is the levels-of-processing model of memory?*

▲ *Why is it that some events, like the death of JFK, Jr., can be etched in memory for a lifetime?*

▲ *H ow is knowledge organized in long-term memory?*

▲ *Why do we sometimes feel that the answer to a question is on the tip of our tongue?*

▲ *Why may it be useful to study in the room in which we will be tested?*

Forgetting

▲ *What types of memory tasks are used in measuring forgetting?*

▲ *Why can learning Spanish make it harder to remember French?*

▲ *What is repression?*

▲ *Can children remember events from the first couple of years of life?*

▲ *Why do people frequently have trouble recalling being in accidents?*

Using the Psychology of Memory to Improve Your Memory

▲ *How can people improve their memory?*

The Biology of Memory: From Engram to Adrenaline

▲ *What neural events are connected with memory?*

READING FOR UNDERSTANDING/REFLECT

The following section provides you with the opportunity to perform 2 of the R's of the PQ4R study method. In this section you are encouraged you to check your understanding of your reading of the text by filling in the blanks in the brief paragraphs that relate to each of the Preview questions. You will also be prompted to rehearse your understanding of the material with periodic Reflection breaks. Remember, it is better to study in more frequent, short sessions than in one long "cram session." Be sure to reward yourself with short study breaks before each Rehearsal/Reflection exercise.

Reading for Understanding About the "Kinds of Memory"

What is meant by explicit memory? Explicit memories, also referred to as (1) _____ memories, are memory for specific information. (2) _____ memories contain specific information that can be clearly stated or "declared." The information may be (3) _____ or refer to general knowledge. In contrast, (4) _____ memory is referred to as nondeclarative memory and is memory on how to do something, like perform a task. Psychologists have identified two types of explicit memories: (5) _____ and (6) _____.

What is meant by episodic memory and semantic memory? An episodic memory, also referred to as (7) _____ memory, is a memory of a specific event that one has observed or participated in. (8) _____ memories are the memories of the things that have happened to us. (9) _____ memory is general-knowledge memory, as in remembering that the United States has 50 states or that Shakespeare wrote *Hamlet*. We are more likely to say that we (10) _____ semantic memories and that we (11) _____ episodic memories.

What is meant by implicit memory? As we mentioned above, implicit memories are memories of (12) _____. Implicit memories are suggested, or implied, but not plainly stated and are illustrated by the things we (13) _____. (14) _____ memory means knowing how to do things, like write with a pencil or ride a bicycle. It is also called (15) _____ memory. Often, implicit memories are repeated so frequently that the associations become relatively (16) _____, a phenomenon that psychologists refer to as (17) _____.

What is the difference between retrospective memory and prospective memory? (18) _____ memories concern events in the past that can be explicit or implicit. (19) _____ memories involve remembering to do things in the future. There are various types of prospective memory; these include (20) _____ tasks, event-based tasks, and (21) _____-based tasks. Prospective memory is affected by factors such as distraction, (22) _____, and age.

Reflection Break 1

Fill in the blanks in the chart below on the relationships between the different types of memory:

_____memories
(remembering things past)

_____ memories
*(remembering things to
do in the future)*

_____memories
*(memories for specific
information)*

_____memories
*(memories of how to
perform tasks)*

_____memories
(memories of things you did)

_____memories
(memories of general information)

Reading for Understanding About "Processes of Memory: Processing Information in Our Most Personal Computers"

What is the role of encoding in memory? (23) _____ information means transforming information from the outside world so that we can place it in memory. We commonly use visual (pictures), auditory (sounds), and semantic (meanings) (24) _____ to convert physical and chemical stimulation into psychological formats that can be remembered.

What is the role of storage in memory? The second stage in the memory process is (25) _____. Storage means the (26) _____ information over time. The main methods of storing information are (27) _____, or rote repetition, in which you repeat information over and over again; and (28) _____, or relating it to things we already know. As we become more aware of the functioning of our memory, our (29) _____ becomes more sophisticated.

What is the role of retrieval in memory? (30) _____, the third memory process, means locating stored information and bringing it back into consciousness. Efficient retrieval requires use of the proper (31) _____ (just as to retrieve information stored on a hard drive, we need to know the filename.) (32) _____ is defined as the processes by which information is encoded, stored, and retrieved.

Reading for Understanding About "Stages of Memory: Making Sense of the Short and Long of It"

What is the Atkinson-Shiffrin model of memory? Atkinson and Shiffrin proposed that there are three stages of memory—(33) _____ memory, (34) _____ memory, and (35) _____ memory—and that the progress of information through these stages determines whether and how long it is remembered.

How does sensory memory function? Each sense is believed to have a sensory (36) _____ that briefly holds the memory traces of stimuli in sensory memory. The traces then (37)

_____ . Visual sensory memory makes discrete visual sensations—produced by (38) _____ eye movements—seem continuous. To demonstrate that visual stimuli are maintained in sensory memory for only a fraction of a (39) _____ , McDougall used the (40) _____ procedure in which he presented subjects 1 to 12 letters arranged in rows for a very brief amount of time and asked them to report every letter they saw. Sperling modified McDougall's procedure and used the (41) _____ procedure to show that we can see more objects than we can report afterward. In (42) _____ procedure, people were asked to report the contents of only one of the three rows, rather than all. Sperling also found that the amount of (43) _____ that elapsed before he indicated the row to report was crucial, and thus he concluded that the memory trace of (44) _____ stimuli decay within a second.

(45) _____ are mental representations of visual stimuli. The sensory memory that holds icons is called (46) _____ memory. Iconic memory appears to hold (47) _____ , photographic memories, but they are very brief. Some people, usually (48) _____ , can maintain icons over long periods of time and are said to have (49) _____ , or the extraordinary ability to "see" the memory trace of a visual stimulus in the sensory register long after the trace would have decayed in most people.

Echoes are representations of (50) _____ stimuli (sounds). The sensory register that holds echoes is referred to as (51) _____ memory. Echoes can be held in sensory memory for several (52) _____ . It has been suggested that the differences in the lasting duration of visual and auditory traces has to do with (53) _____ differences in the ear and eye. Nonetheless, both echoes and icons do (54) _____ with time; if they are to be retained, they must be attended to. Through the use of (55) _____ we sort out certain stimuli from background noise.

How does short-term memory function? (56) _____ memory is the second stage of memory processing. Focusing on a stimulus allows us to maintain it in short-term memory—also called (57) _____ memory—for a minute or so after the trace decays. In short-term memory the image tends to fade significantly after 10 to 12 seconds if it is not repeated or (58) _____ . Rehearsal allows us to maintain information (59) _____ . Once information is in our (60) _____ memory we can "work" on it, but it is not necessarily saved.

Why are we most likely to remember the first and last items in a list? This phenomenon is referred to as the (61) _____ . It has been suggested that this effect may occur because we pay more (62) _____ to the first and last stimuli in a series since they serve as the boundaries for the other stimuli. However, it may be that we tend to remember the initial items in a list because they are rehearsed most often (the (63) _____ effect) and that we tend to remember the final items in a list because they are least likely to have been displaced by the appearance of new information (the (64) _____ effect).

Is seven a magic number, or did the phone company get lucky? Miller showed that the average person can hold (65) _____ chunks of information (plus or minus (66) _____) in short-term memory. The appearance of new information beyond seven (67) _____ the old information.

How does long-term memory function? The third stage of information processing is (68) _____ memory. You can think of your long-term memory as a vast (69) _____ of information. There is no known limit to the amount of information that can be (70) _____ in long-term memory, and memories can be stored for a (71) _____. However, long-term memories have not been shown to be perfectly (72) _____. We might not be able to (73) _____ all of them; some may be lost because of improper (74) _____, or they might be kept unconscious by forces of (75) _____. Elizabeth (76) _____ notes that our long-term memories are frequently distorted and biased because they are reconstructed according to our (77) _____—that is, our ways of mentally organizing our experiences. Loftus and Palmer also showed that the memories of (78) _____ can also be distorted by leading questions.

Information is usually transferred from (79) _____ to (80) _____ memory by one of two paths: (81) _____ rehearsal (rote repetition) and (82) _____ rehearsal (relating information to things that are already known). The more often chunks of information are (83) _____, the more likely they are to be transferred to long-term memory, however, (84) _____ rehearsal is the more effective method. In this type of rehearsal we make information more (85) _____ by purposefully relating the new information to things already well known. It has been suggested that people who use elaborative rehearsal to remember things are processing at a (86) _____ level than people who use maintenance rehearsal.

What is the levels-of-processing model of memory? This model, proposed by Craik and Lockhart, views memory in terms of a single (87) _____-not three stages. It is hypothesized that we encode, store, and retrieve information more (88) _____ when we have processed it more deeply.

Why is it that some events, like the death of JFK. Jr., can be etched in memory for a lifetime? So-called (89) _____ memories, as of the death of a public figure like Princess Diana or JFK Jr., tend to occur within a web of unusual and emotionally arousing circumstances and to preserve experiences in detail. It is suggested that the reason the memory is "etched" is the (90) _____ of the memory; in other words, the events stand out because they are striking in and of themselves. Another suggestion may be that we may (91) _____ the experience more extensively-that is, relate them to many things, or elaboratively rehearse them.

How is knowledge organized in long-term memory? Memories in long-term memory are generally well (92) _____. We tend to organize information according to a (93) _____ structure. That is, we classify or arrange chunks of information into (94) _____ or classes according to common features

Why do we sometimes feel that the answer to a question is on the tip of our tongue? The (95) _____ phenomenon, or feeling-of-knowing experience, refers to the frustrating experience of knowing that you know something but not being able to remember it. Research suggests that the TOT phenomenon often reflects (96) _____ learning.

Why may it be useful to study in the room in which we will be tested? This is because memories are frequently dependent on the (97) _____ in which they were formed. That is, context dependence refers to the finding that we often retrieve information more (98) _____ when we are in the same context we were in when we acquired it. One of the more eerie psychological experiences associated with context-dependent memory is (99) _____, in which we find ourselves in a new place but have the feeling we have been there before. The déjà vu experience seems to occur when we are in a context similar to one we have been in before and the (100) _____ seems to lead us to think "I've been here before." (101) _____ memory is an expansion of context-dependent memory and refers to the finding that we often retrieve information better when we are in the same state of consciousness or mood we were in when we learned it.

Reflection Break 2

Fill in the blanks to review your understanding of the various types of memory and memory processes

Memory Processes:

- Process by which information is modified from one sensory modality so that it can be placed in memory

_____

- Process of maintaining information over time
- Can be done via maintenance or elaborative rehearsal

_____

- Process of finding stored information and bringing it to conscious awareness
- Dependent on cues

_____

Stages of Memory:

- First stage in memory processing
- Type or stage of memory that is first encountered by a stimulus and briefly holds an impression of it

_____Memory

- Second stage in memory processing
- Type or stage of memory that can hold information for up to a minute
- Also referred to as working memory
- Limited to 7 ± 2 chunks

_____Memory

- Third stage in memory processing
- Type or stage of memory that is capable of relatively permanent storage

_____Memory

Reading for Understanding About "Forgetting"

What types of memory tasks are used in measuring forgetting? (102) _____ syllables were developed by Ebbinghaus in the 19th century as a way of studying memory and forgetting. Since nonsense syllables are intended to be (103) _____, remembering them depends on (104) _____ rehearsal rather than elaborative rehearsal and thus makes them well suited for use in measurement of (105) _____. (106) _____ is often tested through three types of memory tasks: recognition, recall, and relearning, and nonsense syllables have been used to study each of them. (107) _____ is the easiest type of memory task used to measure forgetting, and forgetting is demonstrated by a failure to recognize a previously read syllable. (108) _____ is tested by asking the subject to produce syllables from memory or through a (109) _____ task in which subjects are shown pairs of syllables and then asked to recall one item of the pair when shown the other item. (110) _____ is the third assessment method. Ebbinghaus devised the (111) _____ to study the efficiency of relearning in which he measured the number of repetitions required to initially learn, then relearn a list of nonsense syllables. The difference between the first and second sessions is the "savings."

Why can learning Spanish make it harder to remember French? This is an example of (112) _____ interference, in which new learning interferes with old learning. In (113) _____ interference, on the other hand, old learning interferes with new learning. According to (114) _____ theory, people can forget because learning can cause cues (such as English words) to be connected with the wrong information (perhaps a Spanish word when a French word is sought).

What is repression? Repression refers to (115) _____ concept of motivated forgetting. Freud suggested that we are (116) _____ to forget threatening or unacceptable material. Psychoanalysts believe that (117) _____ is at the heart of disorders such as dissociative amnesia. Research on the recovery of repressed memories is quite (118) _____.

Can children remember events from the first couple of years of life? Probably not. This phenomenon is referred to as (119) _____. Freud believed that infantile amnesia is due to (120) _____, but modern psychologists believe that infantile amnesia reflects factors such as immaturity of the (121) _____ and failure to use acoustic and semantic (122) _____ to help remember information. (123) _____ explanations also include the arguments that (a) infants are not particularly interested in remembering the past; (b) infants tend not to weave episodes together into (124) _____ stories; and (c) infants do not make reliable use of (125) _____ to symbolize or classify events.

Why do people frequently have trouble recalling being in accidents? This is because the physical (126) _____ can interfere with memory formation. Two kinds of (127) _____ are caused by physical trauma. In (128) _____ amnesia, a traumatic event such as damage to the hippocampus prevents the formation of new memories. In (129) _____ amnesia, shock or other trauma prevents previously known information from being retrieved.

Reading for Understanding About "Psychology and Modern Life: Using the Psychology of Memory to Improve Your Memory"

How can people improve their memory? People can improve their memory through use of (130) _____ rehearsal, as in drill and practice, or (131) _____ rehearsal, as in relating new information to what is already known, forming unusual and exaggerated associations, using the (132) _____ , using mediation, or using (133) _____ devices or ancronyms.

Reading for Understanding About "The Biology of Memory: From Engrams to Adrenaline"

What neural events are connected with memory? Early in the century many psychologists used the concepts of the (134) _____ in their study of memory. Engrams were viewed as (135) _____ circuits in the brain that corresponded to memory traces-neurological processes that paralleled experiences. (136) _____ is apparently connected with the proliferation of dendrites and synapses in the brain. Learning and memory are also connected with the release of the (137) _____ serotonin and acetylcholine and the (138) _____ adrenaline and vasopressin.

What brain structures are connected with memory? The (139) _____ relays sensory information to the cortex and is therefore vital in formation of new memories. Visual memories appear to be stored in the visual (140) _____ , auditory memories in the auditory cortex, and so on. The (141) _____ is connected with the formation of visual memories.

Reflection Break 3

Matching

a. hippocampus
b. proactive interference
c. adrenaline and noradrenaline
d. recall
e. glutamate
f. relearning
g. method of savings
h. retroactive interference

i. vasopressin
j. paired associates
k. repression
l. nonsense syllables
m. anterograde amnesia
n. recognition
o. method of loci
p. mnemonic devices
q. engram

r. long-term potentiation
s. infantile amnesia
t. acetylcholine
u. retrograde amnesia
v. estrogen and testosterone
w. thalamus
x. interference theory
y. serotonin

_____ 1. Method of measuring retention of learned material by examining whether it is relearned more rapidly when presented a second time.

_____ 2. Electrical circuits in the brain that correspond to hypothetical memory traces.

_____ 3. Brain structure involved in verbal memories.

_____ 4. In Freud's theory, this is the ejection of anxiety producing ideas from conscious awareness.

_____ 5. Memory lapses for the period of time that follow a trauma, blow to the head, or operation.

_____ 6. Sex steroids; these hormones facilitate the functioning of working memory.

_____ 7. Method of memory enhancement that involves forming unusual associations with location.

_____ 8. Inability to remember memories due to older learning interfering with the capacity to retrieve more recently learned material.

_____ 9. Method of testing memory in which a subject is asked to indicate whether or not the nonsense syllable presented was presented before.

_____ 10. Memory device that organizes chunks of information into an acronym, jingle, or phrase.

_____ 11. Also known as antidiuretic hormone; use of this hormone in the form of a nasal spray has shown beneficial effects on memory.

_____ 12. Pairs of nonsense syllables in which memory is tested by presenting the first member of the pair and asking the subject to recall the second.

_____ 13. Failure to remember events that took place before an accident.

_____ 14. Ebbinghaus's method of studying the efficiency of relearning in which he measured the differences in the number of repetitions required to learn a list of nonsense syllables.

_____ 15. Method of testing memory used by Ebbinghaus in which he would ask the subject to recite a list of nonsense syllables.

_____ 16. These hormones work together to heighten memories for stressful events.

_____ 17. The term used to refer to the greater efficiency in neural transmission at synapses as learning progresses.

_____ 18. Increases in this chemical in the brain promote conditioning in mice.

_____ 19. The inability to retrieve old memories due to the interference from new learning.

_____ 20. Neurotransmitter that increases the efficiency of conditioning in sea snails.

_____ 21. Low levels of this neurotransmitter have been connected with Alzheimer's disease.

_____ 22. The inability to remember episodes or events that occurred prior to the age of 3.

_____ 23. The view of memory that argues that we forget material in short-term and long-term memory due to interference from other memories.

_____ 24. Sets of meaningless groups of consonants with a vowel sandwiched between them to make a syllable.

_____ 25. Part of the limbic system, brain structure believed to be responsible for storage of memories.

REVIEW: KEY TERMS AND CONCEPTS

episodic memory	189	eidetic imagery	197	déjà vu	209
declarative memory	189	photographic memory	197	state dependent memory	209
explicit memory	189	echoic memory	197	nonsense syllables	211
implicit memory	189	short-term memory	198	Hermann Ebbinghaus	211
autobiographical memory	189	working memory	198	recognition	211
semantic memory	190	serial position effect	199	recall	211
priming	190	primacy effect	199	paired associates	211
retrospective memory	191	recency effect	199	relearning	212
prospective memory	191	chunks	199	method of saving	212
encoding	193	George Miller	199	savings	212
visual code	193	rote	200	interference theory	212
acoustic code	193	displacement	201	retroactive interference	212
semantic codes	193	long-term memory	201	proactive interference	212
storage	193	repression	201	repression	212
maintenance rehearsal	193	schemas	201	dissociative amnesia	213
metamemory	193	maintenance rehearsal	204	infantile amnesia	215
elaborative rehearsal	194	elaborative rehearsal	205	hippocampus	215
retrieval	194	levels of processing model	205	anterograde amnesia	216
memory	194	flashbulb memories	206	retrograde amnesia	216
Atkinson-Shiffrin model	195	hierarchical structure	207	method of loci	218
saccadic eye movements	196	tip-of-the-tongue (TOT) phenomenon	208	mnemonic devices	219
sensory memory	196	feeling of knowing experience	208	engrams	220
memory trace	196	context dependent memory	209	long-term potentiation (LPT)	220
sensory register	196				
whole-report procedure	196				
partial-report procedure	196				
iconic memory	197				

FINAL CHAPTER REVIEW

Review

Visit the *Psychology in the New Millennium* Web site at www.harcourtcollege.com/psych/PNM/siteresources.html and take the Chapter Quizzes to test your knowledge.

Recite

Go to the Recite section for this chapter in your textbook. Use the tear-off card provided at the back of the book to cover the answers of the Recite section. Read the questions aloud, and recite the answers. This will help you cement your knowledge of key concepts.

Essay Questions

1. In a two-page essay, define short-term memory, and describe it in terms of its temporal duration and capacity. What suggestions would you give to a friend who wanted to improve her short-term memory capacity?

2. Do you know anyone with an extraordinary or photographic memory? In a brief essay to your instructor, describe the behaviors that suggested to you that this person might have such a memory. How did you account for your friend's abilities before you began this chapter? How do psychologists account for it?

3. Imagine that one week ago you moved to a new city. You now have a new address and phone number to remember. For the first few weeks when someone asks for your phone number, you will probably have a hard time remembering it. However, in six months, you will probably have difficulty remembering your old address and phone number. In a three-paragraph essay, name and detail the processes responsible for your failure to remember both the new and eventually old phone number.

4. Describe when police interviews of eyewitnesses to a crime should take place and how they should be structured in order to minimize the possibility that a witness would recall inaccurate information.

5. List and give examples of at least five ways you can apply your new knowledge about memory to improve your study skills and, therefore, your performance on your next psychology exam. Which study aid/method mentioned in your textbook do you find most useful for you in studying psychology? Why? Do you think that this method will work as well in other disciplines? Why or why not? What methods do you find more beneficial for studying for your humanities classes? Your biology classes? Your math classes? Why?

RELATE/EXPAND/INTEGRATE

1. **Psychology and Modern Life: Using the Psychology of Memory to Improve Your Memory:** Your textbook author suggests that the design (PQ4R) of the textbook is set up using the memory principles to enhance/encourage the ability of the student to better remember the material presented. Do you think that this approach has been successful? Has the PQ4R setup of the textbook helped you improve your retention of the course material? Which aspect of the method have you found most beneficial? Why? Which aspect of memory does this target?

2. **The Biology of Memory: From Engrams to Adrenaline:** In recent years the claims for the benefits of so called smart drugs have increased dramatically. Web sites like the one below have sprung up all over the Internet. Gingko, Vinpocetine, and MemRx are just a few herbal or food supplements that have been suggested to enhance your mental sharpness. Examine the Web sites below, and using your critical thinking skills, evaluate the claims made. What do you think? Is there enough evidence to convince you that these products work? Why or why not? Discuss your findings with your study group.

   Smart Products @ Brain.com
   URL: http://www.brain.com/products/nutriceuticals/memrx/

3. **Controversy in Psychology: False Memory:** Have you ever been convinced that you were remembering something accurately only to discover later that your memory was not as accurate as you thought? How did you account for the distorted memory? Why do you think you were so convinced that your memory was accurate? What position do psychologists take as to the accuracy of eyewitness reports? Research the articles on the Web sites below and present a summary of the various viewpoints. Which viewpoint do you feel presents the strongest argument?

   URL: http://faculty.washington.edu/eloftus
   URL: http://www.vcu.edu/hasweb/psy/psy101/forsyth/loftus.htm
   URL: http://www.apa.org/pubinfo/mem.html
   URL: http://www.skeptic.com/02.3.hochman-fms.html
   URL: http://www.jimhopper.com/memory/

4. **Stages of Memory: Gender Differences:** Are girls more likely than boys to remember dolls and teddy bears? Your text cites a study done by Renninger & Wozniak in 1985 that suggests that 2-year-old girls are more likely to remember dolls than cars and puzzles in photographs. Is there more evidence to support this claim? Using your favorite Web search engine, search for support for stereotypical gender patterns in memory. Present your findings to your class in a format specified by your instructor.

   URL: http://www.yahoo.com
   URL: http://www.google.com
   URL: http://www.dogpile.com

5. **Processes and Stages of Memory. Memory and Cognition Demos and Tutorials From Southwest Missouri State University:** Visit this site and explore the wide variety of demonstrations of memory phenomenon. The files are executable files that will run on Window 95, 98, or NT, so you can download them and explore them offline. Included are demonstrations of Sperling's iconic memory, levels of processing and encoding specificity, proactive and retroactive interference, serial position effect, short-term memory decay, and memory span. Download as many as you can and experience the different concepts.

URL: http://courses.smsu.edu/tab293f/mem/mydemos.html

ANSWERS FOR CHAPTER 6: MEMORY

Reading for Understanding About "Kinds of Memory"

1. declarative
2. Explicit
3. autobiographical
4. implicit
5. episodic
6. semantic
7. autobiographical
8. Episodic
9. Semantic
10. know
11. remember
12. doing
13. do
14. Procedural
15. skill
16. automatic
17. priming
18. Retrospective
19. Prospective
20. habitual
21. time
22. mood

Reflection Break 1

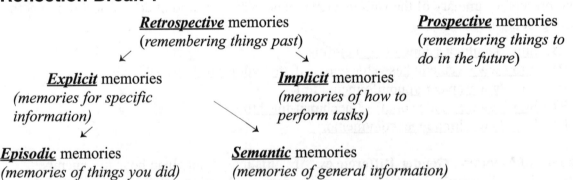

Retrospective memories
(*remembering things past*)

Prospective memories
(*remembering things to do in the future*)

Explicit memories
(*memories for specific information*)

Implicit memories
(*memories of how to perform tasks*)

Episodic memories
(*memories of things you did*)

Semantic memories
(*memories of general information*)

Reading for Understanding About "Processes of Memory: Processing Information in Our Most Personal Computers"

23. Encoding
24. codes
25. storage
26. maintaining
27. maintenance rehearsal
28. elaborative rehearsal
29. metamemory
30. Retrieval
31. cues
32. Memory

Read for Understanding about the "Stages of Memory: Making Sense of the Short and Long of It"

33. sensory
34. short-term
35. long-term
36. register
37. decay
38. saccadic
39. second
40. whole-report
41. partial-report
42. Sperling's
43. time
44. visual
45. Icons
46. iconic
47. accurate
48. children
49. eidetic imagery
50. auditory
51. echoic
52. seconds
53. biological
54. fade
55. selective attention

56. Short-term
57. working
58. rehearsed
59. indefinitely
60. short-term
61. serial-position effect
62. attention
63. primacy
64. recency
65. seven
66. two
67. displaces
68. long-term
69. storehouse
70. stored
71. lifetime
72. accurate
73. retrieve
74. cues
75. repression
76. Loftus
77. schemas
78. eyewitnesses

79. short-term
80. long-term
81. maintance
82. elaborative
83. rehearsed
84. elaborative
85. meaningful
86. deeper
87. dimension
88. efficiently
89. flashbulb
90. distinctiveness
91. elaborate
92. organized
93. hierarchical
94. groups
95. tip-of-the-tongue
96. incomplete
97. context
98. efficiently
99. déjà vu
100. familiarity
101. State-dependence

Reflection Break 2

Memory Processes:

• Process by which information is modified from one sensory modality so that it can be placed in memory *ENCODING*	• Process of maintaining information over time • Can be done via maintenance or elaborative rehearsal *STORAGE*	• Process of finding stored information and bringing it to conscious awareness • Dependent on cues *RITRIEVAL*

Stages of Memory:

• First stage in memory processing • Type or stage of memory that is first encountered by a stimulus and briefly holds an impression of it ***SENSORY*** Memory	• Second stage in memory processing • Type or stage of memory that can hold information for up to a minute • Also referred to as working memory • Limited to 7 ± 2 chunks ***SHORT-TERM*** Memory	• Third stage in memory processing • Type or stage of memory that is capable of relatively permanent storage ***LONG-TERM*** Memory

Reading for Understanding About "Forgetting"

102. Nonsense
103. meaningless
104. maintenance
105. forgetting
106. Retention
107. Recognition
108. Recall
109. paired assoc iates
110. Relearning
111. method of savings

112. retroactive
113. proactive
114. interference
115. Freud's
116. motivated
117. repression
118. controversial
119. infantile amnesia
120. repression
121. hippocampus

122. codes
123. Cognitive
124. meaningful
125. language
126. trauma
127. amnesia
128. anterograde
129. retrograde

Reading for Understanding About "Psychology and Modern Life: Using the Psychology of Memory to Improve Your Memory"

130. maintenance
131. elaborative

132. method of loci
133. mnemonic

Read for Understanding about "The Biology of Memory: From Engrams to Adrenaline"

134. engram
135. electrical
136. Learning

137. neurotransmitters
138. hormones
139. hippocampus

140. cortex
141. thalamus

Reflection Break 3

1. f
2. q
3. w
4. k
5. m
6. v
7. o
8. b
9. n
10. p
11. I
12. j
13. u
14. g
15. d
16. c
17. r
18. e
19. h
20. y
21. t
22. s
23. x
24. l
25. a

Chapter 7
Cognition and Language

PREVIEW

Skim the major headings in this chapter in your textbook. Jot down anything that you are surprised or curious about. After this, write down four or five questions that you have about the material in this chapter.

Things that surprised me/I am curious about from Chapter 7:

Questions that I have about cognition and language:

▲

▲

▲

▲

QUESTION

These are some questions that you should be able to answer after you finish studying this chapter.

Cognition

▲ *What is cognition?*

Cognition Concepts: Building Blocks of Cognition

▲ *How do concepts function as building blocks of cognition?*

Problem Solving

▲ *How do people go about solving problems?*

▲ *It is best to use a tried and true formula to solve a problem?*

▲ *What factors make it easier or harder to solve a problem?*

Creativity

▲ *What are the relationships among creativity, problem solving, and intelligence?*

▲ *What factors other than intelligence are connected with creativity?*

Reasoning

▲ *How do people reason?*

Judgment and Decision Making

▲ *How do people go about making judgments and decisions?*

▲ *How do people frame information in order to persuade others?*

▲ *Why do people tend to be convinced that they are right, even when they are dead wrong?*

Language: "Of Shoes and Ships and Sealing Wax, . . . and Whether Pigs Have Wings"

▲ *How do we define language?*

▲ *What are the properties of a "true" language as opposed to an inborn communication system?*

▲ *What basic concepts are used to discuss language?*

▲ *What does research reveal about the advantages and disadvantages of bilingualism?*

Language and Cognition

▲ *What are the relationships between language and cognition?*

▲ *Is it possible for English speakers to share the thoughts experienced by people who speak other languages?*

READING FOR UNDERSTANDING/REFLECT

The following section provides you with the opportunity to perform 2 of the R's of the PQ4R study method. In this section you are encouraged to check your understanding of your reading of the text by filling in the blanks in the brief paragraphs that relate to each of the Preview questions. You will also be prompted to rehearse your understanding of the material with periodic Reflection breaks. Remember, it is better to study in more frequent, short sessions than in one long "cram session." Be sure to reward yourself with short study breaks before each Reflection exercise.

Reading for Understanding About "Cognition" and "Concepts: Building Blocks of Cognition"

What is cognition? (1) _____ is defined as mental activity that is involved in the understanding, processing, and communicating of information. Cognition is also referred to as thinking, which entails to (2) _____ information, representing it (3) _____, reasoning about it, and making judgments and (4) _____. (5) _____ generally refers to conscious, planned attempts to make sense of the world.

How do concepts function as building blocks of cognition? Concepts are crucial to cognition. (6) _____ provide mental categories that allow for the grouping together of objects, events, or ideas with common properties. We tend to organize concepts in (7) _____. (8) _____ are good examples of particular concepts. Simple prototypes are usually taught by means of (9) _____, or positive and negative instances of the concept. (10) _____ concepts are usually formed through explanations involving more basic concepts.

Reading for Understanding About "Problem Solving" and "Creativity"

How do people go about solving problems? People first attempt to (11) _____ the problem. Successful understanding of a (12) _____ requires three features: the parts of our mental representation of the problem must (13) _____ to one another in a meaningful way; the elements of our mental representation must (14) _____ to the elements of the problem in the outer world; and we must have a (15) _____ of background knowledge that we can apply to the problem.

Once problem solvers (16) _____ the problem successfully, they use various strategies for attacking the problem, including algorithms, (17) _____ devices, and (18) _____. (19) _____ are specific procedures for solving problems (such as formulas) that invariably work as long as they are applied correctly. An example of a useful algorithm is the (20) _____ algorithm, in which you would examine every possible combination of problem elements.

Is it best to use a tried and true formula to solve a problem? Not necessarily. (21) _____ devices often help us "jump" to correct conclusions. Heuristics are rules of thumb that help us (22) _____ and solve problems. Heuristics are less (23) _____ than algorithms, but when they are effective, they allow us to solve problems more (24) _____. One commonly used heuristic device is (25) _____ analysis, in which we assess the difference between our current situation and our goals and do what we can to reduce the discrepancy. An (26) _____ is partial similarity among things that are different in other ways. The (27) _____ heuristic applies the solution of an earlier problem to the solution of a new, similar problem.

What factors make it easier or harder to solve a problem? Three internal factors make problem solving easier or harder. These include your level of (28) _____-experts solve problems more efficiently and rapidly than novices; whether you fall prey to a (29) _____ (mental sets can make our work easier but may (30) _____ us when the similarity between the problems is illusory); and whether you develop (31) _____, or that "Aha!" experience, into the problem. Often we may need to stand back from a problem and allow for the (32) _____ of insight. Other factors influencing the ease of problem solving include (33) _____, the extent to which the elements of the problem are fixed in function, and the way the problem is (34) _____.

What are the relationships among creativity, problem solving, and intelligence? (35) _____ is the ability to make unusual and sometimes remote associations to or among the elements of a problem in order to generate new combinations. Creative problem solving demands (36) _____ rather than convergent thinking. In (37) _____ thinking, thought is limited to present facts and the problem solver narrows his or her thinking to find the best solution. In (38) _____ thinking, the problem solver freely associates to the elements of the problem. There is only a (39) _____ relationship between creativity and academic ability.

What factors other than intelligence are connected with creativity? Creativity is characterized by (40) _____ thinking. Creative people show traits such as (41) _____, fluency, and (42) _____. The pressure of (43) _____ appears to reduce creativity, (44) _____ may foster creativity, and the effects of (45) _____, a group process that is intended to encourage creativity in which the group leader stimulates group members to generate a great number of ideas-even wild ones-and judgment is suspended until a later time, on creativity are debatable.

Reflection Break 1

1. What are the steps that you would go through to solve the problem of finding the best Chinese restaurant in your new town?

2. Why do people often find some problems difficult to solve?

3. What is the connection between creativity and intelligence? Is creativity a necessary aspect of intelligent behavior?

Reading for Understanding About "Reasoning" and "Judgment and Decision Making"

How do people reason? (46) _____ is the transformation of information in order to reach conclusions. Two types of reasoning used by people are (47) _____ and inductive reasoning. In (48) _____ reasoning, one reaches conclusions about premises that are true as long as the premises are true. In (49) _____ reasoning, we reason from individual cases or particular facts to a general conclusion that is not necessarily true. Most psychologists have assumed that all humans engage in the same basic cognitive processes. However, recent research has indicated that there may be (50) _____ differences in thinking. These studies suggest that (51) _____ cultures (Japan and China) tend to think more holistically, while Western cultures (U.S.) tend to think more (52) _____.

How do people go about making judgments and decisions? People sometimes make (53) _____ by carefully weighing the pluses and minuses, but most make decisions on the basis of limited information. Decision makers frequently use rules of thumb or (54) _____, which are shortcuts that are correct (or correct enough) most of the time. According to the (55) _____ heuristic, people make judgments about events according to the populations of events that they appear to represent. According to the (56) _____ heuristic, people's estimates of frequency or probability are based on how easy it is to find examples of relevant events. According to the (57) _____ heuristic, we adjust our initial estimates as we receive additional information-but we often do so unwillingly.

How do people frame information in order to persuade others? People frequently phrase or frame arguments in ways to (58) _____ others. The (59) _____ effect refers to the way in which wording, or the context in which information is presented, can influence decision making. For example, people on both sides of the abortion issue present themselves as being in favor of an important value either pro-life or pro-choice.

Why do people tend to be convinced that they are right, even when they are dead wrong? People tend to be (60) _____ about their decisions, whether they are right or wrong. People tend to retain their convictions, even when proven false, for several reasons. These include that they tend to be unaware of the flimsiness of their assumptions, they tend to focus on events that (61) _____ their judgments, they tend to forget things that run counter to their judgments, and they work to bring about results consistent with their judgments.

Reflection Break 2

Match the term with its proper description.

Terms:

a. deductive reasoning
b. framing effect
c. availability heuristic
d. inductive reasoning

e. heuristic devices
f. reasoning
g. representativeness heuristic
h. anchoring and adjustment heuristic

Descriptions:

_____ 1. Wording or presenting information in such a way as to influence decisions or judgments.

_____ 2. Heuristic in which we base our decisions on initial views or presumptions.

_____ 3. Rules of thumb used in decision making.

_____ 4. Decision-making rule based on how easy it is to find examples of relevant events.

_____ 5. The reorganization of information in order to reach a conclusion.

_____ 6. Reasoning in which general decisions or conclusions are made based on individual cases.

_____ 7. Decision making based on the population of events that a sample represents.

_____ 8. Reasoning that reaches conclusions based on an initial premise.

Reading for Understanding About "Language: 'Of Shoes and Ships and Sealing Wax, . . . and Whether Pigs Have Wings'" and "Language and Cognition"

How do we define language? What are the properties of a "true" language as opposed to an inborn communication system? (62) _____ is the communication of thoughts and feelings by means of symbols that are arranged according to rules of grammar. True language is distinguished from the communication systems of lower animals by properties such as semanticity, infinite creativity, and (63) _____. (64) _____ means that the symbols of a language have meaning. Infinite creativity is the capacity to combine words into (65) _____, never-spoken-before sentences. (66) _____ is the ability to communicate information about events and objects from another time or place.

What basic concepts are used to discuss language? The basic concepts of language include (67) _____ (sounds), (68) _____ (units of meaning), (69) _____ (word order), and (70) _____ (the meanings of words and groups of words). Phonemes are the smallest units of (71) _____ in a language, and morphemes, the smallest units of (72) _____. Morphemes that are tacked onto the ends of nouns and verbs are referred to as (73) _____, or grammatical markers, that change the form of the word to indicate grammatical relationships such as number (singular vs. plural), and tense (present, past, or future). (74) _____ deals with the ways words are strung together, or ordered, to create phrases and sentences. The rules for word order are the (75) _____ of the language.

What does research reveal about the advantages and disadvantages of bilingualism? Most people throughout the world are (76) _____. Contemporary research reveals that bilingualism (77) _____ people's perspectives and often helps them better learn their first language.

What are the relationships between language and cognition? The relationship between language and cognition is complex. Piaget believed that language reflects (78) _____ of the world but that much knowledge can be (79) _____ without language. (80) _____ is not necessary for cognition, but language makes possible cognitive activity that involves use of symbols arranged according to rules of grammar.

Is it possible for English speakers to share the thoughts experienced by people who speak other languages? Perhaps it is. According to the (81) _____ hypothesis, the concepts we use to understand the world are derived from our language. Therefore, speakers of various languages would (82) _____ about the world in different ways. However, modern cognitive scientists suggest that the (83) _____ of a language suggests the range of concepts that the users have traditionally found to be useful, not their cognitive limits.

Reflection Break 3

1. What are the characteristics of language? How do psychologists distinguish true language from the communication systems of lower animals?

2. What special opportunities or problems are connected with bilingualism? What advantages are there for bilingual children? Based on what you have learned about cognition and language, what do you think: should children who do not speak English in the home be taught in their native language in U.S. schools? Why or why not?

REVIEW: KEY TERMS AND CONCEPTS

cognition	230	insight	235	semanticity	246
thinking	230	incubation	235	infinite creativity	246
concepts	230	functional fixedness	236	displacement	246
hierarchies	231	creativity	237	phonology	247
prototypes	231	convergent thinking	237	phoneme	247
exemplars	231	divergent thinking	237	morphemes	247
positive instances	231	brainstorming	239	inflections	247
negative instances	231	reasoning	240	semantics	248
overextension	231	deductive reasoning	240	transitional program	249
understanding	232	inductive reasoning	240	maintenance method	249
algorithm	233	representativeness heuristic	243	two-way immersion	249
systematic random search	233	availability heuristic	243	cognates	249
heuristics	233	anchoring and adjustment heuristic	243	linguistic-relativity hypothesis	251
means-end analysis	233	framing effect	244		
analogy	234	language	245		
mental set	235				

FINAL CHAPTER REVIEW

Review

Visit the *Psychology in the New Millennium* Web site at www.harcourtcollege.com/psych/PNM/siteresources.html and take the Chapter Quizzes to test your knowledge.

Recite

Go to the Recite section for this chapter in your textbook. Use the tear-off card provided at the back of the book to cover the answers of the Recite section. Read the questions aloud, and recite the answers. This will help you cement your knowledge of key concepts.

Essay Questions

1. Have you ever thought about a problem for a long time and then had the solution just "come to you in a flash?" Why do you think that it happened like that? What was the experience like? What do you think happens within us when we stand back from a problem and allow insight to "incubate?" How do psychologists explain the occurrence of insight?

2. Do you know some brilliant people who aren't very creative? Do you know some creative people who are not necessarily brilliant? What do you think is the connection between creativity and intelligence? What does the psychological evidence suggest?

3. Provide two examples of times in your life that you used deductive reasoning. Explain why these examples are deductive reasoning and not inductive reasoning. Now, provide two examples of times when you used inductive reasoning. Explain why these examples are not deductive reasoning and are inductive reasoning.

4. Do you sometimes make decisions without all the information you need? Do you think that you could ever give up, or at least seriously change, your political or religious beliefs? Why or why not? (In your response, remember that we have not asked for you to promote your view, but to examine how strongly you hold it and why it is held that strongly.)

   Do you know people who refuse to change their minds even when they are shown to be wrong? What about you? Do you have beliefs that you refuse to change even though the evidence suggests that you may be wrong? How do you explain the reluctance to make changes? How do psychologists explain this? Explain your answers in a two-page essay for your instructor.

5. Do you think that you can force creativity? How does pressure affect your creative abilities? Does it stimulate you to be more or less creative? Does it make creativity more difficult, or does the pressure make it easier? Why do you think this may be the case? What does the evidence suggest? Present your answers in a two-page essay. Be sure to support your answers with citations of research examples.

RELATE/EXPAND/INTEGRATE

1. **Cognition:** Participate in one of the cognitive psychology experiments online at the Cognitive Psychology Experiments @ Purdue University or the Experimental Psych Lab links. How did participation in this study help expand your understanding of cognitive science? Describe your experience to the members of your study group, and compare your experience to those of the other members of the group.

   Cognitive Psychology Experiments @ Purdue University
   URL: http://coglab.psych.purdue.edu
   Experimental Psych Lab
   URL: http://www.psych.unuzh.ch/genpsy/ulf/lab/webexppsylab.html

2. **Problem Solving:** What is an expert? Are you an expert at something? What are you an expert at? How do you know that you are an expert? Justify your answer by citing the qualities of an expert, and explain how you meet those characteristics. How did you get to be an expert? Do you think that your path to "expert status" is typical or unusual? Why? Research the concept of expertise using your favorite Internet search engine and formulate your answers to these questions. Report your conclusions to your classmates in a format specified by your instructor.

   URL: http://www.yahoo.com
   URL: http://www.google.com
   URL: http://www.dogpile.com

3. **21st-Century Problem Solving:** This site claims that "You have the opportunity to learn to solve problems easily and reliably. You only need to take the time to understand how problems are solved. This site shows you how to do this. Problem solving will no longer be an uphill battle." Visit the 21st Century Problem Solving site and try some of the recommendations. Did you find that your problem-solving abilities improved? Do you find the claims of this site justified? Why or why not? Compare your experience with those of the other members of your study group.

   URL: http://www2.hawaii.edu/suremath/howTo.html

4. **Creativity:** Do you consider yourself to be creative? Why or why not? Justify your answer by describing the characteristics of creativity. Do you think that you could become more creative? Visit the Creativity Web and the information presented to help you become more creative. Resources are numerous and include books, software, and techniques. Additional resources are included to stimulate your thinking: quotations, affirmations, and humor. After examining these resources, did you change your mind? Which resources did you find helpful? Present a report to your study group in how its members might improve their creativity based on your findings.

   URL: http://www.ozemail.com.au/~caveman/Creative/

5. **Psychology and Modern Life: Making Decisions about Self-Help Books: Are There Any Quick Fixes?** Visit *Self-Help Magazine OnLine* at http://www.shpm.com and pick one of the articles in the most recent issues. Does the author of the article provide enough good-quality evidence to support the claims made? What evidence is provided? Why is the evidence sufficient or insufficient? What type of thinking did you use to reach your conclusion? What kind of heuristic devices do most people use when they make judgments as to the reliability of the information found in self-help books? Has your approach to this type of information changed since you began the course? How? Share your article with your study partner. Does he or she reach the same conclusions as you do?

   URL: http://www.shpm.com

6. **Language.** Have you ever known anyone to claim that a pet could "speak" or understand English or another language? Did the pet really "speak?" Did the pet really "understand" language? What was the nature of the evidence presented to convince you? What was your conclusion?

   Do you believe that nonhuman animals are capable of true language? How do psychologists distinguish true language from the communication system of "lower" animals? Visit the Web links on animal language listed below. Did your view on animal language change after your visits to these Web sites? Report your findings in a one-page position paper.

   URL: http://pubpages.unh.edu/~jel/apelang.html
   URL: http://www.cages.org/research/pepperberg/index.html
   URL: http://www.santafe.edu/~johnson/articles.chimp.html

ANSWERS FOR CHAPTER 7

Reading for Understanding About "Cognition" and "Concepts: Building Blocks of Cognition":

1. Cognition
2. attending
3. mentally
4. decisions
5. Thinking
6. Concepts
7. hierarchies
8. Prototypes
9. exemplars
10. Abstract
11. understand
12. problem
13. relate
14. correspond
15. storehouse
16. represent
17. heuristic
18. analogies
19. Algorithms
20. systematic random search
21. Heuristic
22. simplify
23. reliable
24. rapidly
25. means-end
26. analogy
27. analogy
28. expertise
29. mental set
30. mislead
31. insight
32. incubation
33. functional fixedness
34. defined
35. Creativity
36. divergent
37. convergent
38. divergent
39. moderate
40. divergent
41. flexibility
42. independence
43. social evaluation
44. rewards
45. brainstorming

Reflection Break 1

1. You would first attempt to understand the problem. Successful understanding of a problem requires three features: the parts of your mental representation of the problem must relate to one another in a meaningful way; the elements of your mental representation must correspond to the elements of the problem in the outer world; and you must have a storehouse of background knowledge that you can apply to the problem. Once you have represented the problem successfully, you could use various strategies for attacking the problem, including algorithms, heuristic devices, and analogies.

2. Three internal factors make problem solving easier or harder. These include your level of expertise—experts solve problems more efficiently and rapidly than novices; whether you fall prey to a mental set—mental sets can make our work easier but may mislead us when the similarity between the problems is illusory; and whether you develop insight, or that "Aha!" experience, into the problem. Often we may need to stand back from a problem and allow for the incubation of insight. Other factors influencing the ease of problem solving include the extent to which the elements of the problem are fixed in function and the way the problem is defined. Functional fixedness is your tendency to think of objects in terms of its name or it familiar function.

3. Creativity is the ability to make unusual and sometimes remote associations to or among the elements of a problem in order to generate new combinations. Creativity is characterized by divergent thinking. Creative people show traits such as flexibility, fluency, and independence. There is only a moderate relationship between creativity and performance on intelligence tests and academic ability. However, as you will see in the next chapter, at least one psychologist (Robert Sternberg) disagrees and argues that creativity and creative thinking is a very important aspect of intelligence.

Reading for Understanding About "Reasoning" and "Judgment and Decision Making"

46. Reasoning
47. deductive
48. deductive
49. inductive
50. cultural
51. Eastern

52. analytically
53. decisions
54. heuristics
55. representativeness
56. availability
57. anchoring and adjustment

58. persuade
59. framing
60. overconfident
61. confirm

Reflection Break 2

1. b
2. h
3. e

4. c
5. f
6. a

7. g
8. d

Reading for Understanding About "Language: 'Of Shoes and Ships and Sealing Wax, . . . and Whether Pigs Have Wings' " and "Language and Cognition"

62. Language
63. displacement
64. Semanticity
65. original
66. Displacement
67. phonology
68. morphology
69. syntax

70. semantics
71. sound
72. meaning
73. inflections
74. Syntax
75. grammar
76. bilingual
77. broadens

78. knowledge
79. acquired
80. Language
81. linguistic-relativity
82. think
83. vocabulary

Reflection Break 3

1. Language is the communication of thoughts and feelings by means of symbols that are arranged according to rules of grammar. The basic concepts of language include phonology (sounds), morphology (units of meaning), syntax (word order), and semantics (the meanings of words and groups of words). True language is distinguished from the communication systems of lower animals by properties such as semanticity, infinite creativity, and displacement. Semanticity means that the symbols of a language have meaning. Infinite creativity is the capacity to combine words into original, never-spoken-before sentences. Displacement is the ability to communicate information about events and objects from another time or place.

2. Most people throughout the world are bilingual. Contemporary research reveals that bilingualism broadens people's perspectives and often helps them better learn their first language. The research on the benefit of bilingual education is limited, and the topic has become more of a political issue than a scientific one. In your answer you should cite research whenever possible to support your position.

Chapter 8

Intelligence

PREVIEW

Skim the major headings in this chapter in your textbook. Jot down anything that you are surprised or curious about. After this, write down four or five questions that you have about the material in this chapter.

Things that surprised me/I am curious about from Chapter 8:

Questions that I have about intelligence:

▲

▲

▲

▲

QUESTION

These are some questions that you should be able to answer after you finish studying this chapter.

What Is Intelligence?

▲ *Just what is intelligence?*

▲ *What are factor theories of intelligence?*

▲ *What is meant by multiple intelligences?*

▲ *What is Sternberg's triarchic model of intelligence?*

▲ *Just what is "emotional intelligence"?*

The Measurement of Intelligence

▲ *What is the Stanford-Binet Intelligence Scale?*

▲ *What is different about the Wechsler scales of intelligence?*

Socioeconomic and Ethnic Differences in Intelligence

▲ *What are the socioeconomic and ethnic differences in intelligence?*

Extremes of Intelligence

▲ *What is mental retardation?*

▲ *What does it mean to be gifted?*

The Testing Controversy

▲ *Do intelligence tests contain cultural biases against ethnic minority groups and immigrants?*

Determinants of Intelligence: Where Does Intelligence Come From?

▲ *What are the genetic influences on intelligence?*

▲ *What are the environmental influences on intelligence?*

READING FOR UNDERSTANDING/REFLECT

The following section provides you with the opportunity to perform 2 of the R's of the PQ4R study method. In this section you are encouraged to check your understanding of your reading of the text by filling in the blanks in the brief paragraphs that relate to each of the Preview questions. You will also be prompted to rehearse your understanding of the material with periodic Reflection breaks. Remember, it is better to study in more frequent, short sessions than in one long "cram session." Be sure to reward yourself with short study breaks before each Reflection exercise.

Reading for Understanding About "What Is Intelligence?"

Just what is intelligence? The concept of intelligence is closely related to the concept of (1) _____, but is thought of more broadly as the underlying ability to understand the world and cope with its challenges. (2) _____ underlies (provides the cognitive basis for) thinking and academic achievement. It has been defined by (3) _____ as the "capacity . . . to understand the world . . . and . . . resourcefulness to cope with its challenges."

What are factor theories of intelligence? (4) _____ theories of intelligence argue that intelligence is made up of a number of mental abilities. Spearman and (5) _____ are two early psychologists who believed that intelligence is composed of a number of factors. Spearman believed that a common factor, "(6) _____," underlies all intelligent behavior but that people also have specific abilities, or (7) _____ factors. To test his views Spearman developed factor analysis, a (8) _____ technique that allows researchers to determine which items on tests seem to be measuring the same things.

Thurstone suggested that there are nine specific factors, which he labeled (9) _____. These included word fluency, visual and (10) _____ abilities, perceptual (11) _____, and numerical ability.

More recently, J. P. (12) _____ has expanded the number of factors found in intellectual functioning to hundreds. The most significant critique of the (13) _____ theory approach to intelligence is that it seems that the more factors identified, the more (14) _____ there is among them.

What is meant by multiple intelligences? Howard (15) _____ believes that people have several intelligences, not one, and that each is based in a different area of the (16) _____. Two such "intelligences" are language ability and logical-(17) _____ ability, but Gardner also includes bodily-kinesthetic intelligence, (18) _____ intelligence, and inter- and intra-(19) _____ intelligences. Critics of Gardner's approach agree that people function more intelligently in some aspects of life than in others but question whether special (20) _____ like body-kinesthetic and musical abilities are really "intelligences."

What is Sternberg's triarchic model of intelligence? Sternberg's (21) _____ theory proposes three kinds of intelligence: analytical, (22) _____, and practical. (23) _____ intelligence is equated with what we generally think of as academic ability and enables us to solve problems and acquire new knowledge. Analytic intelligence is surprisingly not necessarily the best predictor of (24) _____. (25) _____ intelligence is defined by the ability to cope with novel situations and to profit from experience. Practical intelligence, or "(26) _____," refers to the ability to adapt to the demands of the environment.

Just what is "emotional intelligence"? The theory of (27) _____ intelligence proposed by psychologists Peter Salovey and John Mayer and popularized by Daniel Goleman holds that social and emotional skills are a form of intelligence that helps children avert violence and depression. The theory suggests that emotional skills like self-(28) _____ and social awareness are best learned during childhood. Again, critics of the theory of emotional intelligence do not deny that emotional coping skills like self-awareness, self-control, empathy, and cooperation are important; they do, however, question whether they represent a kind of (29) _____.

Reading for Understanding About "Psychology and Modern Life: Wired—The Awesome Future of Artificial Intelligence"

(30) _____, or A.I., is the duplication of human intellectual functioning in computers. The concept of A.I. has had a long history in both science and (31) _____, but its reality is just being realized. In the 1950s it was predicted that one day (32) _____ would understand spoken language, decipher bad handwriting, solve problems, and make decisions. These

predictions are today's reality. In some ways A.I. goes beyond (33) _____. Today's computers can carry out complex intellectual functions and solve in a flash (34) _____ that would take people years to solve. However, despite these abilities even the most advanced A.I. machines lack the (35) _____ and creativity found in people.

Reflection Break 1

1. Compare and contrast the factor theory, the theory of multiple intelligences, the triarchic theory of intelligence, and the theory of emotional intelligence as to their definitions of intelligence. What are the similarities among the views of intelligence? What are the differences?

2. Are there any of the approaches to intelligence discussed in this section that you would not consider to be intelligence? Why?

Reading for Understanding About "The Measurement of Intelligence"

What is the Stanford-Binet Intelligence Scale? Although there is disagreement as to exactly what intelligence is, thousands of intelligence (36) _____ are administered every day. The (37) _____ Intelligence scale (SBIS) is the test originated by Alfred Binet and Theodore Simon in France and further developed by Louis Terman at Stanford University. (38) _____ assumed that intelligence increased with age, so the scale includes a series of age-graded questions. The original Binet-Simon scale yielded a score called (39) _____, or MA, which showed the intellectual level at which a child was functioning. The current SBIS derives an IQ score by dividing a child's (40) _____ age score by the child's (41) _____ age and then multiplying by (42) _____.

What is different about the Wechsler scales of intelligence? The (43) _____ scales, developed by David Wechsler, use (44) _____ Iqs, which are derived by comparing a person's performance with that of age-mates and contains a number of separate subtests that each measure a different intellectual task. The Wechsler scales contain verbal and (45) _____ subtests that measure general information, (46) _____, similarities (conceptual thinking), vocabulary, (47) _____, block design (copying designs), and (48) _____ (piecing puzzles together). In this way the Wechsler scales highlight children's relative strengths and (49) _____ in addition to measuring overall intellectual functioning.

Both the SBIS and Wechsler scales are (50) _____ tests in that they are administered to one person at a time. This one-to-one ratio is considered (51) _____. But shortage of trained examiners and the need to test large numbers of individuals lead to the development of (52) _____ tests that could be administered to large groups. At first these tests were viewed as remarkable instruments, but as the years passed group tests have come under increasing attack.

Reading for Understanding About "Socioeconomic and Ethnic Differences in Intelligence" and "Extremes of Intelligence"

What are the socioeconomic and ethnic differences in intelligence? There is a body of research suggestive of differences in intelligence between (53) _____ and ethnic groups. Lower-class U.S. children obtain IQ scores some 10 to 15 points (54) _____ than those of middle- and upper-class children. (55) _____ American children tend to obtain IQ scores some 15 to 20 points lower than those of their European American agemates. Latino and Native American children also tend to score (56) _____ the norms for European American children. Asians and Asian Americans usually obtain (57) _____ IQ scores than British or European Americans.

Several studies have confused the factors of social class and (58) _____ because a disproportionate number of African Americans, Latino and Latina Americans, and Native Americans are found among the (59) _____ socioeconomic classes. However, when observations are limited to particular ethnic groups, an effect is still found for social (60) _____. Environmental factors such as parental encouragement and (61) _____, peer support, and stereotype (62) _____ have been suggested to contribute to these differences.

What is mental retardation? Mental retardation is defined as (63) _____ limitation in functioning that is characterized by an IQ score of no more than (64) _____ and problems in (65) _____ skills, including communication, self-care, home living, social skills, or functional academics. Mental retardation is usually assessed through a combination of (66) _____ scores and behavioral (67) _____. Most people who are retarded are (68) _____ retarded; they are capable of adjusting to the demands of educational institutions and eventually to society at large. Children with Down syndrome are most likely to be (69) _____ retarded. Severely and profoundly retarded children may not acquire (70) _____ and self-help skills and are likely to remain (71) _____ on others throughout their lives. Causes of retardation range from (72) _____ abnormalities to other genetic disorders, or (73) _____ damage.

What does it mean to be gifted? (74) _____ involves high scores on intelligence tests along with high performance in a specific academic area, creativity, leadership, or talent in physical activities. Louis (75) _____ longitudinal studies of genius found that gifted children generally turned out to be successful as adults. (76) _____ percent of children are gifted, and there are numerous ways to help gifted children reach their full potential. These include: giving them access to (77) _____ and other resources, being a responsive, sensitive parent, and (78) _____ their school curriculum, all of which are not bad for all children, regardless of their IQ status.

Reflection Break 2

1. What are the similarities and differences in the three types of intelligence tests (SBIS, Wechsler, and group tests)? Do you think that any of these assessments actually measures intelligence? Why or why not?

2. What evidence suggests that ethnic differences in IQ reflect socioeconomic differences rather than racial differences per se?

Reading for Understanding About "The Testing Controversy" and "Determinants of Intelligence: Where Does Intelligence Come From?"

Do intelligence tests contain cultural biases against ethnic minority groups and immigrants? (79) _____ tests were used historically to prevent many Europeans and others from immigrating to the United States. They were administered in (80) _____ to people who did not know English. Most psychologists and educators believe that intelligence tests are (81) _____ against African Americans and people in the lower classes in that they require familiarity with cultural concepts, particularly those that reflect middle-class European American culture. It is now recognized that intelligence tests cannot be considered (82) _____ if used with people who do not understand the language, but most psychologists still consider intelligences tests (83) _____ against African Americans and members of lower socioeconomic classes.

What are the genetic influences on intelligence? Research on the (84) _____ influences on human intelligence is generally based on kinship studies, twin studies, and adoption studies. (85) _____ studies compare the IQ scores of closely and distantly related people. If heratibility is a factor in intelligence, then (86) _____ related people should have IQ scores more similar than (87) _____ related individuals. (88) _____ studies examine the correlation between MZ (identical) and DZ (fraternal) twins reared apart or together. (89) _____ studies compare the IQ scores of adopted children and their biological and adoptive parents. Studies generally suggest that the (90) _____ of intelligence is between 40% and 60%.

What are the environmental influences on intelligence? Research on (91) _____ influences on intelligence considers factors such as stereotype vulnerability, which leads many (92) _____ American test takers to self-destruct; the effects of the home environment, including styles of (93) _____; the effects of education, including (94) _____ programs; and, among adults, links to lifestyle, such as engaging in cultural activities; and even exercise. The majority of psychologists and educators believe that intelligence reflects a complex interaction of (95) _____ factors, (96) _____ experiences, and (97) _____ factors and expectations.

Reflection Break 3

1. What is meant by a culturally biased intelligence test? What types of items do you believe ought to be on intelligence tests? Do you think that the SBIS and Wechsler tests seem to be culturally biased? Do these tests include the types of things that you consider important for measurement of intelligence? Why or why not?

2. Compare the three approaches to researching the genetic influences on intelligence:

Kinship studies   **Twin studies**   **Adoptee studies**

How do the results obtained from each of these studies compare? What are the similarities? Differences?

3. Briefly summarize the findings of research on the Mozart effect. What kind of conclusions can be drawn from this research?

REVIEW: KEY TERMS AND CONCEPTS

FINAL CHAPTER REVIEW

Review

Visit the *Psychology in the New Millennium* Web site at www.harcourtcollege.com/psych/PNM/siteresources.html and take the Chapter Quizzes to test your knowledge.

Recite

Go to the Recite section for this chapter in your textbook. Use the tear-off card provided at the back of the book to cover the answers of the Recite section. Read the questions aloud, and recite the answers. This will help you cement your knowledge of key concepts.

Essay Questions

1. How do you define intelligence? Which of the theories of intelligence discussed in your text is most similar to yours? What are the similarities/differences among the views of intelligence described in the text? Are there any that you would not consider to be intelligence? Why? Write a two-page essay describing your definition of intelligence and comparing it with current psychological theory. In your essay, be sure to clearly explain your ideas.

2. Just what do IQ tests measure? Do you agree or disagree with this statement: "The SBIS and Wechsler scales actually measure achievement rather than intelligence." Why? Be sure to clearly justify your position in your essay and make sure that you clearly define achievement and intelligence.

3. What evidence suggests that ethnic differences in IQ reflect socioeconomic differences rather than racial differences per se? What is your ethnic background? Are there any stereotypes as to how people from your ethnic background perform in school or intelligence tests? If so, what has been your reaction to these stereotypes? Prepare a one-page letter to the editor of your local or school newspaper on the above topic. Be sure that you fully support your position and clearly define your terms in ways that the average newspaper reader will understand.

4. In a two-page essay, respond to the question "How should society respond to people with exceptional intelligence?" In your essay, be sure to compare the educational experiences of the mentally retarded and gifted. What kind of educational or training experiences do mentally retarded individuals receive? What about gifted individuals? Do these experiences seem appropriate? Are the current programs adequate? Why or why not?

5. As you look back on your own childhood, can you point to any kinds of family or educational experiences that seem to have had an impact on your intellectual development, or do you attribute your intelligence level more to genetics?

   Does your own family seem to be generally similar in overall intellectual functioning? Are there one or more family members who appear to stand out from the others because of intelligence? If so, in what ways? Where do you seem to stand in your family in terms of intellectual functioning? Would you say that your background overall was deprived or enriched?

RELATE/EXPAND/INTEGRATE

1. **Psychology and Modern Life: Wired—The Awesome Future of Artificial Intelligence:** Visit the Web site below and read the information on AI presented to gain a more through understanding of how psychologists and cognitive scientists define AI.

   WWW virtual Library: Artificial Intelligence
   URL: http://archive.comlab.ox.ac.uk/comp/ai.html

   AI on the Web
   URL: http://www.cs.cmu.edu/People/ralf/ai.html

   Outsiders Guide to AI
   URL: http://www.robotwisdom.com/ai/index.html

   AI on ThinkQuest
   http://library.thinkquest.org/2705/index.html

Now, visit one of the artificial intelligence ("bot") sites on the Web. (Some links are provided below, but you may find one of your own if you prefer.) Interact with the site. Hold a conversation with it. If you had not known that you were "talking" with a robot, would you have recognized that you were not interacting with a human? Would you award this bot the Loebner Prize? How was your conversation with the bot similar to human computer chats? How was it different? Report your experiences to your classmates in a format specified by your instructor.

Botspot.com—This site provides a central listing of different "bots" available online. URL: http://www.botspot.com

Eliza—This bot claims to be a friend like you've never had before. URL: http://www-ai.ijs.si/eliza/eliza.html

Advice Dummy—This bot offers advice like an advice columnist. URL: http://missinformation.com/AdviceDummy/index.cfm

Brian—This computer thinks "he" is an 18 year old college student URL: http://www.strout.net/info/science/ai/brian/

2. **The Measurement of Intelligence:** You have probably taken a number of intelligence tests—most of which were group tests. What were the experiences like? Were you informed as to how well you did? Do you believe that the test assessed you fairly or arrived at an accurate estimate of your intelligence? Take two of the online IQ tests at the links below. Are the scores the same? How accurate do you think these are?

Cyberia Shrink
URL: http://www.queendom.com/iq.html

"Uncommonly Difficult IQ Tests"
URL: http://www.eskimo.com/~miyaguch/

Q-Tests
URL: http://iqtests.virtualave.net

Wizard Realm
URL: http://www.wizardrealm.com/tests

Self Discovery Workshop
URL: http://www.iqtest.com/

The Intelligence Testing center
URL: http://www.tjhsst.edu/Psych/iq/

3. **Socioeconomic and Ethnic Differences in Intelligence:** Your textbook profiles Claude Steele, who argues that African Americans experience a feeling of racial vulnerability when they observe things in society that are made to match Caucasian skin, and that they also experience stereotype vulnerability when they see standardized tests that are perceived to be designed to match "pink skin." With your study group, prepare a panel discussion on Steele's ideas. Do you agree with Steele's ideas? Why or why not? What is your ethnic background, and how do you think that your ethnicity has influenced your position on this topic?

4. **Do Intelligence Tests Really Measure Intelligence?** With your study group, develop a series of questions for a culturally fair intelligences test. Are you sure that your questions do not provide members of your ethnic group an advantage? What types of items did you include? Would your test be a fair intelligence test—or would it be culturally biased? Give your test to another study group and ask its members to critique it. Your group should critique the other group's. Were either of the tests culturally fair? Do you think that there is such a thing as a truly culturally unbiased intelligence test? Why or why not? Share your experience with the rest of your class in a format specified by your instructor.

5. **Determinants of Intelligence: Where Does Intelligence Come From?** Visit the following Web sites and read the reviews of *The Bell Curve*. Prepare a two-page essay that briefly summarizes and evaluates the major points of each article. In your conclusion, provide a final evaluation of the controversy.

    APA's view
    URL: http://www.apa.org/releases/intell.html

    Howard Gardner on *The Bell Curve*
    URL: http://www.prospect.org/print/V6/20/gardner-h.html

    Robert Sternberg's Views on *The Bell Curve* in *Skeptic* magazine
    URL: http://www.skeptic.com/03.3.fm-sternberg-interview.html

    The bell is cracked-disputed view on *The Bell Curve*
    URL: http://www.mdle.com/WrittenWord/rholhut/holhut27.htm

6. **Psychology and Modern Life: Enhancing Intellectual Functioning:** Controversy in Psychology—The Mozart Effect. Use your favorite Web search engine (http://www.dogpile.com, http://www.google.com, or http://www.ask.com) to conduct a Web search using the term "Mozart Effect" as the key word to research this issue. What do you think? Does the data suggest that early music exposure will provide children with the sweet sounds of success? Prepare a report (in a format specified by your instructor) for your class on your findings.

ANSWERS FOR CHAPTER 8

Reading for Understanding About "What Is Intelligence?"

1. cognition
2. Intelligence
3. Wechsler
4. Factor
5. Thurstone
6. g
7. s
8. statistical
9. primary mental abilities
10. spatial
11. speed
12. Guilford
13. factor
14. overlap
15. Gardner
16. brain
17. mathematical
18. mathematical
19. personal
20. talents
21. triarchic
22. creative
23. Analytical
24. success
25. Creative
26. street smarts
27. emotional
28. awareness
29. intelligence

Reading for Understanding About "Psychology and Modern Life: Wired—The Awesome Future of Artificial Intelligence"

30. Artificial intelligence
31. science fiction
32. computers
33. intelligence
34. problems
35. insight

Reflection Break 1

1. Similarities and differences include:
   - Factor theory argues that intelligence is made up of a number of factors.
   - Both the theory of multiple intelliengences and the triarchic theory propose the existence of several intelligences. They simply disagree as to how many kinds of intelligences exist.
   - All approaches to intelligence include some aspect of reasoning abilities.
   - Only the triarchic theory argues that creative behavior is a type of intelligence.

2. This answer requires support for personal views. The answer should include a discussion of the strengths of the chosen theory and the weaknesses of those not chosen.

Reading for Understanding About "The Measurement of Intelligence"

36. tests
37. Stanford-Binet
38. Binet
39. mental age
40. mental
41. chronological
42. 100
43. Wechsler
44. deviation
45. performance
46. comprehension
47. mathematics
48. object assembly
49. weaknesses
50. individual
51. optimal
52. group

Reading for Understanding About "Socioeconomic and Ethnic Differences in Intelligence" and "Extremes of Intelligence"

53. socioeconomic
54. lower
55. African
56. below
57. higher
58. ethnicity
59. lower
60. class
61. supervision

62. vulnerability
63. substantial
64. 70 to 75
65. adaptive
66. IQ
67. observations
68. mildly
69. moderately
70. speech

71. dependent
72. chromosomal
73. brain
74. Giftedness
75. Terman's
76. Two to three
77. books
78. enriching

Reflection Break 2

1. Both the SBIS and Wechsler tests are individual tests that are administered to one person at a time. Both scales test skills like reasoning, memory, and language. Only the Wechsler scales include a nonverbal "performance" scale. The Wechsler scale contains subtests that measure individual intellectual tasks and can highlight children's strength's and weaknesses. Both types of individual tests are scored by conparing the individual's perfomance to that of his or her agemates.

2. Although several studies have confused the factors of social class and ethnicity because of the high proportion of African American and Latino Americans found among the lower socioeconomic classes, there is an extensive body of research that suggests that differences in intelligence scores among ethnic groups are the result of socoeconomic factors. Middle-class African Americans, Latino and Latina Americans, and Native Americans outscore lower-class members of their own ethnic group.

Reading for Understanding About "The Testing Controversy" and "Determinants of Intelligence: Where Does Intelligence Come From?"

79. Intelligence
80. English
81. biased
82. valid
83. culturally biased
84. genetic
85. Kinship

86. closely
87. distantly
88. Twin
89. Adoptee
90. heritability
91. environmental
92. African

93. parenting
94. Head Start
95. genetic
96. childhood
97. sociocultural

Reflection Break 3

1. Culturally biased tests assume that the individual taking the test is familiar with the language and cultural concepts of the dominant culture in which the test is based. Most currently used intelligence tests reflect middle-class European American culture and thus may not demonstate an accurate representation of the intelligence of an individual unfamiliar with the cultural values. In the rest of your answer, be sure to support your view with concrete references to theories of intelligence.

2. **Kinship studies** compare the IQ scores of closely and distantly related people. If heratibility is a factor in intelligence, then closely related people should have IQ scores more similar than distantly related individuals. Results of these kinds of studies indicate moderate correlations between closely related individuals (twins, siblings, parents) and weak correlations between individuals of distant realtionships (foster children and cousins).

   Twin studies examine the correlation between MZ (identical) and DZ (fraternal) twins reared apart or together. As expected, the correlations between DZ twins is the same as those of other siblings. MZ twins, on the other hand, show that they are more similar than DZ twins in spatial memory and word comprehension. MZ twins reared together show higher correlations than those reared apart.

   Adoptee Studies compare the IQ scores of adopted children and their biological and adoptive parents. Several studies have found a stronger relationship between the IQ scores of adopted children and their biological parents than with their adoptive parents.

3. Numerous studies have shown that early environment is linked to IQ score and academic achievement. Recent research also suggests that listening to and studying music may enchance spatial reasoning in children. However, many psychologists caution that these results are preliminary, and not all studies that have attempted to replicate the orginal studies have succeeded.

Chapter 9

Motivation and Emotion

PREVIEW

Skim the major headings in this chapter in your textbook. Jot down anything that you are surprised or curious about. After this, write down four or five questions that you have about the material in this chapter.

Things that surprised me/I am curious about from Chapter 9:

Questions that I have about motivation and emotion:

▲

▲

▲

▲

QUESTION

These are some questions that you should be able to answer after you finish studying this chapter.

The Psychology of Motivation: The Whys of Why

▲ *What is the psychology of motivation? What are motives, needs, drives, and incentives?*

Theories of Motivation: Which Why Is Which?

▲ *What is meant by species-specific behaviors?*

▲ *What is drive-reduction theory? How is it related to homeostasis?*

▲ *How does humanistic theory differ from the instinct and drive-reduction theories of motivation?*

▲ *What is Maslow's hierarchy of needs?*

▲ *Why are people motivated to eliminate inconsistencies in their worldviews?*

▲ *How do we make sense of all these different views of motivation?*

Hunger: Do You Go by "Tummy-Time"?

▲ *What bodily mechanisms regulate the hunger drive? What psychological processes are at work?*

▲ *If obesity is connected with health problems and unhappiness with the image in the mirror, why are so many people overweight?*

▲ *So what can people do to shed a few pounds?*

Stimulus Motives

▲ *Are all motives aimed at the reduction of tension?*

▲ *Do we need to be active? Do we need to stimulate our senses?*

▲ *Why do puppies and kittens explore their environments when they are brought into new homes?*

Cognitive Dissonance Theory: Making Things Fit

▲ *Why are people who go unrewarded more likely than those who are rewarded to think or say that what they are doing is worthwhile for its own sake?*

The Three A's of Motivation: Achievement, Affiliation, and Aggression

▲ *Why do some people strive to get ahead?*

▲ *Why do people need people?*

▲ *Why do people kill, maim, and injure one another?*

Emotion: Adding Color to Life

▲ *Just what is an emotion?*

▲ *How can we tell when other people are happy or despondent?*

▲ *Can smiling give rise to feelings of good will? Can frowning produce anger?*

▲ *How do the physiological, situational, and cognitive components of emotions interact to produce feelings and behavior?*

▲ *How do lie detectors work? How reliable are they?*

READING FOR UNDERSTANDING/REFLECT

The following section provides you with the opportunity to perform 2 of the R's of the PQ4R study method. In this section you are encouraged to check your understanding of your reading of the text by filling in the blanks in the brief paragraphs that relate to each of the Preview questions. You will also be prompted to rehearse your understanding of the material with periodic Reflection breaks. Remember, it is better to study in more frequent, short sessions than in one long "cram session." Be sure to reward yourself with short study breaks before each Reflection exercise.

Reading for Understanding About "The Psychology of Motivation: The Whys of Why" and "Theories of Motivation: Which Why is Which?"

What is the psychology of motivation? The psychology of motivation corcerns (1) _____ people do certain things. Motives are hypotherical states within an organism that (2) _____ behavior and propel the organism toward (3) _____. Psychologists assume that (4) _____ give rise to behavior and can take the form of (5) _____, drives, and (6) _____. Psychologists speak of (7) _____ *needs*, such as those for oxygen and food, and of (8) _____ needs, such as those for achievement and self-esteem. Needs give rise to (9) _____; for example, depletion of food gives rise to the hunger drive. An (10) _____ is an object, person, or situation that can satisfy a need or is desirable for its own sake.

Although psychologists agree that it is important to understand why humans and animals do things, they do not agree about the precise nature of (11) _____. The chapter examines four theoretical perspectives on motivation: the biological perspective; Hull's (12) _____ theory; Maslow's (13) _____ theory; and (14) _____ theory.

What is meant by species-specific behaviors? The biological perspective considers the role of the (15) _____ and (16) _____ systems and evolution and (17) _____. According to (18) _____ theory, organisms are born with preprogrammed tendencies to behave in certain ways in certain situations. These preprogrammed tendencies are called instincts, or species-specific behaviors, or (19) _____ (FAPs). FAPs occur in the presence of stimuli called (20) _____. Male members of many species are sexually aroused by (21) _____ secreted by females. Psychologists (22) _____ whether humans have instincts, and if so, what they are.

What is drive-reduction theory? How is it related to homeostasis? According to (23) _____ theory, we are motivated to engage in behavior that reduces drives. (24) _____ drives such as hunger and pain are based on the biological makeup of the organism. (25) _____ drives such as the drive for money are learned. Drives trigger (26) _____ and (27) _____ behavior. We learn to do what (28) _____ drives. The body has a tendency called (29) _____ to maintain a steady state; therefore, food deprivation leads to the hunger drive and eating, which reduces the hunger drive.

How does humanistic theory differ from the instinct and drive-reduction theories of motivation? Whereas instincts and drives are mainly (30) _____, aimed at survival and reproduction,

© 2002 Thomson Learning, Inc.

humanistic psychologists argue that people are (31) _____ and that behavior can be (32) _____. Abraham (33) _____ believed that people are motivated by the conscious desire for personal growth. He argued that people are motivated to strive for (34) _____, or our self-initiated striving to become whatever we believe we are capable of being. Maslow hypothesized that people have a (35) _____ of needs. Once lower-level needs such as (36) _____ and (37) _____ needs are satisfied, people strive to meet higher-level needs such as those for love, (38) _____, and self-actualization.

Why are people motivated to eliminate inconsistencies in their worldviews? According to cognitive theory, people are motivated to (39) _____ and (40) _____ events. People must (41) _____ the world accurately in order to accomplish these goals, and therefore their cognitions need to be (42) _____, or consistent with one another.

How do we make sense of all these different views of motivation? There is no question that many animals are born with (43) _____; the question remains as to what instincts people have and how compelling they are. Drive-reduction theory appears to apply to (44) _____ drives such as hunger and. thirst, but people often act to (45) _____ rather than (46) _____ the tension they experience. Although (47) _____ theory has been criticized as unscientific, many psychologists make room for conscious striving in their views of humans. (48) _____ appears to be a fact of human life, although psychologists debate ways of directly assessing it.

Reflection Break 1

Compare each of the theories of motivation by filling in the chart below.

	Biological	Drive-Reduction	Humanistic	Cognitive
Beliefs	✓ ✓ ✓ ✓ ✓	✓ ✓ ✓ ✓	✓ ✓ ✓ ✓	✓ ✓
Critique	✓ ✓	✓ ✓	✓ ✓ ✓	✓ ✓

Reading for Understanding About "Hunger: Do You Go by 'Tummy-Time'?"

What bodily mechanisms regulate the hunger drive? What psychological processes are at work? Hunger is regulated by several (49) _____ mechanisms, including stomach contractions, blood sugar level, receptors in the mouth and liver, and the responses of the hypothalamus. Chewing and swallowing provide some sensations of (50) _____, or satisfaction with the amount eaten. Stomach contractions, or (51) _____, correspond with hunger but do not fully regulate it. The (52) _____ of the hypothalamus functions as a stop-eating center. Damage to the VMN leads to (53) _____ in rats; that is, the animals grow to several times their normal body weight. The (54) _____ may function as a start-eating center. The (55) _____ mechanisms are only a part of the regulation of hunger, however. External stimuli such as the (56) _____ of food can also trigger hunger.

If obesity is connected with health problems and unhappiness with the image in the mirror, why are so many people overweight? More than half of adult Americans are (57) _____. Biological factors in obesity include (58) _____, (59) _____ tissue (body fat), and the (60) _____ rate (the rate at which the individual converts calories to energy). (61) _____ factors such as stress, observational learning, and emotional states can also contribute to overeating. (62) _____ factors like ethnicity and socioeconomic status are also important in obesity. Socioeconomic status plays a role in obesity and is more prevalent among (63) _____ people. Since people of color are typically of lower socioeconomic status than European Americans, rates of obesity tend to be (64) _____ among African and Latino and Latina Americans.

So what can people do to shed a few pounds? Sound weight control programs involve improving (65) _____ knowledge (e.g., eating more fruits and vegetable and fewer fatty foods), (66) _____ calorie intake, exercising, and changing eating habits. (67) _____ helps people construct healthful diets and cope with temptations.

Reflection Break 2

1. Briefly summarize the biological and psychological mechanisms that appear to regulate the hunger drive.

   Biological:
   -
   -
   -
   -

   Psychological:
   -
   -
   -

2. Provide a brief overview of the biological, psychological, and socioeconomic factors in obesity.

Reading for Understanding About "Stimulus Motives"

Are all motives aimed at the reduction of tension? Apparently not. Stimulus motives, like physiological motives, are innate, but they involve motives to (68) _____ rather than (69) _____ "tension" or the amount of stimulation acting on the organism. (70) _____ motives include sensory stimulation, activity, exploration, and manipulation of the environment.

Do we need to be active? Do we need to stimulate our senses? Sensory-deprivation studies suggest that inactivity and lack of stimulation are (71) _____ in humans. People and many lower animals have (72) _____ for stimulation and activity.

Why do puppies and kittens explore their environments when they are brought into new homes? People and many lower animals have needs for (73) _____ and manipulation. The key question is whether people and animals seek to explore and manipulate their environment because these activities help them (74) _____ primary drives, or whether they engage in these activities for their own sake. Many psychologists believe that exploration is (75) _____ in and of itself.

Reading for Understanding About "Cognitive Dissonance Theory: Making Things Fit" and "The Three A's of Motivation: Achievement, Affiliation, and Aggression"

Why are people who go unrewarded more likely than those who are rewarded to think or say that what they are doing is worthwhile for its own sake? (76) _____ theorists argue that organisms are motivated to create realistic mental maps of the world and will adjust their representations, if needed, to make things fit. Cognitive-dissonance theory hypothesizes that people dislike situations in which their attitudes and behavior are (77) _____. Such situations apparently induce (78) _____, which people can reduce by changing their attitudes. For example, people engage in (79) _____, that is, they tend to justify boring or fruitless behavior to themselves by concluding that their efforts are worthwhile, even when they go unrewarded.

Why do some people strive to get ahead? One reason may be that they have more (80) _____ motivation than other people. Achievement motivation is the need to (81) _____ things. McClelland studied achievement motivation by means of people's responses to (82) _____ cards. He found that college graduates with (83) _____ achievement motivation found jobs in occupations characterized by risk, decision making, and the chance for great success. Research also shows that people with high achievement motivation attain higher (84) _____ and earn more (85) _____ than people of comparable ability with lower achievement motivation.

People may be motivated to achieve in school by performance or learning (86) _____. (87) _____ goals are tangible rewards, such as money or getting into graduate school. (88) _____ goals involve the enhancement of knowledge or skills. An understanding of achievement motivation can help psychologists enhance the (89) _____ and job (90) _____ of employees.

Why do people need people? The motive for (91) _____ prompts us to make friends, join groups, and prefer to do things with others rather than alone. This need may have an (92) _____ (instinctive) aspect. Research by Stanley Schachter suggests that (93) _____ tends to increase the need for affiliation, especially with people who share one's predicament.

Why do people kill, maim, and injure one another? Certainly people engage in warfare and other kinds of (94) _____ as members of groups. However, psychological theories also address the problem of (95) _____. (96) _____ theory views aggression as instinctive and linked to brain structures, hormone levels, and the Darwinian concept of the "survival of the fittest." (97) _____ theory views aggression as stemming from inevitable frustrations. According to psychodymanic theory, the best way to prevent harmful aggression may be to encourage less harmful aggression. Psychoanalysts refer to the venting of aggressive impulses as (98) _____. (99) _____ perspectives, on the other hand, predict that people may be aggressive when they see aggression as being appropriate for them, or when they interpret other people's behavior as insults to their honor. (100) _____ theories view aggression as stemming from experience and reinforcement of aggressive skills. The (101) _____ perspective examines the effects of culture-such as the culture of athletic competition-on aggression.

Reflection Break 3

Match the proper motive with its description:

a. Stimulus motives
b. Sensory deprivation
c. Achievement motivation
d. Affiliation motive
e. Theory of social comparison
f. Agression motive

_____ 1. The desire to accomplish things of significance.
_____ 2. The intent to cause physical and/or psychological harm to another person.
_____ 3. Holds that in an ambiguous situation we will affiliate with people with whom we can compare feelings and behavior.
_____ 4. The need for social relations.
_____ 5. Intended to increase stimulation; includes sensory stimulation, activity, exploration, and manipulation of the environment.
_____ 6. Humans find more than a few hours of this extremely unpleasant.

Reading for Understanding About "Emotion: Adding Color to Life"

Just what is an emotion? Emotions add (102) _____ to our lives. An (103) _____ is a state of feeling with physiological, cognitive, and behavioral components. Emotions (104) _____ behavior and also serve as goals. Fear, for example, is connected with arousal of the (105) _____ division of the autonomic nervous system, (106) _____ that one is in danger, and (107) _____ tendencies to escape.

How can we tell when other people are happy or despondent? The expression of many emotions may be (108) _____. (109) _____ are one factor in the expression of emotion. According to (110) _____, there are several basic emotions whose expression is recognized in cultures around the world. However, there is no perfect one-to-one relationship between expressions and emotions. Darwin believed that the universal recognition of facial expressions had (111) _____ value.

Can smiling give rise to feelings of good will? Can frowning produce anger? It does appear that facial expressions can influence one's experience of emotion. The (112) _____ argues that facial expressions can also affect our emotional state. Psychological research suggests that the contraction of facial muscles may be influential in (113) _____ states.

How do the physiological, situational, and cognitive components of emotions interact to produce feelings and behavior? (114) _____ theory suggests that something happens that is interpreted by the person, and the emotion follows. According to the (115) _____ theory, emotions are associated with specific patterns of arousal and action that are triggered by certain external events. The emotion (116) _____ the behavioral response. The (117) _____ theory proposes that processing of events by the brain gives rise simultaneously to feelings and bodily responses. According to this view, feelings (118) _____ bodily responses. According to Schachter and Singer's theory of (119) _____, emotions are associated with similar patterns of arousal, but the level of arousal can differ. The emotion a person experiences in response to an external stimulus reflects that person's appraisal of the stimulus. Research evidence suggests that emotions are not as distinct as the (120) _____ theory would suggest, but that patterns of arousal are more specific than suggested by the theory of (121) _____ and that cognitive appraisal does play a role in determining our responses to events.

How do lie detectors work? How reliable are they? Lie detectors-also called (122) _____- monitor indicators of sympathetic arousal, including heart rate, blood pressure, respiration rate, and electrodermal response (sweating) while a witness or suspect in a crime is being examined. These responses are presumed to indicate the presence of (123) _____-anxiety and/or guilt-that might be induced by lying. Critics find polygraph testing to be (124) _____ and argue that it is sensitive to more emotions than those that might be connected with lying.

Reflection Break 4

Compare the four theories of emotion by completing the following:

Theory	Proposes
Commonsense Theory	
James-Lange Theory	
Cannon-Bard Theory	
Cognitive Appraisal Theory	

REVIEW: KEY TERMS AND CONCEPTS

Leon Festinger and Stanley Schachter	282	drive-reduction theory	285	halo effect	298
cognitive-dissonance theory	282	primary drives	285	affiliation	301
		acquired drives	286	theory of social comparison	301
motive	282	homeostasis	286		
need	283	self- actualization	286	catharsis	303
drive	283	satiety	289	emotion	304
physiological drives	283	hunger pangs	289	sympathetic nervous system	304
incentive	283	ventromedial nucleus (VMN)	289	parasympathetic nervous system	304
species-specific	284	hyperphagic	289		
instincts	284	lateral hypothalamus	290	depression	305
fixed-action patterns FAPs)	284	aphagic	290	facial-feedback hypothesis	306
		stimulus motives	294		
releasers	284	attitude-discrepant behavior	297	James-Lange theory	307
pheromones	284			Cannon-Bard theory	308
vomeronasal organ (VNO)	285	effort justification	297	theory of cognitive appraisal	308
		social motives	298		
instincts	285	Henry A. Murray	298		

FINAL CHAPTER REVIEW

Review

Visit the *Psychology in the New Millennium* Web site at www.harcourtcollege.com/psych/PNM/siteresources.html, and take the Chapter Quizzes to test your knowledge.

Recite

Go to the Recite section for this chapter in your textbook. Use the tear-off card provided at the back of the book to cover the answers of the Recite section. Read the questions aloud, and recite the answers. This will help you cement your knowledge of key concepts.

Essay Questions

1. College students frequently like humanistic theory more than they like instinct theory or drive reductionism. Why do you think this is so? Now that you have studied all of the theories, which one do you feel is the strongest? Why? Answer these questions in a three-paragraph essay for your instructor. Be sure to use the format that he/she specifies.

2. Examine your own eating patterns. Do you need to lose weight? Are you sure? What standard are you using in making this judgment? Do you have difficulty controlling your weight? If so, which of the behavior patterns discussed in the text seem to be contributing to the problem? What does food mean to you? Is food more than a way of satisfying the hunger drive? If so, how? How do you know when you are hungry? What do you experience? Have you ever eaten because you were anxious or bored or because something just "looked good"? Prepare a two-page essay that describes your eating patterns and the effects they have on your health. In your conclusion, be sure to discuss the things that can you do to change your unhealthful eating patterns to healthful ones. Which of the strategies mentioned in the text are likely to work for you? Why?

3. Were you ever subjected to difficult hazing upon joining a sorority, fraternity, or other kind of group? Did the experience affect your feelings about being a member of the group? How? Connect your experience to the concept of effort justification in a one-page essay. Be sure to clearly describe your experience and justify your answer.

4. Why do some people seem satisfied to just get by, whereas other people are driven to work and improve despite their achievements? Do you seem to be driven mainly by performance goals or by learning goals? Explain your answer in a one-page essay for your instructor.

5. Have you ever been able to change the way you *feel* by doing *something?* Have you tried to "keep a stiff upper lip" when you were under stress, or have you preferred to "let it all hang out?" What do the facial-feedback hypothesis and various theories of emotional expression suggest about the effects of one approach or the other? Prepare a brief essay comparing the various theories of emotional expression and the suggestions they make.

RELATE/EXPAND/INTEGRATE

1. **Theories of Motivation: Which Why Is Which?** Survey 20 friends from your other classes as to why they decided to attend college. Keep track of the various answers and the number of times that they occur. Create a summary of the different types of answers that you obtained. Categorize them as to the different motivational theories they represent. Bring your summary to class and compare your findings with those of the other members in your study group. Combine your findings with those of your study group and share them with the rest of the class.

2. *Controversy in Psychology: Do People Respond Instinctively to Pheromones?* Go back to Chapter 3 and review the discussion thread that occurred on the bulletin board in response to the question on whether pheromones make you feel more sexy. Given what you have now learned in this chapter, have you changed your opinions? What do you now think about the impact of pheromones on behavior? Do we respond instinctively to pheromones? Are pheromones involved in human mate selection? Explain your answer. As always, be sure to support your comments with good supporting evidence.

   URL: http://www.cf.ac.uk/biosi/staff/jacob/teaching/sensory/pherom.html

   Society For Neuroscience Brain Briefings On Pheromones
   URL: http://www.sfn.org/briefings/pheromones.html

   Pheromones: An On-Line Resource
   URL: http://www.pheromones.com

3. **Hunger: Do You Go by "Tummy Time"?** Compare the information presented in the advertising of some of the major weight loss programs. (Jenny Craig, Weight Watchers, etc.). How do healthful weight control programs make use of knowledge of the hunger drive? Summarize the information to share with your classmates in a format specified by your instructor.

   URL: http://www.weightwatchers.com
   URL: http://www.jennycraig.com

4. **Stimulus Motives:** How much stimulation do you prefer? Do you like going out for drives or walks and exploring new neighborhoods or countries, or do you prefer quiet evenings at home? Do you have ways of trying to increase the stimulation impacting on you? What are they? Do you go to movies or concerts or listen to music? Can you lie contentedly on the beach for hours, or do you get restless quickly? What do you think this means? What motivates you?
   Take the Sensation Seeking Scale at http://www.calpoly.edu/~epeabody/HSStest.html and compare the results to those you obtained from the sensation seeking scale in your text.

5. **The Three A's of Motivation: Achievement, Affiliation and Aggression:** Using your favorite search engines, research further the ways in which gender, ethnicity, and cultural factors may be related to aggression.

    URL: http://www.google.com
    URL: http://www.dogpile.com
    URL: http://www.ask.com

6. **Emotion: Adding Color to Life:** Your study group has been appointed to a state task force on the use of lie detectors in legal proceedings. It is your task force's responsibility to prepare a report that summaries the research on the reliability and validity of lie detectors in identifying lies. Do lie detectors work? Do they accurately tell when people are lying? How reliable do you think these are? Just what do lie detectors detect? What does your task force recommend? Should lie detectors be used as absolute evidence of truthfulness? Present your "task force's" findings and position to "Congress" (your class).

ANSWERS FOR CHAPTER 9

Reading for Understanding About "The Psychology of Motivation: The Whys of Why" and "Theories of Motivation: Which Why Is Which?"

1. why
2. activate
3. goals
4. motives
5. needs
6. incentives
7. physiological
8. psychological
9. drives
10. incentive
11. motivation
12. drive reduction
13. humanistic
14. cognitive
15. nervous
16. endocrine
17. heredity
18. instinct
19. fixed-action patterns
20. releasers
21. pheromones
22. debate
23. drive-reduction
24. Primary
25. Acquired
26. arousal
27. activate
28. educes
29. homeostasis
30. defensive
31. self-aware
32. growth-oriented
33. Maslow
34. self-actualization
35. hierarchy
36. physiological
37. safety
38. esteem
39. understand
40. predict
41. represent
42. harmonious
43. instincts
44. physiological
45. increase
46. decrease
47. humanistic
48. Cognition

Reflection Break 1

	Biological	**Drive-Reduction**	**Humanistic**	**Cognitive**
Beliefs	✓ Considers the role of the nervous and endocrine systems and evolution and heredity. ✓ Believes that organisms are born with preprogrammed tendencies to behave in certain ways in certain situations. ✓ Preprogrammed tendencies are called instincts, or species-specific behaviors, or fixed-action patterns (FAPs). ✓ FAPs occur in the presence of stimuli called releasers.	✓ Argues that we are motivated to engage in behavior that reduces drives. ✓ Primary drives such as hunger and pain are based on the biological makeup of the organism. ✓ Acquired drives such as the drive for money are learned. ✓ Drives trigger arousal and activate behavior. ✓ We learn to do what reduces drives. ✓ The body has a tendency to maintain a steady state, called homeostasis.	✓ Argues that people are self-aware and that behavior can be growth-oriented. ✓ Maslow believed that people are motivated by the conscious desire for personal growth, or self-actualization ✓ Self-actualization is our self-initiated striving to become whatever we believe we are capable of being. ✓ People have a hierarchy of needs. ✓ Once lower-level needs (physiological and safety) are satisfied, people strive to meet higher-level needs (love, esteem, and self-actualization).	✓ According to cognitive theory, people are motivated to understand and predict events. People must represent the world accurately in order to accomplish these goals, and therefore, their cognitions need to be harmonious or consistent with one another.

	Biological	Drive-Reduction	Humanistic	Cognitive
Critique	✓ There is no question that many animals are born with instincts; the question remains as to what instincts people have and how compelling they are. ✓ Provides circular explanations of human behavior.	✓ Appears to apply to physiological drives such as hunger and, thirst but not psychological needs. ✓ People often act to increase rather than decrease the tension they experience. ✓ Viewed as unscientific.	✓ Allows for too much individual variation for the hierarchy of needs to apply to everyone. ✓ Psychologists do make room for conscious striving in their views of humans.	✓ Relies on unobservable concepts like mental representations and not observable behavior. ✓ It is difficult to represent active behavior without resorting to cognitive concepts. ✓

Reading for Understanding About "Hunger: Do you go by 'Tummy-Time'?"

49. internal
50. satiety
51. hunger pangs
52. ventromedial nucleus (VMN)
53. hyperphagia
54. lateral hypothalamus
55. body
56. aroma
57. overweight
58. heredity
59. adipose
60. metabolic
61. Psychological
62. Sociocultural
63. poorer
64. higher
65. nutritional
66. decreasing
67. Behavior modification

Reflection Break 2

1. Biological:
   - Hunger pangs are stomach contractions that coincide with hunger.
   - The hypothalamus is a key brain structure that appears to regulate hunger. It receives information about blood sugar levels.
   - Two other brain structures are the ventromedial nucleus, which seems to function as a "stop eating" center, and the lateral hypothalamus, which may function as a "start-eating" center.

Psychological:
- Sight and smell of food
- Setting
- Boredom
- Availability of food

2. Biological factors include heredity and metabolic rate.
Psychological factors include observational learning, stress, and emotional states.
Sociocultural factors include socioeconomic status (SES) and acculturation.

Reading for Understanding About "Stimulus Motives"

68. increase
69. decrease
70. Stimulus

71. aversive
72. needs
73. exploration

74. reduce
75. reinforcing

Reading for Understanding About "Cognitive Dissonance Theory: Making Things Fit" and "The Three A's of Motivation: Achievement, Affiliation, and Aggression"

76. Cognitive
77. inconsistent
78. cognitive dissonance
79. effort justification
80. achievement
81. accomplish
82. TAT
83. high
84. grades

85. money
86. goals
87. Performance
88. Learning
89. productivity
90. satisfaction
91. affiliation
92. inborn
93. anxiety

94. combat
95. aggression
96. Biological
97. Psychodynamic
98. catharsis
99. Cognitive
100. Learning
101. sociocultural

Reflection Break 3

1. c
2. f

3. e
4. d

5. a
6. b

Reading for Understanding About "Emotion: Adding Color to Life"

102. color
103. emotion
104. motivate
105. sympathetic
106. cognitions
107. behavioral
108. universal
109. Facial expressions

110. Ekman
111. survival
112. facial-feedback hypothesis
113. emotional
114. Commonsense
115. James-Lange
116. follows
117. Cannon-Bard

118. accompany
119. cognitive appraisal
120. James-Lange
121. cognitive appraisal
122. polygraphs
123. emotions
124. unreliable

Reflection Break 4

Theory	Proposes
Commonsense Theory	Something happens that is interpreted, and the emotion follows.
James-Lange Theory	Emotions follow our behavioral responses to events. Stimuli trigger specific instinctive patterns of arousal and action.
Cannon-Bard Theory	Events trigger bodily responses and the experience of an emotion simultaneously. Emotions accompany body responses but are not caused by the body responses.
Cognitive Appraisal Theory	The label given to an emotion depends on our cognitive appraisal. Emotions are associated with similar patterns of body arousal. Social comparison is used to decide the appropriate emotional response.

Chapter 10

Child Development

PREVIEW

Skim the major headings in this chapter in your textbook. Jot down anything that you are surprised or curious about. After this, write down four or five questions that you have about the material in this chapter.

Things that surprised me/I am curious about from Chapter 10:

Questions that I have about child development:

▲

▲

▲

▲

QUESTION

These are some questions that you should be able to answer after you finish studying this chapter.

Prenatal Development: The Beginning of Our Life Story

▲ *What developments occur from conception through birth?*

Childhood: Physical Development

▲ *What physical developments occur during childhood?*

Childhood: Cognitive Development

▲ *What are Jean Piaget's views of cognitive development?*

▲ *How does language develop?*

▲ *How do children reason about what is right and wrong?*

Childhood: Social and Personality Development

▲ *What are Erikson's stages of psychosocial development?*

▲ *How do feelings of attachment develop? What kinds of experiences affect attachment?*

▲ *What types of parental behavior are connected with variables such as self-esteem, achievement motivation, and independence in children?*

Controversies in Developmental Psychology

▲ *What is the nature-nurture controversy about?*

▲ *How is the nature-nurture controversy applied to language development?*

▲ *Does development occur gradually or in stages?*

READING FOR UNDERSTANDING/REFLECT

The following section provides you with the opportunity to perform 2 of the R's of the PQ4R study method. In this section, you are encouraged to check your understanding of your reading of the text by filling in the blanks in the brief paragraphs that relate to each of the Preview questions. You will also be prompted to rehearse your understanding of the material with periodic Reflection breaks. Remember, it is better to study in more frequent, short sessions than in one long "cram session." Be sure to reward yourself with short study breaks before each Reflection exercise.

Reading for Understanding About "Prenatal Development: The Beginning of Our Life Story"

What developments occur from conception through birth? Within 9 (1) _____ a child develops from a nearly microscopic cell to a (2) _____. (3) _____ development occurs in stages: the germinal, embryonic, and fetal stages. During the germinal stage, the (4) _____, the single cell formed by the union of the sperm and egg divides as it travels through the (5) _____ tube and becomes implanted in the (6) _____ wall. The major organ systems are formed during the (7) _____ stage, which lasts from implantation until about the eighth week of development. By the end of the (8) _____ month the nervous system begins to transmit messages and the sex organs begin to differentiate. The embryo is suspended in the (9) _____ sac and exchanges nutrients and wastes with the mother through the (10) _____. The (11) _____ stage, which lasts from the beginning of the third month until birth, is characterized by maturation and gains in (12) _____. It is during the fetal period that the mother will detect the first fetal (13) _____.

Reading for Understanding About "Childhood: Physical Development"

What physical developments occur during childhood? Childhood begins at (14) _____.
(15) _____ development includes gains in height and weight, maturation of the nervous
system, and development of bones, muscles, and organs. Early physical development-prenatal
and infant-occurs the most (16) _____; babies usually double their birth weight in about
(17) _____ months and (18) _____ it by their first birthday. (19) _____ are
simple, unlearned, inborn responses to stimuli that in many cases are essential to the survival of
the infant. Examples include sucking, rooting, and swallowing.

Newborn babies can (20) _____ quite well and show greater interest in (21) _____
visual stimuli than in simple ones. Infants are capable of (22) _____ perception by the time
they can crawl. Newborns can normally (23) _____ and show a preference for their (24)
_____'s voice. Newborns show preferences for (25) _____ odors and (26)
_____ foods. Motor development usually proceeds in a particular sequence in which
infants roll over and (27) _____ before they creep, (28) _____, stand, and walk.
There is a great deal of variation in the (29) _____ at which infants first engage in motor
activities, but the (30) _____ remains generally the same.

Reflection Break 1

1. Review prenatal developmental changes by filling in the chart below:

	Time Period	**Major Characteristics**
Germinal		
Embryonic		
Fetal		

2. Review the sensory capabilities of the newborn by filling in the chart below.

Sense	Capabilities
Vision	
Hearing	
Taste and Smell	
Touch	

3. Briefly describe the typical pattern of the development of motor skills in infants.

Reading for Understanding About "Childhood: Cognitive Development"

What are Jean Piaget's views of cognitive development? The ways in which children mentally represent and think about the world is their (31) _____ development. The Swiss biologist and psychologist Jean (32) _____ saw children as budding scientists who actively strive to make sense of the perceptual world. He hypothesized that children's cognitive processes develop in an orderly sequence of (33) _____. He defined intelligence as involving the processes of (34) _____ (responding to events according to existing schemes) and (35) _____ (changing schemes to permit effective responses to new events). (36) _____ were a pattern of action or a mental structure involved in acquiring or organizing knowledge. Piaget's view of cognitive development includes four stages: (37) _____ (prior to the use of symbols and language and characterized by the establishment of object permanence); (38) _____ (characterized by egocentric thought, animism, artificialism, and inability to center on more than one aspect of a situation); (39) _____ (characterized by conservation, less egocentrism, reversibility, and subjective moral judgments); and (40) _____ (characterized by abstract logic).

How does language develop? (41) _____ is the communication of thoughts and feelings through symbols that are arranged according to the rules of grammar. Children make the (42) _____ sounds of crying, cooing, and babbling before true language develops. The prelinguistic sounds are not (43) _____, and are therefore not considered language. (44) _____ are vowel-like sounds that resemble "oohs" and "ahs." In (45) _____, babies frequently combine consonants and vowel sounds. Infants usually (46) _____ much more than they can say. Single-word utterances, or (47) _____, occur at about 1 year of age; two-word utterances, known as (48) _____, by the age of 2. Early language is characterized by (49) _____ of familiar words and concepts to unfamiliar objects (calling horses doggies), and by (50) _____ of verbs ("She sitted down"). As time passes, (51) _____ grows larger, and sentence structure grows more (52) _____.

How do children reason about what is right and wrong? Lawrence (53) _____ hypothesized that children's sense of moral reasoning develops through three levels, each of which consists of two stages. Moral decisions develop from being based on pain and pleasure, (54) _____; through necessity to maintain the social order, (55) _____; to reliance on one's own conscience, (56) _____. Not all individuals reach the (57) _____ level.

Reflection Break 2

Match the cognitive concept with its proper description.

a. ebonics	i. preconventional stage	q. overextension
b. concrete operational	j. accommodation	r. scheme
c. assimilation	k. artificialism	s. cooing
d. holophrases	l. center	t. overregularization
e. sensorimotor	m. reversibility	u. animism
f. decentration	n. babbling	v. conservation
g. preoperational	o. object permance	w. conventional stage
h. egocentrism	p. telegraphic speech	

_____ 1. Responding to a new stimulus through a reflex or existing habit.

_____ 2. A pattern of action or mental structure involved in acquiring or organizing knowledge.

_____ 3. The creation of new ways of responding to objects or looking at the world.

_____ 4. Two-word utterances that contain only essential words, in particular nouns and verbs.

_____ 5. The cognitive stage in which thought is characterized by the use of words and symbols to represent objects; thought is limited and tends to be one dimensional.

_____ 6. The belief that environmental events like rain and thunder are human inventions.

_____ 7. The recognition that many processes can be undone, or restored to their previous condition.

_____ 8. The inability of preoperational children to understand that other people do not see things the same way they do.

_____ 9. Stage of moral reasoning in which judgments are based on expectations of rewards and punishments.

_____ 10. Errors in the use of grammatical rules for forming the past tense and plurals.

_____ 11. The realization that objects removed from sight still exist.

_____ 12. Vowel-like sounds linked to feelings of pleasure.

_____ 13. The attribution of life and consciousness to physical objects like the sun.

_____ 14. This laws holds that basic properties of substances such as mass, weight, and volume remain the same when you change superficial properties such as their shape or arrangement.

_____ 15. The inability to think about two aspects of a situation at once.

_____ 16. The stage of cognitive development in which children show the beginnings of the capacity for adult logic.

_____ 17. The first stage of cognitive development in which the infant is capable of assimilating novel stimuli using reflexes and develops object permanence.

_____ 18. Previously called "Black English," or "Black Dialect;" rooted in the remnants of the west African dialects used by slaves.

_____ 19. Combinations of consonants and vowels that sound like speech but are prelinguistic.

_____ 20. The use of a word to refer to other things and actions for which a child does not yet have words.

_____ 21. Children's first linguistic utterances; single words that may express complex meanings.

_____ 22. Stage of reasoning on moral behavior in which right and wrong are judged by conformity to familial, religious, or societal standards.

_____ 23. The ability of concrete-operational children to focus or center on two dimensions of a problem at once.

Reading for Understanding About "Childhood: Social and Personality Development"

What are Erikson's stages of psychosocial development? (58) _____ relationships are crucial to children. Erik (59) _____ hypothesizes that there are eight stages of psychosocial development. Each represents a life (60) _____. The first of these is "(61) _____," during which the crisis centers on the child's learning that the world is a good place that can meet its needs. The second occurs in early childhood, when the child begins to explore the environment and develops (62) _____ (self-direction) or its opposite, feelings of (63) _____ and (64) _____. The third stage, occurring in later childhood, encourages us to develop either (65) _____ or feelings of inferiority.

How do feelings of attachment develop? What kinds of experiences affect attachment? Mary (66) _____ defines attachment as an emotional tie that is formed between a person and another specific person. (67) _____ keeps organisms together and is vital to the survival of infants. According to Ainsworth, there are three stages of attachment: the initial-preattachment phase, which is characterized by (68) _____ attachment; the attachment-in-the-making phase, which is characterized by preference for (69) _____ figures; and the clear-cut attachment phase, which is characterized by intensified dependence on the (70) _____. Ainsworth developed the (71) _____ method to study attachment and identified three types of attachment: secure attachment, avoidant attachment, and ambivalent attachment. In the strange situation, (72) _____ attached infants mildly protest their mother's departure, seek interaction, and are readily comforted; (73) _____ attached infants are least distressed by their mother's departure and ignore their mothers when they return. (74) _____ attached infants show signs of distress when their mother leaves and show ambivalence when she returns by alternately clinging to her and pushing her away.

(75) _____ have argued that children become attached to their mothers through conditioning because their mothers feed them and attend to their other needs. Harry(76) _____'s studies with rhesus monkeys suggest that an innate motive, (77) _____, may be more important than conditioning in the development of attachment. Konrad Lorenz notes that attachment is (78) _____, or inborn. He notes that there are critical developmental periods during which animals such as geese and ducks will become attached instinctively to (or (79) _____ on) an object that they follow.

What types of parental behavior are connected with variables such as self-esteem, achievement motivation, and independence in children? Many psychologists have been concerned with relationships between (80) _____ styles and personality development in children. Diana Baumrind has been interested in the development of (81) _____, or the ability of the child to manipulate the environment, in relation to parenting behavior. Styles of parental behavior include the authoritative, authoritarian, and permissive styles. (82) _____ parents are restrictive and demand mature behavior but temper their strictness with love and support. (83) _____ parents view obedience as a virtue; they have strict guidelines about what is right and wrong and rely on force and poor communication. (84) _____ parents are generally easygoing with their children; they are warm and supportive but poor at communication. Research shows that (85) _____ in parenting is superior in rearing children, but that (86) _____ also pays off . The children of (87) _____ parents are most achievement oriented and well adjusted.

Reflection Break 3

1. Review Erikson's early stages of social development by describing developmental changes that occur.

   Trust versus mistrust:

   Autonomy versus shame and doubt:

   Initiative versus inferiority

2. What is attachment, and how is it demonstrated?

3. Briefly compare and contrast each of the three parenting styles: authoritative, authoritarian, and permissive.

Authoritative:

Authoritarian:

Permissive:

Reading for Understanding About "Controversies in Developmental Psychology"

What is the nature-nurture controversy about? The nature-nurture controversy concerns the relative influences of (88) _____ (nature) and nurture, (89) _____, on development. Development appears to reflect an (90) _____ between nature (genetic factors) and nurture (environmental influences). Maturational theorists focus on the influences of (91) _____, whereas learning theorists focus on (92) _____ influences.

How is the nature-nurture controversy applied to language development? The two main theories of (93) _____ development are learning theories and nativist theories. (94) _____ theories see language as developing according to the laws of learning and thus focus on the roles of reinforcement and imitation. (95) _____ theories assume that innate factors cause children to attend to and perceive language in certain ways. According to psycholinguistic theory, language involves the interaction of environmental influences, such as parental (96) _____ and (97) _____, and an (98) _____ tendency to acquire language. Noam (99) _____ refers to this inborn tendency as a language acquisition device (LAD).

Does development occur gradually or in stages? Another controversy in developmental psychology concerns the question as to whether developmental changes tend to occur gradually (100) _____ or in major leaps (101)_____. (102)_____ theorists like Freud and Piaget view development as discontinuous. According to them, people go through distinct periods of development that differ in (103)_____ and follow an orderly (104)_____. Learning theorists, in contrast, tend to view psychological development as a more (105)_____ process. Some aspects of development, such as the adolescent growth spurt, are (106)_____. There is controversy as to whether (107)_____ development is continuous or discontinuous.

Reflection Break 4

1. Briefly describe the two positions in the nature-nurture debate.

2. Briefly describe the two sides of the continuous-discontinuous debate.

REVIEW: KEY TERMS AND CONCEPTS

FINAL CHAPTER REVIEW

Review

Visit the *Psychology in the New Millennium* Web site at www.harcourtcollege.com/psych/PNM/siteresources.html and take the Chapter Quizzes to test your knowledge.

Recite

Go to the Recite section for this chapter in your textbook. Use the tear-off card provided at the back of the book to cover the answers of the Recite section. Read the questions aloud, and recite the answers. This will help you cement your knowledge of key concepts.

Essay Questions

1. Why do you think babies are born with reflexes? What purpose do reflexes serve? Why do doctors continue to test the reflexes of infants well into the first years of life? Explain your ideas on these issues in a three-paragraph essay.

2. Create a booklet that illustrates examples of the Piagetian concepts of assimilation and accommodation. You might want to use examples from your experience of learning about psychology. In your booklet, also provide examples of your own use of egocentrism, animism, or artificialism in thinking.

3. How do you feel about the Ebonics debate? Do you think that Ebonics should be recognized as a language? Why or why not? Prepare a two-page essay describing your position. Be sure to clearly explain your position and the reasons behind it.

4. How would you characterize your parents' parenting style? Were they warm or cold, restrictive or permissive? How did the parenting style you experienced affect your feelings and behavior? After studying this chapter, how will your own parenting style be similar to your parents? How will it be different? In a one-page essay, characterize your parents' parenting style and compare it with your own. Are you (or will you be) an authoritative parent? How do you know? Provide specific examples of your behavior to support your answer.

5. What is known about the psychological effects of day care? Prepare a report for parents on the psychological impact of day care on children. Does the evidence suggest that a day care experience benefits or harms children? How? If you were a parent, how would (did) you choose the specific day care you use? How does your opinion of day care compare with that of the American Psychological Association's? (You can read about the APA and day care in the *Monitor* article at http://www.apa.org/monitor/mar00/childcare.html.

6. Which side of the developmental controversies do you feel has the most support—nature or nurture? Be sure that you support your answer with good evidence. You might want to complete Web search #4 on the Harcourt Web site before responding to this question so that you can be sure to support your position with good evidence.

RELATE/EXPAND/INTEGRATE

1. **Prenatal Development: The Beginning of Our Life Story**

   Prenatal Screening: What tests and screening measures are available for pregnant women? Which ones are recommended as routine? When would a woman need alternative tests? Investigate the tests recommended for pregnant women and create a one-page summary of your findings. You might want to visit http://www.stanford.edu/~holbrook/. This site provides technical but interesting information about a variety of prenatal tests used to diagnose many different conditions in both the unborn child and the mother. Includes ultrasound, amniocentesis, percutaneous umbilical blood sampling, and Rh disease.

2. **Childhood: Cognitive Development**

   Does research in cognitive development support Piaget's view that children are "budding" scientists? Use your favorite Web search engines to explore the current views on Piaget's theory. Be sure to look for research that takes a cross-cultural approach. Report back to your study group on your findings in a format specified by your instructor.

3. **Childhood: Cognitive Development**

   Have each member of your study group give the following Piagetian conservation tests to a 4-year-old and an 8-year-old child. Summarize the results and report your findings to your whole class in a format specified by your instructor.

   Conservation of number: Place two row of 10 objects (M&M's or Skittles candies work well) so that they line up. Ask the child whether the two rows have the same number of candies. (The child should say yes.) In front of the child, spread out one of the rows of candies so that there is about ½ inch of space between each candy. Ask the child whether the two rows contain the same number of candies now. Record the child's response. Return the candies to their original position and repeat.

   Conservation of length: Cut two pieces of string so that they both are exactly 10 inches long. Place both pieces of string one beneath the other so that the ends line up. Ask the child whether the two strings are the same length. (The child should say yes.) In front of the child, scrunch up one of the strings so that it is looped over itself. Ask the child whether the two strings are the same length now. Record the child's response. Return the strings to their original position and repeat.

   Conservation of substance: Take two identical balls of craft clay. Roll them into balls until the child agrees that they are the same size. Now take one of the balls and roll it into a "hot dog" shape. Ask the child whether the two pieces of clay have the same amount of clay. Record the child's response. Return the balls to their original shape and repeat.

4. **Childhood: Social and Personality Development**

   Child Temperament. Visit http://www.preventiveoz.org/ and use this program to develop a profile of yourself, your own child, or a fictional one. To start using this program, click on

"Image of Your Child" and complete the short temperament questionnaire. You will then see an online profile of your child's temperament. Using the further links, research general strategies for managing the highs or lows of your child's temperament and what specific behavioral issues are normal for your child's temperament. Compare your child's temperament to those of the other members of your study group. Report the similarities and differences to your whole class in a format specified by your instructor.

ANSWERS FOR CHAPTER 10

Reading for Understanding About "Prenatal Development: The Beginning of Our Life Story"

1. months
2. neonate
3. Prenatal
4. zygote
5. fallopian
6. uterine
7. embryonic
8. second
9. amniotic
10. placenta
11. fetal
12. size
13. movements

Reading for Understanding About "Childhood: Physical Development"

14. birth
15. Physical
16. rapidly
17. five
18. triple
19. Reflexes
20. see
21. complex
22. depth
23. hear
24. mother
25. pleasant
26. sweet
27. sit
28. crawl
29. age
30. sequence

Reflection Break 1

1.

	Time Period	**Major Characterisitics**
Germinal	Conception until implantation	The zygote, the single cell formed by the union of the sperm and egg, divides as it travels through the fallopian tube and becomes implanted in the uterine wall.
Embryonic	Implantation to eigthth week	The major organ systems are formed. By the end of the second month, the nervous system begins to transmit messages and the the sex organs begin to differentiate. The embryo is suspended in the amniotic sac and exchanges nutrients and wastes with the mother through the placenta.
Fetal	Eigthth week until birth	Characterized by maturation and gains in size. It is during the fetal period that the mother will detect the first fetal movements.

2.

Sense	**Capabilities**
Vision	Newborn babies can see quite well and show greater interest in complex visual stimuli than in simple ones. Infants are capable of depth perception by the time they can crawl.
Hearing	Newborns can normally hear and show a preference for their mother's voice.
Taste & Smell	Newborns show preferences for pleasant odors and sweet foods.
Touch	Newborns are sensitive to touch but are relatively insensitive to pain.

3. Babies are born with many simple, unlearned stereotypical responses called reflexes. These include the rooting, sucking, startle, and grasping reflexes. Motor development usually proceeds in a particular sequence in which infants roll over and sit before they creep, crawl, stand, and walk. There is a great deal of variation in the age at which infants first engage in motor activities, but the sequence remains generally the same.

Reading for Understanding About "Childhood: Cognitive Development"

31. cognitive
32. Piaget
33. stages
34. assimilation
35. accommodation
36. Schemes
37. sensorimotor
38. preoperational
39. concrete operational

40. formal operational
41. Language
42. prelinguistic
43. symbolic
44. Coos
45. babbling
46. understand
47. holophrases
48. telegraphic speech

49. overextension
50. overregularization
51. vocabulary
52. complex
53. Kohlberg
54. preconventional
55. conventional
56. postconventional
57. postconventional

Reflection Break 2

1. c
2. r
3. j
4. p
5. g
6. k
7. m
8. h

9. i
10. t
11. o
12. s
13. u
14. v
15. l
16. b

17. e
18. a
19. n
20. q
21. d
22. w
23. f

Reading for Understanding About "Childhood: Social and Personality Development"

58. Social
59. Erikson
60. crisis
61. trust versus mistrust
62. autonomy
63. shame
64. guilt
65. industriousness
66. Ainsworth
67. Attachment

68. indiscriminate
69. familiar
70. primary caregiver
71. strange situation
72. securely
73. avoidantly
74. Ambivalently
75. Behaviorists
76. Harlow
77. contact comfort

78. instinctual
79. imprinted
80. parenting
81. instrumental competence
82. Authoritative
83. Authoritarian
84. Permissive
85. warmth
86. strictness
87. authoritative

Reflection Break 3

1. Review Erikson's early stages of social development by decribing developmental that occurs.

   Trust versus mistrust: This first crisis centers on the child's learning that the world is a good place that can meet his or her needs.

Autonomy versus shame and doubt: Occurs in early childhood when the child begins to explore the environment and develops autonomy (self-direction) or its opposite, feelings of shame and guilt.

Initiative versus inferiority: Occurs in later childhood, encourages us to develop either industriousness or feelings of inferiority.

2. What is attachment, and how is it demonstrated?

Ainsworth defines attachment as an emotional tie that is formed between a person and another specific person. Attachments keeps organisms together and are vital to the survival of infants. According to Ainsworth, there are three stages of attachment: the initial-preattachment phase, which is characterized by indiscriminate attachment; the attachment-in-the-making phase, which is characterized by preference for familiar figures; and the clear-cut attachment phase, which is characterized by intensified dependence on the primary caregiver.

3. Briefly compare and contrast each of the three parenting styles: authoritative, authoritarian, and permissive.

Authoritative: Authoritative parents are restrictive and demand mature behavior but temper their strictness with love and support. The children of authoritative parents are most achievement oriented and well adjusted.

Authoritarian: Authoritarian parents view obedience as a virtue, they have strict guidelines about what is right and wrong, and they rely on force and have poor communication skills.

Permissive: Permissive parents are generally easygoing with their children; they are warm and supportive but poor at communication. Research shows that warmth in parenting is superior in rearing children, but that strictness also pays off.

Reading for Understanding About
"Controversies in Developmental Psychology"

88. heredity
89. environmental influences
90. interaction
91. nature
92. environmental
93. language
94. Learning

95. Nativist
96. speech
97. reinforcement
98. inborn
99. Chomsky
100. continuously
101. discontinuously

102. Stage
103. quality
104. sequence
105. continuous
106. discontinuous
107. cognitive

Reflection Break 4

1. The nature-nurture controversy concerns the relative influences of heredity (nature) and nurture (environmental influences) on development. Development appears to reflect an interaction between nature (genetic factors) and nurture (environmental influences).

2. This controversy concerns the question as to whether developmental changes tend to occur gradually (continuously) or in major leaps (discontinuously). Stage theorists like Freud and Piaget view development as discontinuous. According to them, people go through distinct periods of development that differ in quality and follow an orderly sequence. Learning theorists, in contrast, tend to view psychological development as a more continuous process.

Chapter 11

Adolescent and Adult Development

PREVIEW

Skim the major headings in this chapter in your textbook. Jot down anything that you are surprised or curious about. After this, write down four or five questions that you have about the material in this chapter.

Things that surprised me/I am curious about from Chapter 11:

Questions that I have about adolescent and adult development:

▲

▲

▲

▲

QUESTION

These are some questions that you should be able to answer after you finish studying this chapter.

Adolescence: Physical Development

▲ What physical developments occur during adolescence?

Adolescence: Cognitive Development

▲ What cognitive developments occur during adolescence?

Adolescence: Social and Personality Development

▲ What social and personality developments occur during adolescence?

Adulthood: Physical Development

▲ What physical developments occur during adulthood?

▲ Question: What are the gender and ethnic differences in life expectancy?

▲ Why do we age?

Adulthood: Cognitive Development

▲ What cognitive developments occur during adulthood?

▲ What is Alzheimer's disease? What are its origins?

Adulthood: Social and Personality Development

▲ What social and personality developments occur during young adulthood?

▲ Just what is meant by "emerging adulthood"?

▲ What is the "singles scene" like today?

▲ Who cohabits today, and why?

▲ What is the role of marriage today?

▲ How many marriages end in divorce? Why do people get divorced?

▲ Why do people work?

▲ What social and personality developments occur during middle adulthood?

▲ What social and personality developments occur during late adulthood?

▲ How do people in the United States age today?

On Death and Dying

▲ What are psychological perspectives on death and dying?

READING FOR UNDERSTANDING/REFLECT

The following section provides you with the opportunity to perform two of the R's of the PQ4R study method. In this section you are encouraged to check your understanding of your reading of the text by filling in the blanks in the brief paragraphs that relate to each of the preview questions. You will also be prompted to rehearse your understanding of the material with periodic Rehearsal/Reflection breaks. Remember, it is better to study in more frequent, short sessions than in one long "cram session." Be sure to reward yourself with short study breaks before each Rehearsal/Reflection exercise.

Reading for Understanding About "Adolescence: Physical Development"

What physical developments occur during adolescence? (1) _____ is a period of life that begins at puberty and ends with assumption of adult responsibilities. (2) _____ begins with the appearance of secondary sex characteristics and is the period during which the body becomes sexually mature. Changes that lead to (3) _____ capacity and secondary sex characteristics are stimulated by increased levels of (4) _____ in the male and of estrogen and (5) _____ in the female. (6) _____ production becomes cyclical in females and regulates the menstrual cycle. The beginning of menstruation is known as (7) _____. During the (8) _____ growth spurt, young people may grow 6 or more inches in a year.

Reading for Understanding About "Adolescence: Cognitive Development"

What cognitive developments occur during adolescence? (9) _____ thinking appears in adolescence, but not everyone reaches this stage. Formal operational thought is characterized by the ability to deal with the (10) _____ and the hypothetical. Adolescent thought is also marked by a form of (11) _____, in that adolescents can understand the thoughts of others but still have trouble separating things that are of concern to others and those that are concerns only to themselves. Two consequences of adolescent egocentrism are the imaginary audience and the (12) _____. The (13) _____ refers to adolescents' beliefs that they are the center of attention and that other people are as concerned with their appearance and behavior as they are. The (14) _____ refers to the adolescent belief that one's feelings and ideas are special, even unique, and that one is invulnerable.

A number of questions have been raised concerning the (15) _____ of Piaget's views. These include: timing, (16) _____, and sequencing. Some critics argue that children are more (17) _____ than Piaget thought, that he underestimated the abilities of children. Other critics argue that events like egocentrism and conservation appear to develop more (18) _____ than Piaget thought, and still others question the consistency of the (19) _____ of development. In the end, although Piaget's theory has been questioned, it has not been (20) _____.

Another aspect of cognitive development in the adolescent includes changes in (21) _____. Although none of Kohlberg's levels are tied to age, most adolescents and adults reason (22) _____. When (23) _____ thought does emerge, it does so in adolescence. Postconventional moral reasoning is based on person's own moral (24) _____; moral judgments are derived from (25) _____, rather than from conventional standards. Research seems to (26) _____ Kohlberg's developmental sequences of moral development.

Reading for Understanding About "Adolescence: Social and Personality Development"

What social and personality developments occur during adolescence? In terms of social and personality development, adolescence has been associated with (27) _____. Adolescents and parents are often in (28) _____ because adolescents desire more (29) _____ and may experiment with things that can jeopardize their health. However, despite bickering, most adolescents continue to love and respect their (30) _____. Stanley Hall attributed the conflicts and distress of adolescence to (31) _____ changes; however, research evidence suggests that (32) _____ influences have a relatively greater impact.

According to Erik Erikson, adolescents strive to forge an (33) _____, or a sense of who they are and what they stand for. Adolescents who do not develop ego identity may experience (34) _____; they spread themselves too thin, running down one blind alley after another. Erikson's views on the development of identity were intended to apply to (35) _____. Erikson believed that the development of (36) _____ was more important to a woman's identity than (37) _____ issues since women's identities were closely connected to women's roles as wives and mothers. Male identities are more closely connected with (38) _____ issues. However, current research shows that young women's identities are also strongly (39) _____ with occupational issues. Other key aspects in identity formation include (40) _____ and sexual identity. (41) _____ is more complicated for adolescents from ethnic minority groups since they may be faced with two sets of cultural standards. Sexually, the changes of (42) _____ prepare the body for sexual activity, and high (43) _____ levels also stir interest in sex. But most sexually active adolescents do not use (44) _____ reliably. Thus about 1 teenage girl in 10 gets (45) _____ each year.

Reflection Break 1

Part I. Matching: *Match the term with its proper description.*

a. Adolescence
b. Puberty
c. Secondary sex characteristics
d. Menarche
e. Testosterone

f. Estrogen and androgens
g. Formal operations
h. Egocentrism
i. Imaginary audience
j. Personal fable
k. Conventional morality

l. Postconventional morality
m. *Sturm und Drang*
n. Ego identity
o. Role diffusion

_____ 1. Erikson's term for adolescents who spread themselves too thin and place themselves at the mercy of leaders.

_____ 2. A time of transition from childhood to adulthood.

_____ 3. The period during which the body becomes sexually mature.

_____ 4. A firm sense of who one is and what one stands for.

_____ 5. The appearance of body hair, deepening of the voice in males, and rounding of hips and breasts in females.

_____ 6. The final stage in Piaget's theory, characterized by abstract thinking.

_____ 7. The inabilities of adolescents to separate things that are of concern to others and those that are of concern only to themselves.

_____ 8. The belief of adolescents that other people are as concerned with their thoughts and behavior as they are.

_____ 9. G. Stanley Hall's term to characterize the storm and stress of adolescence.

_____ 10. The beginning of menstruation.

_____ 11. The belief of adolescents that their feelings and ideas are special, even unique, and that they are invulnerable.

_____ 12. Male sex hormone.

_____ 13. Moral reasoning based on a person's own moral standards and personal values.

_____ 14. Female sex hormones.

_____ 15. Moral reasoning governed by social rules and conventions.

Part 2. Briefly describe how the physical, cognitive and social/personal aspects of adolescence contribute to an ego identity.

Reading for Understanding About "Adulthood: Physical Development"

What physical developments occur during adulthood? Development continues throughout the (46) _____. The most obvious aspects of development during adulthood are (47) _____. People are usually at the (48) _____ of their physical powers during young adulthood. Middle adulthood is characterized by a gradual (49) _____ in strength. (50) _____, or the cessation of menstruation, usually occurs in the late 40s or early 50s and has been thought to depress many women, but research suggests that most women go through this passage without great (51) _____. Older people show less sensory (52) _____, and their reaction time (53) _____. The (54) _____ system weakens, and changes occur that eventually result in death.

What are the gender and ethnic differences in life expectancy? Women (55) _____ men by nearly 7 years, and (56) _____ and (57) _____ Americans tend to outlive other ethnic groups in the United States. (58) _____ differences also play a role in ethnic differences in life expectancy: members of ethnic minorities are more likely to be poor, and poor people tend to eat less nutritious diets, encounter more (59) _____, and have less access to health care. By and large, the groups who live longer are more likely to seek and make use of (60) _____.

Why do we age? (61) _____ plays a role in longevity. One theory ((62) _____) suggests that aging and death are determined by our genes. Another theory ((63) _____) holds that factors such as pollution, disease, and ultraviolet light weaken the body so that it loses the ability to repair itself. (64) _____ factors such as exercise, proper nutrition, and not smoking also contribute to longevity.

Reading for Understanding About "Adulthood: Cognitive Development"

What cognitive developments occur during adulthood? People are usually at the height of their (65) _____ powers during early adulthood, but people can be (66) _____ for a lifetime. (67) _____ functioning declines with age, but the declines are not usually as large as people assume. People tend to retain (68) _____ ability, as shown by vocabulary and general knowledge, into advanced old age.(69) _____ intelligence, or one's vocabulary and accumulated knowledge, generally increases with age, while (70) _____ intelligence, the ability to process information rapidly, declines more rapidly. However, workers' (71) _____ with solving specific kinds of problems is often more important than their fluid intelligence.

Some developmental theorists have proposed the existence of (72) _____ thought, a stage of cognitive development after formal operational thought that is characterized by creative thinking, the ability to solve complex problems, and the posing of new questions. People usually show postformal thought in their areas of (73) _____.

What is Alzheimer's disease? What are its origins? (74) _____ disease is characterized by a general, gradual cognitive deterioration in memory, language, and problem solving. On a biological level, it is connected with reduced levels of (75) _____ in the brain and with the buildup of (76) _____ in the brain. Alzheimer's disease does not reflect the normal aging process. There are, however, normal, more gradual (77) _____ in intellectual functioning and memory among older people.

Reading for Understanding About "Adulthood: Social and Personality Development"

Changes in (78) _____ and (79) _____ development during adulthood are most likely the most fluid. Research evidence does suggest that people tend to grow psychologically (80) _____ as they advance from adolescence through middle adulthood.

What social and personality developments occur during young adulthood? (81) _____ adulthood is generally characterized by efforts to advance in the business world and the development of intimate ties. Many young adults reassess the directions of their lives during the "(82) _____."

Just what is meant by "emerging adulthood"? (83) _____ is a hypothesized period that exists in wealthy societies. It roughly spans the ages of 18 through 25 and affords young people extended periods of (84) _____. The concept dovetails with (85) _____ concept of a prolonged adolescence we find in industrialized societies, one that permits a period of (86) _____ during which the individual searches for personal identity.

Sheehy proposes that the (87) _____ are a period in which people basically strive to advance their careers and establish their pathways in life. During this time many young adults adopt what Daniel (88) _____ calls the dream, or the drive to "become" someone and to leave a mark on history, this then serves as a tentative blueprint for their life. Erikson characterizes young adulthood as the stage of (89) _____, or the time for the establishment of intimate relationships.

The ages of 28 to 33 have been labeled by Levinson as the "age-30 transition" and by Sheehy as the "Catch 30s" because of the tendency for (90) _____. Often we find that the lifestyles that we adopted during our 20s do not fit as comfortably as we had expected, and the later 30s are characterized by (91) _____.

What is the "singles scene" like today? Being (92) _____ has become the nation's most common lifestyle for people in their early 20s as they delay (93) _____ to pursue education and careers. For some, being single is a stage that precedes marriage; for others, it is an (94) _____ lifestyle. For some, being single means a string of (95) _____. Some engage in serial (96) _____, in which they have a series of exclusive sexual relationships.

Who cohabits today. and why? (97) _____ has become so common in the United States that about 5 million couples cohabit today and at least half of couples who got married during the past decade had cohabited first. Liberal, (98) _____, and divorced people are somewhat more likely to cohabit than are other people. Research suggests that cohabitation is often an alternative to the (99) _____ that can accompany living alone, without the legal entanglements of marriage. (100) _____ factors also seem to be a factor in cohabitation.

What is the role of marriage today? (101) _____ remains the most popular lifestyle in the United States, and people still think of marriage as permanent. Marriage (102) _____ sexual relations, creates a home life, and provides an institution for the rearing of children. People continue to have high expectations of marriage, including feelings of (103) _____. We tend to marry people to whom we are (104) _____, and they are usually like us in age and physical attractiveness and hold similar attitudes on major issues.

How many marriages end in divorce? Why do people get divorced? At least half of today's marriages end in (105) _____, mainly because of problems in communication. But relaxed legal restrictions and women's greater (106) _____ independence have also contributed to the divorce rate. Divorce usually has (107) _____ and emotional repercussions. On the average, a divorced (108) _____ income drops by one quarter whereas a divorced (109) _____ income drops by less than 10 %. People who are divorced also have the highest rates of (110) _____ and psychological disorders, and children of divorced parents are more likely to have (111) _____ problems, engage in (112) _____, and earn lower grades.

Why do people work? People work for (113) _____ (e.g., money, financial security) and (114) _____ reasons (self-identity, the social values of work, a way of structuring one's time). Work provides us with a means to pay our bills along with a (115) _____, self-fulfillment, and self-worth.

What social and personality developments occur during middle adulthood? Erikson labeled the life (116) _____ of middle age as generativity versus stagnation. (117) _____ involves doing things that we believe are worthwhile and enhances and maintains self-esteem. (118) _____ means treading water or moving backwards and has powerful destructive effects on self-esteem.

Many theorists view middle adulthood as a time of crisis (the (119) "_____") and further reassessment. Many adults try to come to terms with the (120) _____ between their achievements and the dreams of their youth during middle adulthood. Some middle-aged adults become depressed when their youngest child leaves home (the so-called (121) _____ syndrome), but many report increased satisfaction, stability, and self-confidence. On a more positive note, many people in middle adulthood experience (122) "_____"-a phase during which they redefine themselves and their goals for the 30 to 40 healthy years they expect lie ahead of them.

What social and personality developments occur during late adulthood? Erikson characterizes late adulthood as the stage of (123) _____. He saw the basic challenge as maintaining the belief that life is worthwhile in the face of (124) _____. Ego integrity derives from (125) _____, which can be defined as expert knowledge about the meaning of life, balancing one's own needs and those of others, and striving for excellence in one's behavior and achievements. Other views of late adulthood stress the importance of creating new (126) _____; however (127) _____ and (128) _____ realities may require older people to become more selective in their pursuits.

How do people in the United States age today? Many (129) _____ about aging are growing less prevalent. Most older Americans report being generally (130) _____ with their lives. Those who experience (131) "_____" reshape their lives to focus on what they find to be important, maintain a positive outlook, and find new challenges.

Reading for Understanding About "On Death and Dying"

What are psychological perspectives on death and dying? (132) _____ has identified five stages of dying among people who are terminally ill: denial, anger, bargaining, depression, and final acceptance. However, other investigators find that psychological reactions to approaching (133) _____ are more varied than Kübler-Ross suggests.

Reflection Break 2

Part I. *Briefly describe the physical and cognitive changes that occur during adulthood by filling in the chart below:*

	Physical	Cognitive	Psychosocial
Early adulthood			
Middle adulthood			
Later adulthood			

REVIEW: KEY TERMS AND CONCEPTS

FINAL CHAPTER REVIEW

Review

Visit the *Psychology in the New Millennium* Web site at www.harcourtcollege.com/psych/PNM/siteresources.html and take the Chapter Quizzes to test your knowledge.

Recite

Go to the Recite section for this chapter in your textbook. Use the tear-off card provided at the back of the book to cover the answers of the Recite section. Read the questions aloud, and recite the answers. This will help you cement your knowledge of key concepts.

Essay Questions

1. Did you undergo puberty early or late as compared with your peers? How did your experience with puberty affect your popularity and your self-esteem? Compare your experience with what is considered "typical" by psychologists in a one-page essay.

2. How do changes in cognitive development during adolescence contribute to the desire for privacy and risk taking? Did you have an intense need for privacy as an adolescent? Do you know adolescents who act as if they believe that they will live forever? Why do you think that adolescents think like this? Does Piaget's theory explain these behaviors? What do you think can be done—based on what you have learned about the thinking of adolescents—to decrease risk-taking behavior in today's adolescents? Prepare a two-page report that describes your recommendations; be sure to support your ideas with evidence from developmental theory.

3. Is there a "manopause?" What do you think? Why? Does the research support your belief? In a two-page essay describe your views and the current research on the topic.

4. Think of the older people that you know. In a three or four-paragraph essay describe how the concepts of crystallized and fluid intelligence apply to their lives. What kind of cognitive changes can you look forward to as you age? Do you think that you will follow the "typical" pattern? Why or why not?

5. Diversity: What factors may contribute to differences in health and longevity among people in different ethnic groups and gender? How do you explain the different patterns of aging in the different ethnic groups? Explain your views on this issue in a two-page essay. Be sure to describe the kind of data would you need to collect to test your theories. Does this data exist?

6. Erik Erikson wrote that one aspect of wisdom is the ability to visualize one's role in the march of history and to accept one's own death. Do you believe that acceptance of death is a sign of wisdom? Why or why not? Present your views in a two-page essay.

RELATE/EXPAND/INTEGRATE

1. **Adolescence: Physical Development**
   Sex and sexuality are important issues for adolescents, yet American parents generally give their children little information about sex. Although both teenagers and parents express the need to talk freely about sex, parents are often reluctant and claim that they lack the knowledge and communication skills to talk openly about sex. One source of information about sex is popular magazines like *Parents,* Parenting.com, *Ladies Home Journal, Redbook,* and for teens *YM and Seventeen* magazines.

   Search the most recent issues of three of these magazines for information on adolescent sexuality. What kind of information is presented? Are issues like homosexuality, contraception, and sexually transmitted diseases discussed? What about values-are they addressed? How are the approaches of the "parent"-oriented magazines different from those directed at teens? Share your findings with your study group. Report your study group's findings to your class in a format specified by your instructor.

2. **Adolescence: Social and Personality Development**
   Consider the stereotype of adolescence as a time of "storm and stress." What findings or occurrences prompted this stereotype? Does this stereotype fit your own experience? How or how not? What does the psychological research suggest-is adolescence a time of "storm and stress?" Visit a teen chat room (http://www.chatweb.net/) and pose this question to those present. Report your findings to your class in a format specified by your instructor.

3. **Adulthood: Physical Development**
   Northwestern Mutual's Longevity Game. This is an interactive lifestyle and health awareness quiz, to get a general idea of how long you may live past retirement. Take the quiz. How long does the site suggest that you will live? The site also claims that you can learn the secrets of longevity by finding out what their centenarians have to say. Are there any behavior patterns that you could change that might add to your life expectancy?

   URL: http://www.northwesternmutual.com/nmcom/NM/longevitygameintro/toolbox—calculator—longevitygameintro—longevity intro

4. **Adulthood: Cognitive Development**
   Have the movements towards gender equity changed the workplace for women? The data cited in your text in the work's diversity section is from 1998; research more current data on gender distribution of labor. How have salaries changed? Use your favorite Web search engine to research more current data, and prepare a report for your classmates on your findings. Do you think that we will ever reach a point of true gender equity? Why or why not?

   URL: http://www.ask.com
   URL: http://www.dogpile.com
   URL: http://www.google.com

5. **Adulthood: Social and Personality Development**
   Do women experience "empty-nest syndrome" when their youngest child leaves home? Interview five women whose children have recently left. Do they report experiencing "empty nest syndrome?" Combine your findings with those of your study group. After you have completed your interviews, use your favorite Web search engine to research the factors that predict the occurrence of "empty nest syndrome." Report your findings to the class.

   URL: http://www.ask.com
   URL: http://www.dogpile.com
   URL: http://www.google.com

ANSWERS FOR CHAPTER 11

Reading for Understanding About "Adolescence: Physical Development"

1. Adolescence
2. Puberty
3. reproductive
4. testosterone
5. androgens
6. Estrogen
7. menarche
8. adolescent

Reading for Understanding About "Adolescence: Cognitive Development"

9. Formal operational
10. abstract
11. egocentrism
12. personal fable
13. imaginary audience
14. personal fable
15. accuracy
16. stages
17. capable
18. continuously
19. sequence
20. rejected
21. moral reasoning
22. conventionally
23. postconventional
24. standards
25. personal values
26. support

Reading for Understanding About "Adolescence: Social and Personality Development"

27. turbulence
28. conflict
29. independence
30. parents
31. biological
32. sociocultural
33. ego identity
34. role diffusion
35. males
36. interpersonal relationships
37. occupational
38. occupational
39. connected
40. ethnicity
41. Identity formation
42. puberty
43. hormone
44. contraceptives
45. pregnant

Reflection Break 1

Part 1. Matching

1. o	6. g	11. j
2. a	7. h	12. e
3. b	8. I	13. l
4. n	9. m	14. f
5. c	10. d	15. k

Part 2

Biologically, cognitively, and socially, the adolescent is undergoing change. Physically, adolescents begin to look like adults. The sex hormones surge and stimulate a new interest in sexuality. Cognitively, their thinking is expanding and they can think about new possibilities. Socially, they are striving to be independent but are cognitively aware of their limitations. Since different systems in the body grow at different rates, their coordination and body control may be awkward. This may lead them to question themselves, impacting the formation of their self-concept and self-esteem; thus impacting their social interactions.

Reading for Understanding About "Adulthood: Physical Development"

46. lifespan	53. lengthens	60. health care
47. physical	54. immune	61. Heredity
48. height	55. outlive	62. programmed senescence
49. decline	56. European	63. wear-and-tear theory
50. Menopause	57. Asian	64. Lifestyle
51. difficulty	58. Socioeconomic	
52. acuity	59. stress	

Reading for Understanding About "Adulthood: Cognitive Development"

65. cognitive	70. fluid	75. acetylcholine
66. creative	71. familiarity	76. plaque
67. Memory	72. postformal	77. declines
68. verbal	73. expertise	
69. Crystallized	74. Alzheimer's	

Reading for Understanding About "Adulthood: Social and Personality Development"

78. social
79. personality
80. healthier
81. Young
82. age-30 transition
83. Emerging adulthood
84. role exploration
85. Erikson's
86. moratorium
87. 20s
88. Levinson
89. intimacy versus isolation
90. reassessment
91. settling down
92. single
93. marriage
94. open-ended
95. affairs
96. monogamy
97. ohabitation
98. well-educated
99. loneliness
100. Economic
101. Marriage
102. legitimizes
103. romantic love
104. attracted
105. divorce
106. economic
107. financial
108. women's
109. man's
110. physical illness
111. behavior
112. substance abuse
113. extrinsic
114. intrinsic
115. self-identity
116. crisis
117. Generativity
118. Stagnation
119. midlife crisis
120. discrepancies
121. empty-nest
122. middlescence
123. ego integrity versus despair
124. physical deterioration
125. wisdom
126. challenges
127. biological
128. social
129. stereotypes
130. satisfied
131. successful aging

Reading for Understanding About "On Death and Dying"

132. Kübler-Ross
133. death

Reflection Break 2

Briefly describe the physical and cognitive changes that occur during adulthood by filling in the chart below:

	Physical	**Cognitive**	**Psychosocial**
Early adulthood	People are usually at the height of their physical powers during young adulthood. Sexually, most young adults become easily aroused, and men are more likely to think about ejaculating too quickly than whether or not they will be able to maintain an erection.	People are usually at the height of their cognitive powers during early adulthood, but people can be creative for a lifetime. Some developmental theorists have proposed the existence of postformal thought, a stage of cognitive development after formal operational thought that is characterized by creative thinking, the ability to solve complex problems, and the posing of new questions.	Young adulthood is generally characterized by efforts to advance in the business world and the development of intimate ties. Many young adults reassess the directions of their lives during the "age-30 transition." Emerging adulthood is a hypothesized period that exists in wealthy societies. It roughly spans the ages of 18 through 25 and affords young people extended periods of role exploration. The concept dovetails with Erikson's concept of a prolonged adolescence we find in industrialized societies, one that permits a period of moratorium during which the individual searches for personal identity.

Sheehy proposes that the 20s are a period in which people basically strive to advance their careers and establish their pathway in life. During this time many young adults adopt what Daniel Levinson call the dream, or the drive to "become" someone and to leave a mark on history; this then serves as a tentative blueprint for their life. Erikson characterizes young adulthood as the stage of intimacy versus isolation, or the time for the establishment of intimate relationships.

The ages of 28 to 33 have been labeled by Levinson as the age-30 transition and by Sheehy as the |

			Catch 30s because of the tendency for reassessment. Often we find that the lifestyles that we adopted during our 20s do not fit as comfortably as we had expected, and the later 30s are characterized by settling down.
Middle adulthood	Middle adulthood is characterized by a gradual decline in strength. Menopause, or the cessation of menstruation, usually occurs in the late 40s or early 50s and has been thought to depress many women, but research suggests that most women go through this passage without great difficulty. Menopause is the final stage of the climacteric, a falling off in the secretion of the hormones estrogen and progesterone that women experience.	Memory functioning declines with age, but the declines are not usually as large as people assume. People tend to retain verbal ability, as shown by vocabulary and general knowledge, into advanced old age. Crystallized intelligence, or one's vocabulary and accumulated knowledge, generally increases with age; while fluid intelligence, the ability to process information rapidly, declines more rapidly.	Erikson labeled the life crisis of middle age as generativity versus stagnation. Generativity involves doing things that we believe are worthwhile and enhances and maintains self-esteem. Stagnation means treading water or moving backwards and has powerful destructive effects on self-esteem. Many theorists view middle adulthood as a time of crisis (the "midlife crisis") and further reassessment. Many adults try to come to terms with the discrepancies between their achievements and the dreams of their youth during middle adulthood. Some middle-aged adults become depressed when their youngest child leaves home (the so-called empty-nest syndrome), but many report increased satisfaction, stability, and self-confidence. On a more positive note, many people in middle adulthood experience "middlescence"-a phase during which they redefine themselves and their goals for the 30 to 40 healthy years they expect lie ahead of them. Marriage remains the most popular lifestyle in the United States, and people still think of marriage as permanent.

Later adulthood	Older people show less sensory acuity, and their reaction time lengthens. Older people develop wrinkles and gray hair due to the decline in melanin, collagen, and elastin. Although people are capable of enjoying sexual experiences throughout their lifetime, changes do occur. Older men and women experience less interest in sex and men may have difficulty reaching and maintaining an erection. Women may experience less vaginal lubrication. The immune system weakens, and changes occur that eventually result in death.	Alzheimer's disease is characterized by a general, gradual cognitive deterioration in memory, language, and problem solving. On a biological level, it is connected with reduced levels of acetylcholine in the brain and with the build-up of plaque in the brain. Alzheimer's disease does not reflect the normal aging process. There are, however, normal, more gradual declines in intellectual functioning and memory among older people.	Erikson characterizes late adulthood as the stage of ego integrity versus despair. He saw the basic challenge as maintaining the belief that life is worthwhile in the face of physical deterioration. Ego integrity derives from wisdom, which can be defined as expert knowledge about the meaning of life, balancing one's own needs and those of others, and striving for excellence in one's behavior and achievements. Other views of late adulthood stress the importance of creating new challenges; however, biological and social realities may require older people to become more selective in their pursuits. Many stereotypes about aging are growing less prevalent. Most older Americans report being generally satisfied with their lives. Those who experience "successful aging" reshape their lives to focus on what they find to be important, maintain a positive outlook, and find new challenges.

Chapter 12

Personality

PREVIEW

Skim the major headings in this chapter in your textbook. Jot down anything that you are surprised or curious about. After this, write down four or five questions that you have about the material in this chapter.

Things that surprised me/I am curious about from Chapter 12:

Questions that I have about personality:

▲

▲

▲

▲

QUESTION

These are some questions that you should be able to answer after you finish studying this chapter.

Introduction to Personality: "Why Are They Sad and Glad and Bad?"

▲ *Just what is personality?*

▲ *What is Freud's theory of psychosexual development?*

▲ *Who are some other psychodynamic theorists? What are their views on personality?*

The Psychodynamic Perspective

▲ *What are the strengths and weaknesses of the psychodynamic perspective?*

The Trait Perspective

▲ *What are traits?*

▲ *What is the history of the trait perspective?*

▲ *How have contemporary researchers used factor analysis to reduce the universe of traits to smaller lists of traits that show common features?*

▲ *What are the strengths and weaknesses of trait theory?*

Learning Theory Perspective

▲ *What does learning theory have to contribute to our understanding of personality?*

▲ *What is Watson's contribution to personality theory?*

▲ *How did Skinner develop Watson's views?*

▲ *How does social-cognitive theory differ from the behaviorist view?*

▲ *What are the strengths and weaknesses of learning theories as they apply to personality?*

The Humanistic-Existential Perspective

▲ *What is humanism? What is existentialism?*

▲ *How do humanistic psychologists differ from psychodynamic theorists?*

▲ *Just what is your self? What is self theory?*

▲ *What are the strengths and weaknesses of humanistic-existential theory?*

Personality and Diversity: The Socio-cultural Perspective

▲ *Why is the sociocultural perspective important to the understanding of personality?*

▲ *What does it mean to be individualistic? What is meant by individualism and collectivism?*

▲ *How do sociocultural factors affect the self-concept and self-esteem?*

▲ *How does acculturation affect the psychological well-being of immigrants and their families?*

Measurement of Personality

▲ *How are personality measures used?*

▲ *What are objective personality tests?*

▲ *How do projective tests differ from objective tests?*

▲ *What are some of the more widely used projective tests?*

READING FOR UNDERSTANDING/REFLECT

The following section provides you with the opportunity to perform 2 of the R's of the PQ4R study method. In this section, you are encouraged you to check your understanding of your reading of the text by filling in the blanks in the brief paragraphs that relate to each of the preview questions. You will also be prompted to rehearse your understanding of the material with periodic Reflection breaks. Remember, it is better to study in more frequent, short sessions than in one long "cram session." Be sure to reward yourself with short study breaks before each Reflection exercise.

Reading for Understanding About "Introduction to Personality: 'Why Are They Sad and Glad and Bad?' "

Just what is personality? (1) _____ is defined as the reasonably stable patterns of behavior, including thoughts and emotions, that distinguish one person from another. Psychologists seek to explain how personality (2) _____ and to (3) _____ how people with certain personality traits respond to life's demands. This chapter discusses five (4) _____ on personality: the psychodynamic, trait, learning, humanistic-existential, and sociocultural.

Reading for Understanding About "The Psychodynamic Perspective"

What is Freud's theory of psychosexual development? Freud's theory is termed (5) _____ because it assumes that we are driven largely by unconscious motives and by the movement of unconscious forces within our minds. Freud labeled the region that pokes through into awareness the (6) _____; the (7) _____ mind contains elements of the mind that are out of awareness but that can be made conscious by focusing on them, and the (8) _____ contains biological instincts such as sex and aggression and cannot be experienced consciously. According to psychodynamic theory, people experience (9) _____ as basic instincts of hunger, sex, and aggression come up against social pressures to follow laws, rules, and moral codes. At first this conflict is (10) _____, but as we develop, it is (11) _____. The unconscious (12) _____ represents psychological drives and seeks instant gratification. The (13) _____, or the sense of self or "I," is governed by the reality principle and develops through experience. The ego takes into account what is (14) _____ and possible in gratifying the impulses of the (15) _____. Defense mechanisms such as repression protect the ego from (16) _____ by repressing unacceptable ideas or distorting reality. The (17) _____ is the conscience and develops largely through the Oedipus complex and identification with others. People undergo psychosexual development as psychosexual energy, or (18) _____, is transferred from one erogenous zone to another during childhood. There are (19) _____ stages of development: oral, anal, phallic, latency, and genital. (20) _____ in a stage leads to development of traits associated with the stage.

Who are some other psychodynamic theorists? What are their views on personality? Carl Jung's theory, (21) _____ psychology, features a (22) _____ unconscious and numerous (23) _____, both of which reflect the history of our species. Alfred Adler's theory, (24) _____ psychology, features the (25) _____ self, the inferiority complex, and the compensating drive for (26) _____. Karen Horney's theory focuses on (27) _____ relationships and the possible development of feelings of anxiety and (28) _____. Erik Erikson's theory of (29) _____ development highlights the importance of early social relationships rather than the gratification of childhood (30) _____ impulses. Erikson extended (31) _____'s five developmental stages to eight, including stages that occur in adulthood.

What are the strengths and weaknesses of the psychodynamic perspective? Freud fought for the idea that personality is subject to (32) _____ analysis at a time when many people still viewed psychological problems as signs of (33) _____. He also focused attention on the importance of (34) _____, the effects of child rearing, and the fact that people distort perceptions according to their needs. On the other hand, there is no evidence for the existence of (35) _____, and his theory is fraught with (36) _____ about child development.

Reflection Break 1

Part I. *Match the terms with their correct descriptions.*

a. Pleasure principle
b. Identification
c. Preconscious
d. Repression
e. Psychoanalysis
f. Resistance
g. Psychic structures
h. Id
i. Reality principle
j. Defense mechanism
k. Superego
l. Moral principle

m. Libido
n. Unconscious
o. Erogenous zones
p. Oral stage
q. Fixation
r. Anal stage
s. Conscious
t. Phallic stage
u. Oedipus complex
v. Electra complex
w. Displacement
x. Latency

y. Genital stage
z. Incest taboo
aa. Analytical psychology
bb. Collective unconscious
cc. archetypes
dd. Eros
ee. Inferiority complex
ff. Creative self
gg. Individual psychology
hh. ego

_____ 1. The portion of the mind that enters into awareness.

_____ 2. Principle that guides the superego; sets moral standards and holds examples of an ideal self.

_____ 3. Ideas or thought that is beneath awareness but that can be made conscious by focusing on it.

_____ 4. The portion of the mind that contains biological instincts such as sex and aggression and is shrouded in mystery.

_____ 5. The automatic ejection of anxiety-evoking ideas from awareness.

_____ 6. The cultural prohibition against marrying or having sexual relations with a close blood relative.

_____ 7. A conflict of the phallic stage in which a boy wishes to have sexual relations with his mother and perceives his father as a rival.

_____ 8. The mature stage of psychosexual development, characterized by preferred expression of libido through intercourse with an adult of the opposite sex.

_____ 9. Psychic structure that develops throughout early childhood, usually incorporating the moral standards and values of the parents.

_____ 10. The stage of psychosexual development in which sexual gratification is obtained through contraction and relaxation of the muscles that control elimination of bodily waste.

_____ 11. The conflict of the phallic stage of development in which a female child longs for her father and resents her mother.

_____ 12. Jung's psychodynamic theory, which emphasizes the collective unconscious and archetypes.

_____ 13. The unconscious assumption of the behavior of another person.

_____ 14. Adler's psychodynamic theory, which emphasizes feelings of inferiority and the creative self.

_____ 15. The transfer of emotions or feelings to more socially appropriate objects.

_____ 16. Freud's term for the energy of the Eros or sexual instinct.

_____ 17. The desire to avoid thinking about or discussing anxiety-evoking ideas.

_____ 18. Freud's method of exploring the unconscious mind.

_____ 19. An area of the body that is sensitive to sexual sensations.

_____ 20. Freud's term for the mental structures used to describe the clashing forces of the personality.

_____ 21. Psychic structure present at birth; represents physiological drives; is entirely unconscious.

_____ 22. The stage of psychosexual development characterized by the development of a sexual attachment to the parent of the opposite gender.

_____ 23. An unconscious function of the ego that protects it from anxiety-evoking material by preventing accurate recognition of this material.

_____ 24. Basic primitive images that reflect the history of our species.

_____ 25. The stage of psychosexual development in which sexual feelings remain unconscious.

_____ 26. The principle used by the id to give its desires; it demands instant gratification without consideration of law, social custom, or the needs of others.

_____ 27. The stage of psychosexual development in which gratification is hypothesized to be obtained through activities such as sucking and biting.

_____ 28. Jung's hypothesized storehouse of primitive images that reflect the history of our species.

_____ 29. Arrested development; failure to move onward to the next stage of psychosexual development.

_____ 30. Freud's term for the basic instinct to preserve life and perpetuate life.

_____ 31. Psychic structure that begins to develop in the first year of life and stands for reason and good sense.

_____ 32. Feelings of inadequacy hypothesized by Adler to serve as a central motivating force.

_____ 33. Principle that guides the desires of the ego; takes into account what is practical.

_____ 34. Self-aware aspect of personality that strives to overcome obstacles and develop the individual's potential.

2. *Match the psychodynamic theorist with the proper description of his or her view.*

a. Erik Erickson   c. Alfred Adler
b. Karen Horney   d. Carl Jung

_____ 1. Argued that little girls do not feel inferior to boys, that these views were based on Western cultural prejudice.

_____ 2. Became a member of Freud's inner circle but fell into disfavor over the importance of sexual instinct; believed in a collective unconscious.

_____ 3. Asserted that social relationships were more crucial determinants of personality than sexual urges; proposed eight stages of psychosocial development throughout the lifespan.

_____ 4. Believed that people are motivated by an inferiority complex and the need to compensate for these feelings; self-awareness plays a key role; spoke of a creative self.

Reading for Understanding About "The Trait Perspective"

What are traits? What is the history of the trait perspective? (37) _____ are reasonably stable personality elements that are inferred from behavior and that account for behavioral consistency. Trait theory adopts a (38) _____ approach to personality. Trait theory dates back to (39) _____, the ancient Greek physician who believed that personality reflects the balance of liquids or (40) "_____" in the body. Sir Francis (41) _____ in the 19th century and Gordon (42) _____ in the 20th century surveyed traits by studying words that referred to them in dictionaries.

How have contemporary researchers used factor analysis to reduce the universe of traits to smaller lists of traits that show common features? Hans Eysenck used (43) _____ to arrive at two broad, independent personality dimensions: introversion–(44) _____ and emotional stability-instability (also known as (45) _____). More recent mathematical analyses point to the existence of (46) _____ key factors: extraversion, agreeableness, conscientiousness, emotional stability, and openness to experience. (47) _____ research suggests that these five factors appear to define personality in numerous cultures.

What are the strengths and weaknesses of trait theory? (48) _____ theorists have helped develop personality tests and used them to predict (49) _____ in various lines of work. Critics argue that trait theory is (50) _____, not explanatory, and that the explanations that are provided by trait theory are (51) _____ in that they restate what is observed and do not explain it.

Reading for Understanding About "Learning Theory Perspective"

What does learning theory have to contribute to our understanding of personality? What is Watson's contribution to personality theory? Behaviorists believe that we should focus on (52) _____ behavior rather than hypothesized (53) _____ forces and that we should emphasize the situational determinants of behavior. John B. (54) _____, the "father" of modern behaviorism, rejected notions of mind and personality altogether. He also argued that he could train any child to develop into a professional or a criminal by controlling the child's (55) _____.

How did Skinner develop Watson's views? B.F. (56) _____ adopted Watson's view in the 1930s. B. F. Skinner opposed the idea of personal (57) _____ and emphasized the effects that (58) _____ have on behavior. In his book, (59) _____, Skinner argued that environmental contingencies can (60) _____ people into wanting to do the things that are required of them. Critics of behavioral theory argue that the view downplays the importance of (61) _____ and (62) _____.

How does social-cognitive theory differ from the behaviorist view? (63) _____ theory, developed by Albert Bandura, has a cognitive orientation and focuses on learning by observation. Bandura proposes a pattern of (64) _____ in which people influence the environment just as much as the environment influences them. To predict behavior, social-cognitive theorists consider (65) _____ variables (rewards and punishments) and (66) _____ variables (competencies, encoding strategies, expectancies, emotions, and self-regulatory systems and plans).

What are the strengths and weaknesses of learning theories as they apply to personality? (67) _____ theorists have highlighted the importance of referring to publicly observable behaviors in theorizing. However, behaviorism does not describe, explain, or suggest the richness of (68) _____ human experience. Critics of social-cognitive theory note that it does not address (69) _____ or adequately account for the development of (70) _____. It may also not pay enough attention to (71) _____ variation in explaining individual differences in behavior.

Reflection Break 2

Compare and contrast the trait, learning, and social-cognitive theories of personality in the chart below:

	Premise	Critique
Trait		
Behavioral		
Social-Cognitive		

Reading for Understanding About "The Humanistic-Existential Perspective"

What is humanism? What is existentialism? How do humanistic psychologists differ from psychodynamic theorists? (72) _____ puts people and self-awareness at the center and argues that we are capable of free choice, self-fulfillment, and ethical behavior. (73) _____ argue that our lives have meaning when we give them meaning. Whereas Freud wrote that people are motivated to gratify (74) _____ drives, humanistic psychologists believe that people have a conscious need for (75) _____, or to become all that they can be.

Just what is your self? What is self theory? According to Carl Rogers, the (76) _____ is an organized and consistent way in which a person perceives his or her "I" in relation to others. Self theory begins by assuming the existence of the self and each person's unique (77) _____, or our own way of looking at ourselves. The self attempts to (78) _____ (develop its unique potential) and best does so when the person receives (79) _____, or acceptance based on intrinsic merit regardless of the person's behavior at the moment. Rogers also argues that (80) _____, the belief that you may have merit only if you behave in a specific way, may lead to a distorted self-concept, to disowning of parts of the self, and to anxiety.

What are the strengths and weaknesses of humanistic-existential theory? Humanistic-existential theory is appealing because of its focus on (81) _____ and freedom of (82) _____, but critics argue that concepts such as conscious experience and self-actualization are (83) _____. Self-actualization, like trait theories, yields (84) _____ explanations for behavior and (85) _____ theories, like learning theories, have very little to say about the development of different personality traits or types.

Reading for Understanding About "Personality and Diversity: The Sociocultural Perspective"

Why is the sociocultural perspective important to the understanding of personality? One cannot fully understand the personality of an individual without understanding the (86) _____ beliefs and (87) _____ conditions that have affected that individual. The sociocultural perspective encourages us to consider the roles of ethnicity, (88) _____, culture, and socioeconomic status in personality formation, behavior, and mental processes.

What does it mean to be individualistic? What is meant by individualism and collectivism? (89) _____ define themselves in terms of their personal identities and give priority to their personal goals. (90) _____ define themselves in terms of the groups to which they belong and give priority to the group's goals. Cross-cultural studies suggest that many (91) _____ societies are individualistic and foster individualism in personality while many (92) _____ societies are collectivist and foster collectivism in personality.

How do sociocultural factors affect the self-concept and self-esteem? Members of the (93) _____ culture in the United States are likely to have positive self-concepts because they share expectations of (94) _____ and respect. Members of ethnic groups that have been subjected to (95) _____ and poverty tend to have poorer self-concepts and lower self-esteem. *How does acculturation affect the psychological well-being of immigrants and their families?* Another sociocultural issue for personality is that of (96) _____, the process of adaptation in which immigrants and native groups identify with a new dominant culture by making behavioral and attitudinal changes. Research suggests that immigrants who (97) _____ the customs and values of their country of origin but who also (98) _____ those of their new host country, and blend the two, tend to have (99) _____ self-esteem than immigrants who either become completely assimilated or who maintain complete separation from the new dominant culture.

Reflection Break 3

Compare and contrast the humanistic-existential and sociocultural perspectives on personality in the chart below.

	Premise	Critique
Humanistic-Existential		
Sociocultural		

Reading for Understanding About "Measurement of Personality"

How are personality measures used? Personality measures are used in many ways, including (100) _____ psychological disorders, predicting the likelihood of (101) _____ in various lines of work, measuring (102) _____, and determining academic placement. Methods of personality assessment typically take a (103) _____ of current behavior to (104) _____ future behavior. (105) _____ scales access behavior in settings such as classrooms or mental hospitals, and students may take tests to gain insight. There are two widely used types of personality (106) _____ : objective and projective tests.

What are objective personality tests? (107) _____ tests present test takers with a standardized set of test items to which they must respond in specific, limited ways (as in (108) _____ or true-false tests). A (109) _____ format asks respondents to indicate which of two or more statements is true for them or which of several activities they prefer. The Minnesota Multiphasic Personality Inventory (MMPI) is presented in a true-false format and is widely used in the assessment of psychological (110) _____ .

How do projective tests differ from objective tests? What are some of the more widely used projective tests? (111) _____ tests do not have specific correct answers. They present (112) _____ stimuli and allow the test taker to give a range of responses that reflect individual differences. Examples include the (113) _____ inkblot test, developed by Hermann Rorschach, and the Thematic Apperception Test. The Rorschach is thought to provide insight into a person's intelligence, interests, cultural background, and many other variables, while the (114) _____ is widely used in clinical practice and research on motivation.

Reflection Break 4

Match the personality assessment technique with its correct description.

a. behavior-rating scales
b. objective tests
c. forced-choice format

d. MMPI
e. projective tests
f. standardized test

g. Rorschach Inkblot test
h. Thematic Apperception Test

_____ 1. A true-false formatted test that contains hundreds of items; is used in clinical and counseling psychology to help diagnose psychological disorders.

_____ 2. A psychological test that presents ambiguous stimuli onto which the test taker projects his or her own personality.

_____ 3. A method of presenting test questions that requires the test taker to select one of a number of possible answers.

_____ 4. A projective test that contains 10 cards of ambiguous images, five of which are in color.

_____ 5. A test that is given to a large number of test takers so that data concerning the typical responses can be accumulated and analyzed.

_____ 6. Tests whose items have concrete answers that are considered correct.

_____ 7. A systematic method for recording the frequency with which a target behavior occurs.

_____ 8. Projective test that presents drawings that are open to interpretations.

REVIEW: KEY TERMS AND CONCEPTS

FINAL CHAPTER REVIEW

Review

Visit the *Psychology in the New Millennium* Web site at www.harcourtcollege.com/psych/PNM/siteresources.html and take the Chapter Quizzes to test your knowledge.

Recite

Go to the Recite section for this chapter in your textbook. Use the tear-off card provided at the back of the book to cover the answers of the Recite section. Read the questions aloud, and recite the answers. This will help you cement your knowledge of key concepts.

Essay Questions

1. How do you describe personality? Think of a friend who is single. How did you describe his or her personality the last time you were trying to fix him or her up on a date and you were asked what kind of "personality" he or she had? What would your answer be now? Has your response changed now that you have a more through understanding of personality and personality theory? How? Compose a brief essay that compares the two descriptions of your friend. Explain which personality concepts prompted you change your description.

2. Write a short story about a person with an overdeveloped superego. Include a depiction or description of that person's personality, the problems that the person's personality creates, and how the person copes with the difficulties of daily living. Use psychodynamic concepts to explain why your character acts or behaves in the way he or she does.

3. Do you have a favorite team? How strongly are you attached to the team? Do you feel more positive about yourself when your team is winning? Have you let the "team" become your social life? What benefits do you think college students who strongly identify with the school team gain? Are there disadvantages? What might they be? Your textbook author presents the argument that team identification serves as a method for meeting unconscious needs and desires. Do you agree? Why or why not?

4. How would you describe yourself in terms of traits? Where would you place yourself on the dimensions of introversion-extraversion and emotional stability? Are you conscientious? Are you open to experience? Is there such a thing as being too conscientious? As being too open to experience? Explain your descriptions in a two-page essay for your instructor. In your essay be sure to provide the evidence for your list of traits.

5. In a brief paper explain the concept of self-esteem. You will want to visit the home page of the National Association for Self-Esteem at http://www.self-esteem-nase.org/ and follow some of its links. After visiting the site, address the following questions in your essay: Do you think that self-esteem is constant or variable? Do you have higher self-esteem in some situations than in others? How do different environments and conditions affect you? How does your self-concept affect how you think, feel, and behave when you try on a bathing suit, go for a job interview, or have dinner with your boss for the first time? Why?

   URL: http://www.self-esteem-nase.org/links.shtml

6. Should employers use personality tests in employee screening? Read the two reports at the following links:

   • "Personality and Aptitude Tests: A Good Idea for Employers?" By Michael Delikat and Rene Kathawala. *The New York Law Journal,* December 29, 1997, at http://www.ljx.com/practice/laboremployment/1229labtest.html.
   • Which traits predict job performance from APA at http://helping.apa.org/work/personal.html.

   Based on your understanding of each of these articles and your text readings on personality testing, would you recommend the use of personality testing in hiring employees? Why or why not? In a format specified by your instructor, prepare a report with your recommendations and the reasoning behind them.

RELATE/EXPAND/INTEGRATE

1. **Introduction to Personality: "Why Are They Sad and Glad and Bad"?**
   Is personality stable? Before you answer this question, read the following articles; then report your findings to your classmates in a format specified by your instructor.

   - *How do parents matter? Let us count the ways, APA Monitor* at http://www.apa.org/monitor/julaug00/parents.html
   - *Elderly people not as 'set in their ways' as is popularly believed, studies show, APA Monitor* at http://www.apa.org/monitor/feb99/set.html
   - *Study on working moms gets widespread press, APA Monitor* at http://www.apa.org/monitor/apr99/mom.html

2. **The Psychodynamic Perspective**
   Beyond The Inkblot. What Do You See? Take the online Thematic Apperception Test (TAT) at http://www.learner.org/exhibits/personality/activity2/. You'll look at a picture and tell a short story about it. The test claims that the story you tell reflects your personality. Post your story to the Web site and obtain an interpretation of it. Now read an online version of the Inkblot Test manual at http://www.dur.ac.uk/~dps0dk/oh.id9b. How would you interpret your story? Is your interpretation the same as the Web site's? Why or why not? How do you think a third person would interpret your story? Which interpretation is correct? Can you really know which interpretation is correct? Report on your experience to your classmates in a format specified by your instructor.

3. **The Trait Perspective**
   Visit the Great Ideas in Personality site at http://www.personalityresearch.org/ and look up further information on the trait theory. Based on your reading, do you think that traits exist? What are the advantages and disadvantages of trait theory? Prepare a report of your findings for your classmates in a format specified by your instructor.

4. **Learning-Theory Perspective**
   Do you expect that you will succeed? Do you believe in your abilities? What is your expectation for success? Take the Generalized Self-Efficacy Scale at *http://www.yorku.ca/faculty/ academic/schwarze/selfscal.htm* and the Expectancy for Success Scale on page 403 of your textbook. Do the measurements coincide? Do they agree with your perceptions of yourself? Compare your results with those of the other members of your study group. Discuss the similarities and differences and try to explain why.

5. **The Humanistic-Existential and the Sociocultural Perspective**
   Visit the Great Ideas in Personality site at http://www.personalityresearch.org/ and look up further information on the humanistic and sociocultural theories. Prepare an essay that compares the two approaches. Can you "believe in" more than one theory of personality?

6. **Searching for the Self Online**

Have you created a "fake" identity for online chat? Do you find that the Internet allows you to let your guard down and say things that you might not say "in person"? Why do you think people do this? Do you think this is "healthy"? Interview 20 college students and ask them the above question; then ask 20 middle-aged adults the same question. Are there age related differences? Compare and discuss your results with your study group.

7. **Measurement of Personality: Online Personality Tests**

Take the *Keirsey Temperament Sorter* personality test at http://www.advisorteam.com/user/kts.asp or http://www.keirsey.com/. (The Keirsey Temperament Sorter scores results according to the Myers-Briggs system and will provide a personality profile similar to one obtained using the Myers-Briggs.)

- What was the test designed to measure?
- Briefly describe the elements of personality that are being measured and how appropriate you think the test is for measuring those personality characteristics.
- Were the descriptions of personality offered specific or very general?
- Do you agree with the test's assessment of your personality?

Now take another personality test at one of the following Web sites. How do the two assessments compare? Report your findings to your class.

URL: http://www.wizardrealm.com/tests
URL: http://www.2h.com/Tests/personality.phtml
URL: http://www.learner.org/exhibits/personality/activity1/
URL: http://www.queendom.com/tests/index.html
URL: http://www.2h.com/Tests/personality.phtml
URL: http://test3.thespark.com/person/
URL: http://www.personalitypage.com/
URL: http://www.usnews.com/usnews/edu/college/cpq/coquiz.htm
URL: http://www.davideck.com/online-tests.html

ANSWERS FOR CHAPTER 12

Reading for Understanding About "Introduction to Personality: 'Why Are They Sad and Glad and Bad?' "

1. Personality
2. develops
3. predict
4. perspectives
5. psychodynamic
6. conscious
7. preconscious
8. unconscious
9. conflict
10. external
11. internalized
12. id
13. ego
14. practical
15. id
16. anxiety
17. superego
18. libido
19. five
20. Fixation
21. analytical
22. collective
23. archetypes
24. individual
25. creative
26. superiority
27. parent-child
28. hostility
29. psychosocial
30. sexual
31. Freud
32. scientific
33. possession
34. sexuality
35. psychic structures
36. inaccuracies

Reflection Break 1

Part I.

1. s
2. l
3. c
4. n
5. d
6. z
7. u
8. y
9. k
10. r
11. v
12. aa
13. b
14. gg
15. w
16. m
17. f
18. e
19. o
20. g
21. h
22. t
23. j
24. cc
25. x
26. a
27. p
28. bb
29. q
30. dd
31. hh
32. ee
33. i
34. ff

Part II.

1.   b
2.   d
3. a
4. c

Reading for Understanding About "The Trait Perspective"

37. Traits
38. descriptive
39. Hippocrates
40. humors
41. Galton

42. Allport
43. factor analysis
44. extraversion
45. neuroticism
46. five

47. Cross-cultural
48. Trait
49. adjustment
50. descriptive
51. circular

Reading for Understanding About "Learning Theory Perspective"

52. observable
53. unconscious
54. Watson
55. environment
56. Skinner
57. freedom
58. reinforcements

59. *Walden Two*
60. shape
61. consciousness
62. choice
63. Social-cognitive
64. reciprocal determinism
65. situational

66. person
67. Learning
68. inner
69. self-awareness
70. traits
71. genetic

Reflection Break 2

Compare and contrast the trait, learning, and social-cognitive theories of personality in the chart below:

	Premise	Critique
Trait	Traits are personality elements that are inferred from behavior and that account for behavioral consistency. Trait theory adopts a descriptive approach to personality.	Critics argue that trait theory is descriptive, not explanatory, and that the explanations that are provided by trait theory are circular in that they restate what is observed and do not explain it.
Behavioral	Behaviorists believe that we should focus on observable behavior rather than hypothesized psychic forces and that we should emphasize the situational determinants of behavior. John B. Watson, the "father" of modern behaviorism, rejected notions of mind and personality altogether. He also argued that he could train any child to develop into a professional or a criminal by controlling the child's environment. B.F. Skinner adopted Watson's view in the 1930s. B. F. Skinner opposed the idea of personal freedom and emphasized the effects that reinforcements have on behavior.	Behavioral theorists have highlighted the importance of referring to publicly observable behaviors in theorizing. However, behaviorism does not describe, explain, or suggest the richness of inner human experience.

Social-cognitive	Developed by Albert Bandura, this theory has a cognitive orientation and focuses on learning by observation. Bandura proposes a pattern of reciprocal determinism in which people influence the environment just as much as the environment influences them. To predict behavior, social-cognitive theorists consider situational variables (rewards and punishments) and person variables (competencies, encoding strategies, expectancies, emotions, and self-regulatory systems and plans).	Critics of social-cognitive theory note that it does not address self-awareness or adequately account for the development of traits It may also not pay enough attention to genetic variation in explaining individual differences in behavior.

Reading for Understanding About "The Humanistic-Existential Perspective"

72. Humanism
73. Existentialists
74. unconscious
75. self-actualization
76. self
77. frame of reference
78. actualize
79. unconditional positive regard
80. conditions of worth
81. self-awareness
82. choice
83. unscientific
84. circular
85. humanistic-existential

Reading for Understanding About "Personality and Diversity: The Sociocultural Perspective"

86. cultural
87. socioeconomic
88. gender
89. Individualists
90. Collectivists
91. Western
92. Eastern
93. dominant
94. achievement
95. discrimination
96. acculturation
97. retain
98. learn
99. higher

Reflection Break 3

Compare and contrast the humanistic-existential and sociocultural perspectives on personality in the chart below.

	Premise	Critique
Humanistic-Existential	Humanisim puts people and self-awareness at the center and argues that we are capable of free choice, self-fulfillment, and ethical behavior. Existentialism argues that our lives have meaning when we give them meaning. Whereas Freud wrote that people are motivated to gratify unconscious drives, humanistic psychologists believe that people have a conscious need for self-actualization, or to become all that they can be.	Humanistic-existential theories have tremendous appeal because of their focus on the importance of personal experience. Self-actualization, like trait theories, yields circular explanations for behavior. Humanistic theories, like learning theories, have little to say about the development of traits and personality types.
Sociocultural	The sociocultural perspective encourages us to consider the roles of ethnicity, gender, culture, and socioeconomic status in personality formation, behavior, and mental processes.	The sociocultural perpective provides valuable insights into the roles of ethnicity, gender, culture, and socioeconomic status in personality formation. Without reference to sociocultural factors we may not be able to understand generalities about behvaior and cognitive processes. However, we will not be able to understand how individuals think, behave, and feel about themsleves within a cultural setting.

Reading for Understanding About "Measurement of Personality"

100. assessing
101. adjustment
102. aptitudes
103. sample
104. predict

105. Behavior-rating
106. tests
107. Objective
108. multiple-choice
109. forced-choice

110. disorders
111. Projective
112. ambiguous
113. Rorschach
114. TAT

Reflection Break 4

1. d
2. e
3. c

4. g
5. f
6. b

7. a
8. h

Chapter 13

Gender and Sexuality

PREVIEW

Skim the major headings in this chapter in your textbook. Jot down anything that you are surprised or curious about. After this, write down four or five questions that you have about the material in this chapter.

Things that surprised me/I am curious about from Chapter 13:

Questions that I have about gender and sexuality:

▲

▲

▲

▲

QUESTION

These are some questions that you should be able to answer after you finish studying this chapter.

Gender Polarization: Gender Stereotypes and Their Costs

▲ *What are gender-role stereotypes?*

▲ *What are the costs of gender polarization?*

Psychological Gender Differences: Vive la Différence or Vive la Similarité?

▲ *What are the gender differences in cognitive abilities?*

▲ *What are the gender differences in social behavior?*

Gender Typing: On becoming a Woman or a Man

▲ *What are some biological views of gender-typing?*

▲ *What are some psychological views of gender-typing?*

Attraction: On Liking, Loving, and Relationships

▲ *What factors contribute to attraction in our culture?*

▲ *Just what is love? What is romantic love?*

▲ *What is meant by the term "sexual orientation"?*

▲ *How do researchers explain gay male and lesbian sexual orientations?*

Sexual Response

▲ *What is the sexual response cycle?*

▲ *What are sexual dysfunctions?*

▲ *What are the origins of sexual dysfunctions?*

▲ *How are sexual dysfunctions treated?*

Sexual Coercion

▲ *Why do men rape women?*

▲ *How can we prevent rape?*

▲ *What is sexual harassment?*

▲ *What do you do if you are sexually harassed on campus or in the workplace?*

AIDS and Other Sexually Transmitted Infections

▲ *What kinds of sexually transmitted infections are there?*

▲ *How is HIV transmitted? What does it do?*

▲ *How is HIV infection diagnosed? How is HIV/AIDS treated?*

▲ *What can you do to prevent the transmission of HIV and other STI-causing organisms?*

READING FOR UNDERSTANDING/REFLECT

The following section provides you with the opportunity to perform 2 of the R's of the PQ4R study method. In this section, you are encouraged to check your understanding of your reading of the text by filling in the blanks in the brief paragraphs that relate to each of the Preview questions. You will also be prompted to rehearse your understanding of the material with periodic Reflection breaks. Remember, it is better to study in more frequent, short sessions than in one long "cram session." Be sure to reward yourself with short study breaks before each Reflection exercise.

Reading for Understanding About "Gender Polarization: Gender Stereotypes and Their Costs"

What are gender-role stereotypes? (1) _____ are fixed, conventional ideas about a group of people that can give rise to prejudice and discrimination. Cultures have broad expectations of men and women that are termed (2) _____ stereotypes. In our culture, (3) _____ are expected to be gentle, dependent, kind, helpful, patient, and submissive. (4) _____ are expected to be tough, competitive, gentlemanly, and protective. (5) _____ in the United States is linked to the traditional view of men as breadwinners and women as homemakers. Gender polarization can be extremely costly for both genders in terms of education, activities, (6) _____, psychological well-being, and interpersonal relationships.

What are the costs of gender polarization? Polarization has historically worked to the (7) _____ of women. For example, (8) _____, women have until recent years been excluded from careers in medicine and law, and math and science courses in the schools are still seen as mainly in the male "domain." (9) _____ tests show that boys and girls are about equal in overall learning ability; yet girls are expected to excel in language arts and boys in math and science. In the (10) _____ domain, women who adhere to traditional feminine gender roles are likely to take a back seat to men in the workplace and in the home. Gender polarization also interferes with (11) _____ well-being and relationships. For example, (12) "_____" men may not be able to ask for help when they need it or to express tender feelings.

Reading for Understanding About "Psychological Gender Differences: Vive la Différence or Vive la Similarité?"

What are the gender differences in cognitive abilities? Throughout history, it has been assumed that women and men must be (13) _____ different in order to fulfill different roles in family and society. However, psychological differences are not as obvious as (14) _____ gender differences, and in many ways women and men are more (15) _____ than different. (16) _____, boys have historically been seen as excelling in math and spatial relations skills, whereas girls have been viewed as excelling in language skills. However, these differences are (17) _____ and growing narrower.

What are the gender differences in social behavior? In the area of social behavior, females are more (18) _____ and nurturant than males. Male friendship with other men also appear to be (19) _____ and less (20) _____ than women's friendships with other women. Males are more tough-minded and (21) _____ than females. Men are more interested than women in (22) _____ and multiple sex partners. Women are more willing than men to marry someone who is not (23) _____, but less willing to marry someone who is unlikely to hold a (24) _____.

Reading for Understanding About "Gender Typing: On Becoming a Woman or a Man"

What are some biological views of gender-typing? The process by which psychological gender differences develop is termed (25) _____. (26) _____ views of gender-typing focus on the roles of evolution, genetics, and prenatal influences in predisposing men and women to gender-linked behavior patterns. According to evolutionary psychologists, gender differences were fashioned by (27) _____ in response to problems in adaptation that were repeatedly encountered by humans over thousands of generations. This (28) _____ process is expressed through structural differences between males and females. For example, research has suggested that although males and females have the same (29) _____ in the brain, they seem to use them somewhat differently. Gender differences in brain (30) _____ might explain, in part, why women excel in verbal skills and men excel in specialized spatial-relations. Sex (31) _____ are responsible for prenatal differentiation of sex organs. (32) _____ in the brains of male fetuses spurs greater growth of the right hemisphere of the brain, which may be connected with the ability to manage spatial-relations tasks. Testosterone is also connected with (33) _____.

What are some psychological views of gender-typing? Psychologists have attempted to explain (34) _____ in terms of psychodynamic, social-cognitive, and gender-schema theories. Freud explained gender-typing in terms of (35) _____ with the parent of the same gender through resolution of the (36) _____ and (37) _____ complexes. (38) _____ theorists explain gender-typing in terms of the ways in which experience helps the individual create concepts of gender-appropriate behavior, and how the individual is motivated to engage in such behavior. Social-cognitive theorists use terms such as observational learning, (39) _____, or the continuous learning process in which children are influenced by rewards to imitate the behavior of same-sex adults, and (40) _____, in which parents and other adults inform children about how they are expected to behave. Research shows that. women can behave as (41) _____ as men when they are provoked, have the means, and believe that the social climate will tolerate their aggression. (42) _____ theory proposes that once children learn the gender schema of their culture, their self-esteem becomes tied up in how well they express the traits considered relevant to their gender. Sandra Bem argues that people look at the social world through (43) "_____." She argues that our (44) _____ polarizes females and males by organizing social life around mutually exclusive (45) _____. No pressure is required; once children understand the (46) _____ boy and girl, they have a basis for blending their self-concepts with the gender (47) _____ of their culture.

Reflection Break 1

1. What is a stereotype? How do gender-role stereotypes influence behavior? What are the costs of gender polarization?

2. Briefly review the biological and psychological influences on gender-typing by completing the following chart.

Biological Influences	Psychological Influences
Brain Organization:	Psychodynamic Theory:
Sex Hormones:	Social-Cognitive Theory:
	Gender-Schema Theory:

Reading for Understanding About "Attraction: On Liking, Loving, and Relationships"

What factors contribute to attraction in our culture? Sexual interactions usually take place within (48) _____. Feelings of (49) _____, or an attitude of liking or disliking, can lead to liking and perhaps to love, and to a more lasting relationship. Attraction is influenced by factors such as physical (50) _____ and attitudes. Physically, (51) _____ seem to find large eyes and narrows jaws to be attractive in women. Women, on the other hand, place greater emphasis on traits like (52) _____, consideration, (53) _____, kindness, and fondness for children. In our culture, (54) _____ is considered attractive in both men and women, and (55) _____ is valued in men. Women tend to see themselves as being heavier than the (56) _____. We are more attracted to (57) _____ people. Similarity in (58) _____ and (59) _____ factors (ethnicity, education, and so on), and (60) _____ in feelings of admiration also enhance attraction. According to the (61) _____, we tend to seek dates and mates at our own level of attractiveness, largely because of fear of rejection. (62) _____ is a powerful determinant of attraction; we tend to return feelings of admiration.

Just what is love? What is romantic love? Sternberg's (63) _____ theory of love suggests that love has three components: intimacy, passion, and commitment. (64) _____ refers to a couple's closeness, (65) _____ means romance and sexual feelings, and (66) _____ means deciding to enhance and maintain the relationship. Different kinds of (67) _____ combine these components in different ways. (68) _____ love is characterized by the combination of passion and intimacy. (69) _____ is most critical in short-term relationships. (70) _____ love has all three factors.

What is meant by the term sexual orientation? (71) _____, which should not be confused with sexual activity, refers to the direction of one's erotic interests. (72) _____ people are sexually attracted to people of the other gender and interested in forming romantic relationships with them. (73) _____ people are sexually attracted to people of their own gender and interested in forming romantic relationships with them. Homosexual males are referred to as (74) _____ and homosexual women are referred to as (75) _____ . (76) _____ people are sexually attracted to, and interested in forming romantic relationships with, both men and women.

How do researchers explain gay male and lesbian sexual orientations? (77) _____ theory connects sexual orientation with improper resolution of the Oedipus and Electra complexes. Learning theorists focus on the role of (78) _____ of early patterns of sexual behavior. Evidence of a (79) _____ contribution to sexual orientation is accumulating. (80) _____ are known to have both organizing and activating effects, but research has (81) _____ to connect sexual orientation with differences in adult levels of sex hormones. However, sex hormones may play a role in determining sexual orientation during (82) _____ development. In sum, the determinants of sexual orientation are mysterious and complex, and the precise (83) _____ among biological and social factors is not yet understood.

Reading for Understanding About "Sexual Response"

What is the sexual response cycle? The sexual response cycle describes the body's response to sexual stimulation and is characterized by (84) _____, the swelling of the genital tissues with blood, and (85) _____, or muscle tension. The cycle consists of (86) _____ phases: excitement, plateau, orgasm, and resolution. (87) _____ is characterized by erection in the male and lubrication in the female. During the (88) _____ phase, the level of sexual arousal remains somewhat stable, breathing may become rapid, and heart rate my increase to 100 to 160 beats per minute. (89) _____ is characterized by muscle contractions and release of sexual tension. In the male there are two stages of (90) _____; in the first, seminal fluid collects at the base of the (91) _____, and in the second, the (92) _____ is propelled out of the body. In the female, (93) _____ is manifested by 3 to 15 contractions of the pelvic muscles. During the (94) _____ phase, and following orgasm, males enter a (95) _____ period during which they are temporarily unresponsive to sexual stimulation.

What are sexual dysfunctions? What are the origins of sexual dysfunctions? Sexual (96) _____ are persistent or recurrent problems in becoming sexually aroused or reaching orgasm. They include (97) _____ disorder (lack of interest in sex), (98) _____ disorder, and (99) _____ disorder (characterized by inadequate vasocongestion), orgasmic disorder, premature ejaculation, (100) _____ (pain during sex), and (101) _____ (involuntary contraction of the muscles of the vaginal barrel, making intercourse difficult).

Sexual dysfunctions may be caused by (102) _____ problems, (103) _____ toward sex, lack of (104) _____ and skills, problems in the relationship, and (105) _____.

How are sexual dysfunctions treated? Sexual dysfunctions are treated by (106) _____, which focuses on reducing performance anxiety, changing self-defeating attitudes and expectations, teaching sexual skills, enhancing sexual knowledge, and improving sexual communication. There are also some (107) _____ treatments, such as drugs that enhance the physical aspects of sexual response.

Reflection Break 2

1. Clearly differentiate between sexual orientation and sexual activity. What are the different types of sexual orientation?

2. Matching:
   Review your understanding of theories of love, the sexual response cycle, and sexual dysfunctions by matching the terms with their correct descriptions.

   a. hypoactive sexual desire disorder
   b. plateau phase
   c. orgasm
   d. male erectile disorder
   e. passion
   f. orgasmic disorder
   g. excitement phase
   h. resolution phase
   i. female sexual arousal disorder
   j. intimacy
   k. premature ejaculation
   l. dyspareunia
   m. consummate love
   n. refractory period
   o. Romantic love
   p. vaginismus

   _____ 1. Involuntary contraction of the muscles surrounding the vaginal opening.
   _____ 2. Sternberg's term for the ideal form of love; involves commitment, passion, and intimacy.
   _____ 3. The phase of the sexual response cycle in which vasocongestion causes erection in men and the vaginal wall lubricates in females.
   _____ 4. Painful sexual activity.
   _____ 5. The phase of the sexual response cycle in which the female experiences 3 to 15 contractions of the pelvic muscles that surround the vaginal barrel.
   _____ 6. Sternberg's term for a couple's closeness, or their mutual concern and sharing of feelings and resources.
   _____ 7. Disorder in which the male ejaculates after minimal sexual stimulation too soon to permit his partner to have full sexual enjoyment.
   _____ 8. Sternberg's term for love that is characterized by passion and intimacy, but not commitment.
   _____ 9. The period immediately following orgasm in which men cannot experience another orgasm or ejaculate.

_____ 10. The inability of a women to become or remain lubricated during sexual activity.

_____ 11. Sternberg's term for romance and sexual feelings.

_____ 12. Phase of the sexual response cycle in which the testes return to their normal size and the clitoris and vaginal barrel shrink to their normal size.

_____ 13. In men or women this disorder occurs when the person, though sexually excited, takes a long time to reach orgasm or does not reach it at all.

_____ 14. The inability of a male to attain or maintain an erection during intercourse.

_____ 15. Disorder in which a person lacks interest in sexual activity and reports a lack of sexual fantasies.

_____ 16. The phase of the sexual response cycle in which the level of sexual arousal remains somewhat stable.

Reading for Understanding About "Sexual Coercion"

Why do men rape women? (108) _____ is common—too common. (109) _____ is a pressing concern on college campuses. Research suggests that as many as 1 in 4 women in the United States has been raped. Social critics argue that men are (110) _____ into sexual aggression by being generally (111) _____ for aggressiveness and competitiveness. Social attitudes such as (112) _____, seeing sex as adversarial, and myths that tend to blame the (113) _____ all help create a climate that encourages rape.

How can we prevent rape? From a (114) _____ perspective, the prevention of rape involves publicly examining and challenging the widely held cultural attitudes and ideals that contribute to rape. Rape can be prevented by social change and by cautionary measures such as avoiding (115) _____ areas and-in dating-by dating in (116) _____ and being (117) _____ in expressing one's sexual intentions and limits.

What is sexual harassment? What do you do if you are sexually harassed on campus or in the workplace? (118) _____ occurs frequently on college campuses, in the business world, and in the military. Sexual harassment consists of deliberate or repeated unwanted comments, (119) _____, or physical contact of a sexual nature that is (120) _____ to the recipient. Sexual harassment is often stopped by means such as imparting a (121) _____, avoiding being (122) _____ with the harasser, keeping a (123) _____ of incidents, notifying the harasser that you recognize the harassment for what it is and that you want it to stop, filing (124) _____ with appropriate campus offices, and consulting a lawyer about the problem.

Reading for Understanding About "AIDS and Other Sexually Transmitted Infections"

What kinds of sexually transmitted infections are there? Sexual relationships can carry (125) _____. (126) _____ is the most feared of the sexually transmitted infections (STI) because it is fatal. However, STIs such as (127) _____ and (128) _____ (caused by HPV) are more widespread and also harmful.

How is HIV transmitted? What does it do? HIV is transmitted by infected (129) _____, (130) _____ (through male/female and male/male sexual activity), vaginal and cervical secretions, and breast milk. HIV kills (131) _____ blood cells (CD4 lymphocytes) in the immune system that recognize viruses and instruct other white blood cells to make the antibodies that combat disease. When the (132) _____ system is depleted of CD4 cells, the body is left vulnerable to opportunistic diseases such as certain forms of cancer and pneumonia.

How is HIV infection diagnosed? How is HIV/AIDS treated? The presence of HIV is detected by blood, (133) _____, and urine tests. HIV/AIDS is treated by a "cocktail" of (134) _____ drugs that includes a protease inhibitor. While the cocktail can reduce HIV in the (135) _____ to undetectable levels, it does not eradicate HIV and therefore is not a (136) _____. Current drug therapy has given rise to the hope that (137) _____ will become increasingly manageable, a chronic disease but not a terminal illness. However, treatment is (138) _____, and many people who could benefit from it cannot afford it. In addition, some people do not respond to the drug cocktail. Therefore, the most effective way of dealing with AIDS is (139) _____.

What can you do to prevent the transmission of HIV and other STI-causing organisms? First, don't close your eyes to the real threat of HIV and other disease-causing organisms. In addition, know your sex partner well, or remain (140) _____, and have regular health checkups.

Reflection Break 3

Part I.   Compare rape and sexual harassment. What can be done to prevent each of these?

Part II.   Briefly match the following STIs with their correct symptoms:

a. syphilis	d. chlamydia	g. pubic lice
b. genital herpes	e. genital Warts	
c. HIV/AIDS	f. gonorrhea	

_____ 1. May not show symptoms for a long time after exposure; may mimic mild flulike symptoms; transmitted via sexual intercourse or contaminated body fluids.

_____ 2. Frequent urination and lower abdominal pain in females; in males, a burning sensation during urination and a slight penile discharge.

_____ 3. Painful reddish bumps around the genitals that may become blisters or sores that fill with pus.

_____ 4. In men, a yellowish thick penile discharge and burning on urination; in females an increased vaginal discharge, burning on urination, and irregular menstrual bleeding.

_____ 5. In primary stage, a hard round, painless sore or chancre that appears within 2 to 4 weeks of infection.

_____   6. Intense itching in hairy areas.

_____   7. Appearance of painless warts resembling cauliflowers on the penis, foreskin, and scrotum in men and on the vulva, labia, and vagina in women.

REVIEW: KEY TERMS AND CONCEPTS

Sandra Lipsitz Bem	423	heterosexual	439	sexual dysfunction	443
stereotype	423	homosexual	439	hypoactive sexual	444
gender	423	gay male	439	desire disorder	
gender role	423	lesbian	439	female sexual arousal	444
gender-typing	428	bisexual	439	disorder	
gender identify	429	Oedipus complex	440	male erectile disorder	444
testosterone	429	organizing effect	440	orgasmic disorder	444
observational	429	activating effect	440	premature ejaculation	444
identification	429	androgens	441	dyspareunia	444
socialization	430	adrenaline	441	vaginismus	444
gender-schema theory	431	cortisol	441	performance anxiety	444
attraction	432	sexual response cycle	442	sex therapy	444
matching hypothesis	436	vasocongestion	442	sexual harassment	448
reciprocity	437	myotonia	442	AIDS	450
triangular model of	437	excitement phase	442	HIV	450
love		clitoris	442	chlamydia	450
intimacy	437	ejaculation	442	genital Warts	450
passion	437	seminal fluid	443	syphilis	451
consummate love	437	orgasm	443	genital herpes	451
romantic love	437	resolution phase	443	opportunistic diseases	451
sexual orientation	439	refractory period	443		

FINAL CHAPTER REVIEW

Review

Visit the *Psychology in the New Millennium* Web site at www.harcourtcollege.com/psych/PNM/siteresource.html and take the Chapter Quizzes to test your knowledge.

Recite

Go to the Recite section for this chapter in your textbook. Use the tear-off card provided at the back of the book to cover the answers of the Recite section. Read the questions aloud, and recite the answers. This will help you cement your knowledge of key concepts.

Essay Questions

1. *What does it mean to be masculine or feminine in the United States?* How are these definitions different in different cultures? Prepare a report briefly describing the characteristics of masculine and feminine behavior in the United States and comparing these

gender-role stereotypes to those in two other cultures. How do gender stereotypes influence your answer? Submit your essay to your instructor.

2. *Are there possible social or political problems connected with attributing gender differences in cognitive abilities to organization of the brain?* What might they be? In a letter to your instructor suggest the possible social or political issues that might arise if society accepted the idea that the brains of males and females are structurally and functionally different.

3. *Is there an evolutionary reason why you are attracted to a specific person?* In a brief essay compare the features that males tend to find most attractive to those that females tend to find most attractive. How might the features found attractive by males and females provide humans with an evolutionary advantage?

4. *Do the changes experienced by women and men during the sexual response cycle seem to be more different or more alike? How do you account for gender differences in the incidence of sexual dysfunctions?* In a short essay compare and contrast the differences and similarities in the sexual responses of males and females, and discuss how these similarities and differences account for gender differences in sexual dysfunctions.

5. *Controversy in psychology: Why do men rape women?* Prepare a two-page essay that examines the various psychological theories that attempt to explain why men engage in sexual abuse. In addition to your textbook, you may find information on the Men Stopping Violence WebLinks at http://www.menstoppingviolence.org/information_for_men_on_abuse.htm useful.

6. *Ethnic differences in the spread of HIV/AIDS.* Summarize the information presented in the textbook that attempts to explain why there are ethnic differences in the transmission of the HIV virus in a one-page essay, and suggest methods that might be used to change these trends.

RELATE/EXPAND/INTEGRATE

1. **Gender Polarization: Gender Stereotypes and Their Costs**
   Are you masculine or feminine? Take the Bem Sex Role Inventory at http://eval1.crc.uiuc.edu/cgi-bin/bem-survey.cgi?show=1&id=9999. What are your sex role ratings? Are you classified as masculine or feminine? Report your results to your classmates in a format specified by your instructor.

2. **Psychological Gender Differences: Vive La Différence or Vive La Similarité?**
   Controversy in psychology: Are men really more aggressive than women? Your textbook tells you that despite the stereotype of male aggressiveness, a meta-analysis of the research revealed that women were actually slightly more likely to hit, kick, use a weapon, and so on against their spouses, cohabitants, or dating partners (Archer, 2000). Interview 20 male college students and 20 female college students as to their use of aggressive behavior. What

does your survey suggest? Combine your results with those of your study group and report the overall outcome to your class in a format specified by your instructor.

3. Gender-Typing: On Becoming a Woman or a Man

Do you think that masculinity and femininity are inborn, or are these behavioral tendencies learned? Read the following two articles and report your conclusions to your classmates.

- Gender and Society: Is It a Matter of Nature or Nurture? at http://www.trinity.edu/~mkearl/gender.html
- Psychological Foundations for Rearing Masculine Boys and Feminine Girls by George Alan Rekers, on Leadership U's site at http://www.leaderu.com/orgs/cbmw/rbmw/chapter17.html.

4. Attraction: On Liking, Loving, and Relationships

Does the research suggest that people choose their sexual orientation? In your search for the answer to this question, you might want to begin by exploring the APA's Public Interest site at http://www.apa.org/pubinfo/answers.html. Here you will find the APA's answers to questions like: "What Is Sexual Orientation?" "What Causes a Person to Have a Particular Sexual Orientation?" "Is Sexual Orientation a Choice?" "Can Therapy Change Sexual Orientation?" and "Is Homosexuality a Mental Illness or Emotional Problem?" Summarize your findings for your classmates in a format specified by your instructor.

5. Sexual Response

Gender differences in sexual response. Your text suggests that women are more likely than men to find sex painful or unenjoyable and that men are more likely to be anxious about their performance. Is this the case? Visit the chat room on the Harcourt Psychology Web site and ask the women and men that are online their opinions on sexual pain. Report your findings and explain which cultural attitudes and expectations you think heighten the stress of erectile dysfunction in men. Be sure to clearly explain the rationale for your answers.

6. Sexual Coercion

What is sexual assault? Prepare a brief (5-minute) informational speech that introduces the definitions of sexual assault and rape and offers suggestions for what to do prevent these forms of sexual coercion. You may want to visit the Web page of the Sexual Assault Center of Knoxville, TN, at http://www.cs.utk.edu/~bartley/sacc/whatIsSA.html to help you prepare your essay.

7. Controversy in Psychology

Where does normal male-female interaction end and sexual harassment begin, and how do we resist sexual harassment? Before answering this question, visit the sexual harassment information page at http://www.de.psu.edu/harassment/. This Web page on sexual harassment invites you to explore the concept of sexual harassment interactively from a variety of perspectives. Examine the issues and topics presented before you post your reply to this question. How would your initial response have been different? Discuss sexual harassment with the members of your study group. Have any of them experienced sexual harassment? What did they do about it?

8. **Psychology in Modern Life: Preventing Rape**
What can you do to minimize the risk of rape? Visit the "Friends Raping Friends" Web link at http://www.cs.utk.edu/~bartley/acquaint/acquaintRape.html. Prepare a promotional brochure that details the important aspects of date rape, how to prevent it, and danger signals. Submit the brochure to your instructor.

9. **Psychology in Modern Life: Preventing STIs**
How much did you really know about AIDS and HIV? Take the AIDS Awareness Inventory on the textbook's Web site. Do you engage in risky behaviors that are connected with the transmission of HIV? Does your partner? Are you sure? Discuss your inventory results and the things you can you do to decrease your risk of AIDS and other sexually transmitted infections with your study group.

ANSWERS FOR CHAPTER 13

Reading for Understanding About "Gender Polarization: Gender Stereotypes and Their Costs"

1. Stereotypes
2. gender-role
3. women
4. Men
5. Gender polarization
6. careers
7. disadvantage
8. educationally
9. Intelligence
10. career
11. psychological
12. masculine

Reading for Understanding About "Psychological Gender Differences: Vive la Différence or Vive la Similarité?"

13. psychologically
14. biological
15. similar
16. Cognitively
17. small
18. extraverted
19. shallower
20. supportive
21. aggressive
22. casual sex
23. good-looking
24. steady job

Reading for Understanding About "Gender Typing: On Becoming a Woman or a Man"

25. gender-typing
26. Biological
27. natural selection
28. evolutionary
29. structures
30. organization
31. hormones
32. Testosterone
33. aggressiveness
34. gender typing
35. identification
36. Oedipus
37. Electra
38. Social-cognitive
39. identification
40. socialization
41. aggressively
42. Gender-schema
43. lenses of gender
44. culture
45. gender roles
46. labels
47. schema

Reflection Break 1

1. What is a stereotype? How do gender-role stereotypes influence behavior? What are the costs of gender polarization?

   Stereotypes are fixed, conventional ideas about a group of people that can give rise to prejudice and discrimination. Cultures have broad expectations of men and women that are termed gender-role stereotypes. Gender polarization can be extremely costly for both genders in terms of education, activities, careers, psychological well-being, and interpersonal relationships. Polarization has historically worked to the disadvantage of women. For example, educationally, women have until recent years been excluded from careers in medicine and law, and math and science courses in the schools are still seen as mainly in the male "domain." Gender polarization also interferes with psychological well-being and relationships. For example, "masculine" men may not be able to ask for help when they need it or to express tender feelings.

2. Briefly review the biological and psychological influences on gender-typing by completing the following chart.

Biological Influences	Psychological Influences
Brain Organization: According to evolutionary psychologists, gender differences were fashioned by natural selection in response to problems in adaptation that were repeatedly encountered by humans over thousands of generations. This evolutionary process is expressed through structural differences between males and females. For example, research has suggested that although males and females have the same structures in the brain, they seem to use them somewhat differently. Gender differences in brain organization might explain, in part, why women excel in verbal skills and men excel in specialized spatial-relations.	**Psychodynamic Theory:** Freud explained gender-typing in terms of identification with the parent of the same gender through resolution of the Oedipus and Electra complexes.

Sex Hormones:
Sex hormones are responsible for prenatal differentiation of sex organs. Testosterone in the brains of male fetuses spurs greater growth of the right hemisphere of the brain, which may be connected with the ability to manage spatial-relations tasks. Testosterone is also connected with aggressiveness.

Social-Cognitive Theory:
Social-cognitive theorists explain gender-typing in terms of the ways in which experience helps the individual create concepts of gender-appropriate behavior, and how the individual is motivated to engage in such behavior.

Social-cognitive theorists use terms such as observational learning, identification, or the continuous learning process in which children are influenced by rewards to imitate the behavior of same sex adults, and socialization, in which parents and other adults inform children about how they are expected to behave.

Gender Schema Theory:
Gender-schema theory proposes that once children learn the gender schema of their culture, their self-esteem becomes tied up in how well they express the traits considered relevant to their gender.

Sandra Bem argues that people look at the social world through "lenses of gender." She argues that our culture polarizes females and males by organizing social life around mutually exclusive gender roles. No pressure is required—once children understand the labels boy and girl, they have a basis for blending their self-concepts with the gender schema of their culture.

Reading for Understanding About "Attraction: On Liking, Loving, and Relationships"

48. relationships
49. attraction
50. appearance
51. men
52. professional status
53. dependability
54. slenderness
55. tallness
56. cultural ideal
57. good-looking
58. attitudes
59. sociocultural

60. reciprocity
61. matching hypothesis
62. Reciprocity
63. triangular
64. Intimacy
65. passion
66. commitment
67. love
68. Romantic
69. Passion
70. Consummate
71. Sexual orientation

72. Heterosexual
73. Homosexual
74. gay males
75. lesbians
76. Bisexual
77. Psychodynamic
78. reinforcement
79. genetic
80. Sex hormones
81. failed
82. prenatal
83. interaction

Reading for Understanding About "Sexual Response"

84. vasocongestion
85. myotonia
86. four
87. Excitement
88. plateau
89. Orgasm
90. muscle contractions
91. penis

92. ejaculate
93. orgasm
94. resolution
95. refractory
96. dysfunctions
97. hypoactive sexual desire
98. female sexual arousal
99. male erectile

100. dyspareunia
101. vaginismus
102. physical
103. negative attitudes
104. sexual knowledge
105. performance anxiety
106. sex therapy
107. biological

Reflection Break 2

Part I. Clearly differentiate between sexual orientation and sexual activity. What are the different types of sexual orientation?

Sexual orientation, which should not be confused with sexual activity, refers to the direction of one's erotic interests. Just engaging in sexual activity with someone of your own gender does not mean that you or that person has a homosexual orientation.

Heterosexual people are sexually attracted to people of the other gender and interested in forming romantic relationships with them. Homosexual people are sexually attracted to people of their own gender and interested in forming romantic relationships with them. Homosexual males are referred to as gay males and homosexual women are referred to as lesbians. Bisexual people are sexually attracted to and interested in forming romantic relationships with both men and women.

Part II. Matching:

1. p	7. k	13. h
2. m	8. o	14. d
3. g	9. n	15. a
4. l	10. i	16. b
5. c	11. e	
6. j	12. h	

Reading for Understanding About "Sexual Coercion"

108. Rape
109. Date rape
110. socialized
111. reinforced
112. gender-role stereotyping
113. victims
114. sociocultural
115. deserted
116. groups
117. assertive
118. Sexual harassment
119. gestures
120. unwelcome
121. professional attitude
122. alone
123. record
124. complaints

Reading for Understanding About "AIDS and Other Sexually Transmitted Infections"

125. risks
126. HIV/AIDS
127. chlamydia
128. genital warts
129. blood
130. semen
131. white
132. immune
133. saliva
134. antiviral
135. blood
136. cure
137. AIDS
138. expensive
139. prevention
140. abstinent

Reflection Break 3

Part I. Compare rape and sexual harassment. What can be done to prevent each of these?

Sexual harassment consists of deliberate or repeated unwanted comments, gestures, or physical contact of a sexual nature that is unwelcome to the recipient. Rape is the coercion of someone into having sexual intercourse or sex play through the use of arguments, pressure or force. Sexual harassment is often stopped by means such as imparting a professional attitude, avoiding being alone with the harasser, keeping a record of incidents, notifying the harasser that you recognize the harassment for what it is and that you want it to stop, filing complaints with appropriate campus offices, and consulting a lawyer about the problem. From a sociocultural perspective, the prevention of rape involves publicly examining and challenging the widely held cultural attitudes and ideals that contribute to rape. Rape can be prevented by social change and by cautionary measures such as avoiding deserted areas and-in dating-by dating in groups and being assertive in expressing one's sexual intentions and limits.

Part II: Matching:

1. c   4. f   7. e
2. d   5. a
3. b   6. g

Chapter 14

Stress and Health

PREVIEW

Skim the major headings in this chapter in your textbook. Jot down anything that you are surprised or curious about. After this, write down four or five questions that you have about the material in this chapter.

Things that surprised me/I am curious about from Chapter 14:

Questions that I have about stress and health:

▲

▲

▲

▲

QUESTION

These are some questions that you should be able to answer after you finish studying this chapter.

Health Psychology

▲ *What is health psychology?*

Stress: Presses, Pushes, and Pulls

▲ *What is stress?*

▲ *What are daily hassles?*

▲ *How is it that too much of a good thing can make you ill?*

▲ *What is conflict?*

▲ *How do irrational beliefs create or compound stress?*

▲ *What is the Type A behavior pattern?*

Psychological Moderators of Stress

▲ *How do our self-efficacy expectations affect our ability to withstand stress?*

▲ *What characteristics are connected with psychological hardiness?*

▲ *Is there any evidence that "A merry heart doeth good like a medicine"?*

▲ *How do predictability and control help us cope with stress?*

▲ *Is there evidence that social support helps people cope with stress?*

Stress and the Body

▲ *What is the general adaptation syndrome?*

▲ *How does the immune system work?*

▲ *How does stress affect the functioning of the immune system?*

A Multifactorial Approach to Health

▲ *What is the multifactorial approach to health?*

▲ *What are the relationships among ethnicity, gender, socioeconomic status, and health?*

Health Problems and Psychology

▲ *How has psychology contributed to our understanding of the origins and treatment of headaches?*

▲ *How has psychology contributed to our understanding of origins and treatment of coronary heart disease?*

▲ *How has psychology contributed to our understanding of the origins and treatment of cancer?*

Psychology and Modern Life: Coping With Stress

▲ *How do we change the irrational thoughts that create and compound stress?*

▲ *How can we lower our levels of arousal? How can we turn down the inner alarm?*

▲ *How does exercise help people cope with stress?*

READING FOR UNDERSTANDING/REFLECT

The following section provides you with the opportunity to perform 2 of the R's of the PQ4R study method. In this section, you are encouraged to check your understanding of your reading of the text by filling in the blanks in the brief paragraphs that relate to each of the Preview questions. You will also be prompted to rehearse your understanding of the material with periodic Reflection breaks. Remember, it is better to study in more frequent, short sessions than in one long "cram session." Be sure to reward yourself with short study breaks before each Reflection exercise.

Reading for Understanding About "Health Psychology"

What is health psychology? (1) _____ psychology studies the relationships between psychological factors and the prevention and treatment of physical health problems. Health psychologists study the ways in which: (2) _____ factors such as stress, behavior patterns, and attitudes can lead to or aggravate (3) _____; people can cope with (4) _____; and the way that stress and pathogens interact to influence the (5) _____ system.

Reading for Understanding About "Stress: Presses, Pushes, and Pulls"

What is stress? (6) _____ is the demand made on an organism to adapt, cope, or adjust. Whereas some stress-called (7) _____-is desirable to keep us alert and occupied, too much stress can tax our adjustive capacities and contribute to (8) _____ health problems. There are many sources of (9) _____, including: daily hassles, life changes, conflict, irrational beliefs, and Type A behavior.

What are daily hassles? (10) _____ are regularly occurring experiences that threaten or harm our well-being. There are several kinds of hassles, including (11) _____, health, (12) _____, inner concern, environmental, (13) _____ responsibility, work, and future security hassles. Daily hassles are linked to psychological variables such as nervousness, (14) _____, inability to get started, and feelings of sadness and (15) _____.

How is it that too much of a good thing can make you ill? Too many positive life changes can affect one's (16) _____ because life changes require adjustment, whether they are positive or negative. In contrast to daily hassles, (17) _____ occur irregularly. Research shows that hassles and life changes are connected with health problems such as (18) _____ and (19) _____. However, the demonstrated connection between life changes and health is (20) _____; thus causality remains clouded.

What is conflict? (21) _____ is the stressful feeling of being pulled in two or more directions by opposing motives. Conflict is (22) _____. There are four kinds of conflict: (23) _____, in which each of the two goals is desirable; (24) _____, in which you are motivated to avoid both goals; (25) _____ (in the case of a single goal), and (26) _____, when each alternative has its pluses and minuses. Approach-approach conflicts are the (27) _____ stressful since each of the two goals is desirable. Avoidance-avoidance conflicts are (28) _____ stressful since avoiding one goal requires approaching the other.

Approach-avoidance conflicts produce mixed motives and may seem more (29) _____ from a distance, but (30) _____ up close. The most (31) _____ conflict is the multiple approach-avoidance since each of several alternative courses of action have pluses and minuses.

How do irrational beliefs create or compound stress? Albert Ellis notes that our (32) _____ about events, as well as the events themselves, can be stressors. He shows that negative (33) _____ events (A) can be made more aversive (C) when (34) _____ (B) compound their effects. People often (35) _____ negative events. Two common irrational beliefs are excessive needs for (36) _____ and (37) _____. Both set the stage for (38) _____ and increased stress.

What is the Type A behavior pattern? Some people create stress for themselves through the (39) _____ behavior pattern. Type A behavior is connected with a sense of (40) _____ and characterized by competitiveness, (41) _____, and aggressiveness. Type A people find it difficult to just do things for fun; they often watch their form, perfect their technique, and demand continual (42) _____. (43) _____ people relax more readily and focus more on the quality of life. Type B people are less (44) _____ and less impatient and pace themselves.

Reading for Understanding About "Psychological Moderators of Stress"

How do our self-efficacy expectations affect our ability to withstand stress? There is no (45) _____ relationship between stress and physical or psychological health problems. Nonetheless, psychological factors do play a role in influencing, or (46) _____, the effects of stress. (47) _____ moderators of stress include: self-efficacy expectations, psychological hardiness, a sense of humor, predictability, and social support. (48) _____ encourage us to persist in difficult tasks and to endure discomfort. Self-efficacy expectations are also connected with lower levels of adrenaline and noradrenaline, thus having a braking effect on bodily (49) _____.

What characteristics are connected with psychological hardiness? Kobasa found that psychological hardiness among business executives is characterized by (50) _____, they involved themselves rather then feeling alienated; (51) _____, they believe that change rather than stability is normal in life; and (52) _____, they felt and behaved as though they were influential and demonstrated what Julian Rotter termed an internal locus of control. Kosbasa argues that (53) _____ people are more resistant to stress because they choose to face it and interpret stress as making life more interesting.

Is there any evidence that "A merry heart doeth good like a medicine"? Yes. Another psychological moderator of stress appears to be a (54) _____. Research evidence shows that students who produce humor under adversity experience (55) _____ stress. Moreover, watching humorous videos apparently enhances the functioning of the (56) _____ system. How exactly humor helps people (57) _____ with stress is uncertain. One possibility is that laughter stimulates the output of (58) _____, which could benefit the functioning of the immune system.

How do predictability and control help us cope with stress? (59) _____ allows us to brace ourselves, and (60) _____ permits us to plan ways of coping with it. Control, even the (61) _____ of being in control, helps people cope with stress.

Is there evidence that social support helps people cope with stress? (62) _____ has been shown to help people resist infectious diseases such as colds. (63) _____, people who lack social skill and live by themselves, seem more prone to developing infectious diseases. Social support also helps people cope with the stress of (64) _____ and other health problems. Kinds of social support include expression of (65) _____ concern, instrumental aid, information, appraisal, and simple (66) _____.

Reflection Break 1

1. Briefly explain how your cognitions (beliefs and attitudes) affect the way external stressors like daily hassles and conflict affect your well-being.

2. What psychological factors can you use to moderate the effect that stress has on your health?

Reading for Understanding About "Stress and the Body"

What is the general adaptation syndrome? The GAS, or (67) _____, is a cluster of bodily changes triggered by stressors. The GAS consists of (68) _____ stages: alarm, resistance, and exhaustion. During the (69) _____ reaction stage, the body prepares itself for defense. This reaction involves a number of body changes that are initiated by the (70) _____ and further regulated by the (71) _____ system and the (72) _____ division of the autonomic nervous system (ANS). (73) _____ help resist stress by fighting inflammation and allergic reactions. Adrenaline (74) _____ the body by activating the sympathetic nervous system, which is highly active during the alarm and resistance stages of the GAS. (75) _____ activity is characterized by rapid heartbeat and respiration rate, release of stores of sugar, muscle tension, and other responses that deplete the body's supply of energy. The (76) _____ division of the ANS predominates during the exhaustion stage of the GAS and is connected with depression and inactivity. Prolonged stress is (77) _____.

How does the immune system work? Research shows that stress (78) _____ the immune system. The (79) _____ system has several functions that combat disease. One of these is the production of (80) _____, or white blood cells, that engulf and kill pathogens, worn-out body cells, and cancerous cells. The immune system also "remembers" how to battle (81) _____ by maintaining their antibodies in the bloodstream. The immune system also facilitates (82) _____, which increases the number of white blood cells that are transported to a damaged area. (83) _____ is a subspecialty of biology, psychology, and medicine in which the relationships between psychological factors, the nervous system, the endocrine system, the immune system, and disease are examined. One of the major areas of concern in psychoneuroimmunology is the effect of (84) _____ on the immune system.

How does stress affect the functioning of the immune system? Stress (85) _____ the functioning of the immune system by stimulating the release of corticosteroids. (86) _____ counter inflammation and interfere with the formation of antibodies; they also suppress the functioning of the immune system.

Reading for Understanding About "A Multifactorial Approach to Health"

What is the multifactorial approach to health? The (87) _____ approach to health recognizes that many factors, including biological, psychological, sociocultural, and environmental factors, affect our health. Nearly 1 million preventable (88) _____ occur each year in the United States. Measures such as quitting (89) _____, eating properly, exercising, and controlling (90) _____ intake would prevent nearly 80% of them.

What are the relationships among ethnicity, gender, socioeconomic status, and health? (91) _____ Americans live about 7 years less than (92) _____ Americans, largely because of sociocultural and (93) _____ factors that are connected with less access to health care and greater likelihood of eating high-fat diets, smoking, and living in unhealthful neighborhoods. (94) _____ are less likely than men to have heart attacks in early and middle adulthood due to the protective effects of estrogen. Women outlive men by (95) _____ years on the average. One reason is that (96) _____ are more likely than (97) _____ to consult health professionals about health problems.

Reading for Understanding About "Health Problems and Psychology"

How has psychology contributed to our understanding of the origins and treatment of headaches? Psychologists participate in research concerning the origins of (98) _____, including stress and tension. Psychologists help people alleviate headaches by reducing (99) _____. They have also developed (100) _____ training methods for helping people cope with migraines.

How has psychology contributed to our understanding of origins and treatment of coronary heart disease? Psychologists have participated in research that shows that the risk factors for (101) _____ disease include family history; physiological conditions such as hypertension and high levels of serum cholesterol; behavior patterns such as heavy drinking, smoking, eating fatty foods, and Type A behavior; work overload; chronic tension and fatigue; and physical inactivity.

They help people achieve healthier cardiovascular systems by stopping (102) _____, controlling (103) _____, reducing (104) _____, lowering (105) _____ levels, changing Type (106) _____ behavior, reducing (107) _____, and exercising.

How has psychology contributed to our understanding of the origins and treatment of cancer? Psychologists have participated in research that shows that the risk factors for (108) _____ include family history, smoking, drinking alcohol, eating animal fats, sunbathing, and stress. The following measures can be helpful in (109) _____ and (110) _____ cancer: controlling exposure to behavioral risk factors for cancer, having regular medical checkups, regulating exposure to stress, and vigorously fighting cancer if it develops.

Reading for Understanding About "Psychology and Modern Life: Coping With Stress"

(111) _____ takes many forms and can harm our psychological well-being and physical health. Three ways for coping with stress include: controlling (112) _____, lowering arousal, and (113) _____.

How do we change the irrational thoughts that create and compound stress? People often feel pressure from their own (114) _____. In order to keep thoughts from producing stress, we must (115) _____ them. (116) _____ psychologists have outlined a three-step process for doing so. It involves becoming (117) _____ of the thoughts, preparing and practicing (118) _____ thoughts, and (119) _____ oneself for changing.

How can we lower our levels of arousal? How can we turn down the inner alarm? Stress tends to trigger (120) _____. Arousal serves as a sign that something may be (121) _____. However, once we are aware that a (122) _____ is acting on us, high levels of (123) _____ are not helpful. Psychologists have developed many methods for teaching people to (124) _____ arousal including meditation, biofeedback training, and progressive relaxation. In (125) _____, people purposefully tense and then relax muscle groups to develop awareness of muscle tensions and learn how to let the tensions go.

How does exercise help people cope with stress? (126) _____ enhances our psychological well-being and also strengthens the (127) _____ system, our fitness, or "condition" so that we can better (128) _____ the bodily effects of stress.

Reflection Break 2

1. Briefly summarize the physical effects of prolonged stress on the body.

2. How can an understanding of health psychology help a person remain healthy?

3. After reading this chapter what can you do to cope with the stresses of your life?

REVIEW: KEY TERMS AND CONCEPTS

FINAL CHAPTER REVIEW

Review

Visit the *Psychology in the New Millennium* Web site at www.harcourtcollege.com/psych/PNM/siteresources.html and take the Chapter Quizzes to test your knowledge.

Recite

Go to the Recite section for this chapter in your textbook. Use the tear-off card provided at the back of the book to cover the answers of the Recite section. Read the questions aloud, and recite the answers. This will help you cement your knowledge of key concepts.

Essay Questions

1. *What is stress?* In a three-paragraph essay describe the definition of stress you had before reading the chapter, and compare it with the psychological definition provided in your textbook.

2. *Controversy in Psychology: Just how are daily hassles and life changes connected with health problems?* How many daily hassles do you experience? Are they temporary or permanent? How many are connected with your role as a student? Can you think of any positive life changes in your own life that caused your stress? Make a list of your hassles and hangups that you must cope with in your daily life, and group them in the following categories:

Household hassles	Work hassles
Time pressure hassles	School hassles
Health hassles	Future/security hassles
Family hassles	Social hassles
Financial responsibility hassles	Other

After you complete your list, rank your hassles on a scale of 1 to 10, with 1 representing the least important; 10 the most important. Which category of daily hassles are the most pressing for you? How can you decrease the stress they produce? Present your information to your classmates on a posterboard in a format specified by your instructor, and compare your profile with those of your classmates. Are you more or less stressed than your peers?

5. *How do your attitudes and beliefs affect the impact that external stressors have?* In a two-page essay explain how our cognitions—our attitudes and beliefs—affect the impact that external stressors have on us, and how we can moderate these effects through psychological mechanisms. In your essay be sure to address the role of irrational beliefs in our interpretation of events and how we can use changes in self-efficacy expectations, a sense of humor, and social support. Format your essay as specified by your instructor.

6. *Controversy in Psychology: Does it matter if your physician is a woman or a man?* How would you further research the question as to whether or not the sex of your physician influences the type of preventative care that you receive? Your textbook reports on two studies that suggest that female patients whose physicians are also female are more likely to receive screening for cancer than those whose physicians are male. However, it is unclear whether this was due to the tendency for female patients with female doctors to seek out preventative care, or whether the doctors themselves are more likely to encourage the tests. Suggest a possible research study that might help clarify this issue. Remember that there are numerous possibilities for this research; there is no right or wrong answer. However, you must be clear as to what your variables are (clearly state your operational definitions) and how you will measure them. Present your proposed research to your instructor. Be careful not to confuse correlation with causation!

7. *Does your behavior pattern influence your risk of CHD, and can you reduce your risk?* In a short report, differentiate between Type A and Type B behavior patterns, and discuss the link between Type A behavior and coronary heart disease (CHD). Conclude your report with recommendations for reducing the risk of CHD. Format your report as specified by your instructor.

RELATE/EXPAND/INTEGRATE

8. **Health Psychology**
What is health psychology? What type of career opportunities are available in health psychology? Read about careers in health psychology on the "Careers in Health Psychology" page from West Chester University at http://www.wcupa.edu/_ACADEMICS/ sch_cas.psy/Career_Paths/Health/Career02.htm. Pick one of the subfields presented, and prepare a 3-minute oral report on it. Be sure to describe the specialization's emphasis and the types of job responsibilities that someone might have if he or she chose this career.

9. **Sources of Stress: Don't Hassle Me? (Right)**
Controversy in psychology: Just how are daily hassles and life changes connected with health problems? Do you find that the more life hassles you have, the more likely you are to get sick? How often do you find that you get sick during, or right after, exam week? Or spring break? Have each member of your study group interview 20 college students with the above questions. Tabulate the results. Do the data suggest that stressful times tend to be correlated with illness? Prepare a report for your class that describes your findings and outlines the different ways that college students can try to prevent becoming ill during peak stress periods.

10. **Stress and Diversity: Acculturative Stress**
Have you experienced "acculturative stress"? Have you ever (or do you now) live(d) in a culture where you were a minority? If so, describe your experience to your class in a format specified by your instructor. Was it similar to Don Terry's? How was it similar? How was it different? To what do you attribute the differences? How did you reduce the stress that you felt? What impact did it have on your health?

11. **Psychology and Modern Life: Alleviating the Type A Behavior Pattern**
What type of behavior pattern do you display? Are you a Type A? Take the "Are You a Type A or Type B" self-assessment on page 473 of your textbook. In a brief essay, report your results on the self-assessment. If you are a Type A person, also describe the advantages and disadvantages (i.e., health risks) of this behavior pattern. If you are a Type B person, offer some advice to a Type A as to how to alleviate Type A tendencies. After reading this chapter, are you convinced that you should change your Type A behavior? If so, how will you do it? If not, why?

12. **Psychological Moderators of Stress**
How resilient are you? Your textbook discusses the role of psychological factors in our experience of stress. Factors such as self-efficacy expectations, psychological hardiness, and a sense of humor are all important in determining how stressful life events are. How resilient are you? Take the quiz by Al Siebert at http://www.thrivenet.com/articles/resilien. html. How do you react to unexpected difficulties? Healthy, resilient people have stress-resistant personalities and learn valuable lessons from rough experiences-are you one of these? If not, how can you become more resilient? Report your findings to your classmates in a format specified by your instructor.

13. **Stress and the Body**
    What are the biological consequences of stress? What do you experience happening in your body when you are under stress? How do those sensations fit the description of the general adaptation syndrome? After reading the textbook's description, you might want to start your search at the "Medical Basis of Stress, Depression, Anxiety, Sleep Problems, and Drug Use" page at http://www.teachhealth.com. Summarize the effects of stress on brain chemistry and the physical symptoms of overstress. Why do people often turn to caffeine, alcohol, and other drugs when they become stressed? Report back to your classmates on your findings in a format specified by your instructor.

14. **A Multifactorial Approach to Health: Health and Diversity: Nations Within the Nation**
    Are we truly "nations within a nation"? Are there ethnic and gender differences in health? Using your favorite Web search tool (Ask Jeeves, Google, Dogpile), research the data on ethnic and gender differences in health in the United States. What does your research tell you? What do you think can be done to change any inequities that exist? Report your findings and recommendations for change to your classmates in a format specified by your instructor.

15. **Psychology and Modern Life: Coping With Stress**
    How can you help yourself to better cope with stress? Visit the following Web sites on stress and stress management, and with your study group prepare an informational brochure for your class that outlines the various stress management techniques suggested
    Mind Tools Website-Stress at http://www.demon.co.uk/mindtool/smpage.html
    Stress Management Site (by Wesley E. Sime, Ph.D./MPH./Ph.D.) http://www.unl.edu/stress/mgmt/
    How To Fight & Conquer Stress (Rose Medical Center in Denver, CO)
    http://www.coolware.com/health/medical_reporter/stress.html

ANSWERS FOR CHAPTER 14

Reading for Understanding About "Health Psychology"

1. Health
2. psychological
3. illness
4. stress
5. immune

Reading for Understanding About "Stress: Presses, Pushes, and Pulls"

6. Stress
7. eustress
8. physical
9. stress
10. Daily hassles
11. household
12. time-pressure
13. financial
14. worrying
15. loneliness
16. health
17. life changes
18. heart disease
19. cancer

20. correlational
21. Conflict
22. frustrating
23. approach-approach
24. avoidance-avoidance
25. approach-avoidance
26. multiple approach-avoidance
27. least
28. more
29. attractive
30. undesirable
31. complex
32. beliefs

33. activating
34. irrational beliefs
35. catastrophize
36. social approval
37. perfectionism
38. disappointment
39. Type A
40. time urgency
41. impatience
42. self-improvement
43. Type B
44. ambitious

Reading for Understanding About "Psychological Moderators of Stress"

45. one-to-one
46. moderating
47. Psychological
48. Self-efficacy expectations
49. arousal
50. commitment
51. challenge

52. control
53. psychologically hardy
54. sense of humor
55. less
56. immune
57. cope
58. endorphins
59. Predictability

60. control
61. illusion
62. Social support
63. Introverts
64. cancer
65. emotional
66. socializing

Reflection Break 1

1. Briefly explain how your cognitions (beliefs and attitudes) affect the way external stressors like daily hassles and conflict affect your well-being.

   Stress is the demand made on an organism to adapt, cope or adjust. Whereas some stress—called eustress—is desirable to keep us alert and occupied, too much stress can tax our adjustive capacities and contribute to physical health problems. Albert Ellis argues that our beliefs about events, as well as the events themselves, can be stressors. He shows that negative activating events (A) can be made more aversive (C) when irrational beliefs (B) compound their effects. People often catastrophize negative events. Two common irrational beliefs are excessive needs for social approval and perfectionism. Both set the stage for disappointment and increased stress.

2. What psychological factors can you use to moderate the effect that stress has on your health?

There is no one-to-one relationship between stress and physical or psychological health problems. Nonetheless, psychological factors do play a role in influencing or moderating the effects of stress. Psychological moderators of stress include: self-efficacy expectations, psychological hardiness, a sense of humor, predictability, and social support.

Self-efficacy expectations: Self-efficacy expectations encourage us to persist in difficult tasks and to endure discomfort. Self-efficacy expectations are also connected with lower levels of adrenaline and noradrenaline, thus having a braking effect on bodily arousal.

Psychological hardiness: Psychological hardiness among business executives is characterized by commitment, they involve themselves rather then feeling alienated; challenge, they believe that change, rather than stability, is normal in life; and control, they feel and behave as though they are influential and demonstrate what Julian Rotter termed an internal locus of control. Kosbasa argues that psychologically hardy people are more resistant to stress because they choose to face it and interpret stress as making life more interesting.

A sense of humor: Research evidence shows that students who produce humor under adversity experience less stress. Moreover, watching humorous videos apparently enhances the functioning of the immune system. How exactly humor helps people cope with stress is uncertain. One possibility is that laughter stimulates the output of endorphins, which could benefit the functioning of the immune system.

Predictability: Predictability allows us to brace ourselves, and control permits us to plan ways of coping with it. Control, even the illusion of being in control, helps people cope with stress.

Social support: Social support has been shown to help people resist infectious diseases such as colds. Introverts, people who lack social skill and live by themselves, seem more prone to developing infectious diseases. It also helps people cope with the stress of cancer and other health problems. Kinds of social support include expression of emotional concern, instrumental aid, information, appraisal, and simple socializing.

Reading for Understanding About "Stress and the Body"

67. general adaptation syndrome
68. three
69. alarm
70. brain
71. endocrine
72. sympathetic

73. Corticosteroids
74. arouses
75. Sympathetic
76. parasympathetic
77. dangerous
78. suppresses
79. immune

80. Leukocytes
81. antigens
82. inflammation
83. Psychoneuroimmunology
84. stress
85. depresses
86. Steroids

Reading for Understanding About "A Multifactorial Approach to Health"

87. multifactorial
88. deaths
89. smoking
90. alcohol

91. African
92. European
93. economic
94. Women

95. 7
96. women
97. men

Reading for Understanding About "Health Problems and Psychology"

98. headaches
99. tension
100. biofeedback
101. coronary heart
102. smoking

103. weight
104. hypertension
105. LDL
106. A
107. hostility

108. cancer
109. preventing
110. treating

Reading for Understanding About "Psychology and Modern Life: Coping With Stress"

111. Stress
112. irrational thoughts
113. exercising
114. thoughts
115. change
116. Cognitive-behavioral

117. aware
118. incompatible
119. rewarding
120. arousal
121. wrong
122. stressor

123. arousal
124. reduce
125. progressive relaxation
126. Exercise
127. cardiovascular
128. resist

Reflection Break 2

1. Briefly summarize the physical effects of prolonged stress on the body.

   Research shows that stress suppresses the immune system. The immune system has several functions that combat disease. The general adaptation syndrome (GAS) is a cluster of bodily changes triggered by stressors. The GAS consists of three stages: alarm, resistance, and exhaustion. During the alarm reaction stage, the body prepares itself for defense. This reaction involves a number of body changes that are initiated by the brain and further regulated by the endocrine system and the sympathetic division of the autonomic nervous system. Corticosteroids help resist stress by fighting inflammation and allergic reactions. Adrenaline arouses the body by activating the sympathetic nervous system, which is highly active during the alarm and resistance stages of the GAS. Sympathetic activity is characterized by rapid heartbeat and respiration rate, release of stores of sugar, muscle tension, and other responses that deplete the body's supply of energy. The parasympathetic division of the ANS predominates during the exhaustion stage of the GAS and is connected with depression and inactivity. Prolonged stress is dangerous.

   Psychoneuroimmunology is a subspecialty of biology, psychology, and medicine in which the relationships between psychological factors, the nervous system, the endocrine system, the immune system, and disease are examined. One of the major areas of concern in psychoneuroimmunology is the effect of stress on the immune system.

2. How can an understanding of health psychology help a person remain healthy?

The multifactorial approach to health and coping with stress recognizes that many factors, including biological, psychological, sociocultural, and environmental factors, affect our health. Nearly 1 million preventable deaths occur each year in the United States. Measures such as quitting smoking, eating properly, exercising, and controlling alcohol intake would prevent nearly 80% of them.

Health psychologists participate in research concerning the origins of headaches, including stress and tension. Health psychologists help people alleviate headaches by reducing tension. They have also developed biofeedback training methods for helping people cope with migraines.

Health psychologists have participated in research that shows that the risk factors for coronary heart disease include family history; physiological conditions such as hypertension and high levels of serum cholesterol; behavior patterns such as heavy drinking, smoking, eating fatty foods, and Type A behavior; work overload; chronic tension and fatigue; and physical inactivity. They help people achieve healthier cardiovascular systems by stopping smoking, controlling weight, reducing hypertension, lowering LDL levels, changing Type A behavior, reducing hostility, and exercising.

Health psychologists have participated in research that shows that the risk factors for cancer include family history, smoking, drinking alcohol, eating animal fats, sunbathing, and stress. The following measures can be helpful in preventing and treating cancer: controlling exposure to behavioral risk factors for cancer, having regular medical checkups, regulating exposure to stress, and vigorously fighting cancer if it develops.

3. After reading this chapter, what can you do to cope with the stresses of your life?
Three ways for coping with stress include: controlling irrational thoughts, lowering arousal and exercising.

- *Control irrational thinking:* People often feel pressure from their own thoughts. In order to keep them from producing stress, we must change them. Cognitive-behavioral psychologists have outlined a three-step process for doing so. It involves becoming aware of the thoughts, preparing and practicing incompatible thoughts, and rewarding oneself for changing.

- *Relax:* Stress tends to trigger arousal. Arousal serves as a sign that something may be wrong; however, once we are aware that a stressor is acting on us, high levels of arousal are not helpful. Psychologists have developed many methods for teaching people to reduce arousal, including meditation, biofeedback training, and progressive relaxation. In progressive relaxation, people purposefully tense and then relax muscle groups to develop awareness of muscle tensions and learn how to let the tensions go.

- *Exercise:* Exercise enhances our psychological well-being and also strengthens the cardiovascular system, our fitness, or "condition" so that we can better resist the bodily effects of stress.

Chapter 15

Psychological Disorders

PREVIEW

Skim the major headings in this chapter in your textbook. Jot down anything that you are surprised or curious about. After this, write down four or five questions that you have about the material in this chapter.

Things that surprised me/I am curious about from Chapter 15:

Questions that I have about psychological disorders:

▲

▲

▲

▲

QUESTION

These are some questions that you should be able to answer after you finish studying this chapter.

Historic Views of Psychological Disorders: "The Devil Made Me Do It"?

▲ *How have people historically explained psychological disorders?*

What Are Psychological Disorders?

▲ *How, then, do we define psychological disorders?*

Classifying Psychological Disorders

▲ *How are psychological disorders grouped or classified?*

Anxiety Disorders

▲ *What kinds of anxiety disorders are there?*
▲ *What is known about the origins of anxiety disorders?*

Dissociative Disorders

▲ *What kinds of dissociative disorders are there?*
▲ *What is known about the origins of dissociative disorders?*

Somatoform Disorders

▲ *What kinds of somatoform disorders are there?*
▲ *What is known about the origins of somatoform disorders?*

Mood Disorders

▲ *What kinds of mood disorders are there?*
▲ *Why are women more likely than men to be depressed?*
▲ *What is known about the origins of mood disorders?*
▲ *Why do people commit suicide?*
▲ *What sociocultural factors are connected with suicide?*
▲ *What are some of the myths and realities about suicide?*

Schizophrenia

▲ *What is schizophrenia?*
▲ *What kinds of schizophrenia are there?*
▲ *What is known about the origins of schizophrenia?*

Personality Disorders

▲ *What kinds of personality disorders are there?*
▲ *What is known about the origins of personality disorders?*

Eating Disorders

▲ *What kinds of eating disorders are there?*
▲ *What is known about the origins of eating disorders?*

READING FOR UNDERSTANDING/REFLECT

The following section provides you with the opportunity to perform 2 of the R's of the PQ4R study method. In this section, you are encouraged to check your understanding of your reading of the text by filling in the blanks in the brief paragraphs that relate to each of the Preview questions. You will also be prompted to rehearse your understanding of the material with periodic Reflection breaks. Remember, it is better to study in more frequent, short sessions than in one long "cram session." Be sure to reward yourself with short study breaks before each Reflection exercise.

Reading for Understanding About "Historic Views of Psychological Disorders: 'The Devil Made Me Do It'?"

How have people historically explained psychological disorders? People throughout history have mainly attributed psychological disorders to some sort of (1) _____. The ancient (2) _____ believed that people with such disorders were being punished by the gods. Since the Middle Ages, Europeans mainly attributed these disorders to possession by the (3) _____. We still see remnants of this history in our phraseology; for example, we often hear the expressions "Something got into me" or "The Devil made me do it."

Reading for Understanding About "What Are Psychological Disorders" and "Classifying Psychological Disorders"

How do we define psychological disorders? Psychological disorders are behaviors, or mental processes, that are connected with various kinds of (4) _____. Psychological (5) _____ are characterized by unusual behavior, socially unacceptable behavior, faulty perception of reality, personal distress, dangerous behavior, or self-defeating behavior.

How are psychological disorders grouped or classified? The most widely used (6) _____ scheme is found in the Diagnostic and Statistical Manual (DSM) of the American Psychiatric Association. The current edition of the DSM, the DSM IV, groups disorders on the basis of (7) _____ and no longer uses the category of neuroses. The DSM uses a (8) _____ system of assessment. There are five axes: Axis (9) _____ presents the primary clinical syndrome; Axis (10) _____ presents developmental and personality disorder; Axis (11) _____ provides information on the general medical conditions; Axis (12) _____ examines the psychosocial and environmental problems; and Axis (13) _____ examines the global assessment of functioning. People may receive an Axis I or Axis II (14) _____ or a combination of the two.

Reflection Break 1

Match the DSM axis with its proper description.

I. Axis I   IV. Axis IV
II. Axis II   V. Axis V
III. Axis III

_____ 1. Presents developmental and personality disorders; includes deeply ingrained, maladaptive ways of perceiving others.

_____ 2. An overall judgment of the current functioning and the highest level of functioning the past year according to social, psychological, and occupational criteria.

_____ 3. Includes psychological disorders that impair functioning and are stressful to the individual.

_____ 4. Includes chronic and acute illnesses, injuries, allergies that affect functioning and treatment.

_____ 5. Describes stressors that occurred during the past year that may have contributed to the development of a new mental disorder.

Reading for Understanding About "Anxiety Disorders"

What kinds of anxiety disorders are there? (15) _____ disorders are characterized by motor tension, feelings of dread, and overarousal of the sympathetic branch of the autonomic nervous system. These disorders include irrational, excessive fears, or (16) _____, or persistent (17) _____ of specific objects; (18) _____ disorder, characterized by sudden attacks in which people typically fear that they may be losing control or going crazy; generalized or pervasive anxiety, in which the central feature is (19) _____; obsessive-compulsive disorder, in which people are troubled by intrusive thoughts, or (20) _____, and impulses to repeat some activity, (21) _____; and (22) _____ disorders, in which a stressful event is followed by persistent fears and intrusive thoughts about the event. (23) _____ stress disorder can occur 6 months or more after the event, whereas (24) _____ stress disorder occurs within a month.

What is known about the origins of anxiety disorders? The (25) _____ perspective tends to view anxiety disorders as conflicts originating in childhood. Generalized anxiety disorder is explained as difficulty in (26) _____ primitive impulses, and obsessions are explained as leakage of (27) _____. Many (28) _____ theorists view phobias as conditioned fears. Social-cognitive learning theorists note that (29) _____ plays a role in acquisition of fears. (30) _____ theorists focus on ways in which people interpret threats. (31) _____ factors also play a role in anxiety disorders. Some people may be (32) _____ to acquire certain kinds of fears. (33) _____ disorders tend to run in families. Some psychologists suggest that (34) _____ factors-which could be inherited-may create a predisposition toward anxiety disorders. One such factor is faulty regulation of (35) _____.

Reading for Understanding About "Dissociative Disorders"

What kinds of dissociative disorders are there? (36) _____ disorders are characterized by sudden, temporary changes in consciousness or self-identity. They include dissociative (37) _____, in which individuals forget their past; dissociative (38) _____, which involves forgetting plus fleeing and adopting a new identity; dissociative (39) _____ disorder, otherwise known as multiple personality disorder, in which a person behaves as if more than one personality occupies his or her body; and (40) _____, characterized by feelings that one is not real or that one is standing outside oneself.

What is known about the origins of dissociative disorders? Dissociative disorders are some of the (41) _____ psychological disorders, and there is some (42) _____ about their existence. In any event, the different theoretical perspectives have offered suggestions as to the origins of dissociative disorders. (43) _____ theory proposes that people with dissociative disorders use massive repression to keep disturbing memories or ideas out of mind. (44) _____ theories propose that people with dissociative disorders have learned not to think about bad memories or disturbing impulses to avoid feelings of guilt and (45) _____. Surveys find that the memories being avoided may involve episodes of childhood (46) _____ or physical abuse.

Reading for Understanding About "Somatoform Disorders"

What kinds of somatoform disorders are there? People with (47) _____ disorders exhibit or complain of physical problems, although no medical evidence of such problems can be found. The somatoform disorders include conversion disorder and hypochondriasis. In (48) _____ disorder, stress is converted into a physical symptom, and the individual may show (49) "_____," or an indifference to the symptom. In (50) _____, people insist that they are suffering from a serious physical illness, even though no medical evidence of illness can be found.

What is known about the origins of somatoform disorders? These disorders were once called (51) "_____" and expected to be found more often among women. However, they are also found among men and may reflect the relative benefits of focusing on (52) _____ symptoms rather than fears and conflicts. (53) _____ theory proposes that symptoms of somatoform disorders protect the individual from feelings of shame and guilt, or another source of stress.

Reflection Break 2

Compare and contrast the anxiety, dissociative, and somatoform disorders by completing the following chart.

	Characteristic Symptoms	Theoretical Origins
Anxiety Disorders		
Dissociative Disorders		
Somatoform Disorders		

Reading for Understanding About " Mood Disorders"

What kinds of mood disorders are there? (54) _____ disorders involve disturbances in expressed emotions. (55) _____ is the most common of the psychological disorders. (56) _____ depression is characterized by persistent feelings of sadness, loss of interest, feelings of worthlessness or guilt, and inability to concentrate. Physical symptoms of depression may include disturbances in regulation of (57) _____ and sleeping. Feelings of unworthiness and guilt may be so excessive that they are considered (58) _____. (59) _____ disorder, formerly known as manic-depressive disorder, is characterized by dramatic swings in mood between elation and depression; (60) _____ episodes include pressured speech and rapid flight of ideas.

Why are women more likely than men to be depressed? (61) _____ are two times more likely to be diagnosed with depression than (62) _____. Part of the (63) _____ difference may reflect hormonal factors, but women also experience greater (64) _____ than men in our culture-including the stresses that accompany second-class citizenship. (65) _____ are more likely to experience physical and sexual abuse, poverty, single parenthood, and sexism and are more likely to help other people who are under stress.

What is known about the origins of mood disorders? Research emphasizes possible roles for (66) _____, (67) _____ styles, and underutilization of (68) _____ in depression.

From the (69) _____ perspective, bipolar disorder may be seen as alternating states in which the personality is dominated by the superego and ego. (70) _____ theorists, on the other hand, suggest that depressed people behave as though they cannot obtain reinforcement and point to links between depression and learned helplessness. (71) _____ theorists note that people who tend to ruminate about feelings of depression are more likely to prolong them. And Seligman notes that people who are depressed are more likely than other people to make internal, or (72) _____, stable, and (73) _____ (large) attributions for failures, factors that they are relatively powerless to change. Researchers are also searching for (74) _____ factors in mood disorders. (75) _____ factors involving regulation of neurotransmitters may also be involved in mood disorders. For example, bipolar disorder has been linked to inappropriate levels of the neurotransmitter (76) _____. Moreover, people with severe depression often respond to drugs that heighten the action of (77) _____.

Why do people commit suicide? What are some of the myths and realities about suicide? It is mythical that people who truly intend to kill themselves do it without (78) _____ and that those who fail at the attempt are just seeking attention. Many people who committed (79) _____ had issued warnings, and many had made prior attempts. Suicide usually reflects feelings of helplessness and (80) _____ due to stressful events, especially events that involve loss of social support. Suicide tends to run in families, but it is unclear whether the reasons are (81) _____ or (82) _____.

What sociocultural factors are connected with suicide? Older and better-educated people are (83) _____ to commit suicide. More women (84) _____ suicide, but more men (85) "_____" because they use more lethal means. (86) _____ Americans are twice as likely as (87) _____ Americans to commit suicide. (88) _____ Americans are at the greatest risk. Suicide attempts are more common after (89) _____ events, especially events that entail loss of social support.

Reading for Understanding About "Schizophrenia"

What is schizophrenia? Schizophrenia is a most severe psychological disorder that is characterized by disturbances in thought and language, such as loosening of associations and (90) _____; in perception and attention, as found in (91) _____; in motor activity, as shown by a (92) _____ or by excited behavior; in (93) _____, as in flat or inappropriate emotional responses; and in (94) _____, as in social withdrawal and absorption in daydreams or fantasy.

What kinds of schizophrenia are there? The major types of (95) _____ are paranoid, disorganized, and catatonic. (96) _____ schizophrenia is characterized largely by systematized delusions and frequently related auditory hallucinations. They often have (97) _____ of grandeur and persecution. (98) _____ schizophrenia is characterized by incoherence, loosening of associations, disorganized behavior, and delusions, and flat or highly inappropriate emotional responses; extreme social impairment is common with disorganized schizophrenia. (99) _____ schizophrenia is characterized by a striking motor impairment; often, it is a slowing of activity into a stupor that may suddenly change into an agitated phase.

Catatonic schizophrenics may also show a (100) _____, in which the person maintains positions into which he or she has been manipulated by others, and mutism.

What is known about the origins of schizophrenia? The (101) _____ view argues that schizophrenia occurs because the ego is overwhelmed by sexual or aggressive impulses from the id and the person regresses to an early phase of the oral stage. (102) _____ theorists explain schizophrenia in terms of conditioning and observational learning. (103) _____, schizophrenia is connected with smaller brains, especially fewer synapses in the prefrontal region, and larger ventricles in the brain. According to the (104) _____ theory of schizophrenia, people with schizophrenia use more dopamine than other people do, perhaps because they have more dopamine in the brain along with more dopamine receptors than other people. According to the (105) _____ model, genetic vulnerability to schizophrenia may interact with other factors, such as stress, complications during pregnancy and childbirth, and quality of parenting, to cause the disorder to develop.

Reading for Understanding About "Personality Disorders"

What kinds of personality disorders are there? (106) _____ disorders are inflexible, maladaptive behavior patterns that impair personal or social functioning and cause distress for the individual or others. There are a number of (107) _____ disorders, including paranoid, schizotypal, schizoid, antisocial, and avoidant personality disorders. The defining trait of (108) _____ personality disorder is suspiciousness. People with (109) _____ personality disorders show oddities of thought, perception, and behavior, but the bizarre behaviors of schizophrenia are absent. (110) _____, indifference to relationships, and flat emotional response are the major characteristic of schizoid personality disorder. People with (111) _____ personality disorders persistently violate the rights of others and are in conflict with the law. They show little or no guilt or (112) _____ over their misdeeds and are largely undeterred by punishment. People with (113) _____ personality disorder tend to avoid entering relationships for fear of rejection and criticism.

What is known about the origins of personality disorders? (114) _____ theory connected many personality disorders with hypothesized Oedipal problems. (115) _____ theorists suggest that childhood experiences can contribute to maladaptive ways of relating to others. (116) _____ psychologists find that antisocial adolescents encode social information in ways that bolster their misdeeds. (117) _____ factors may be involved in some personality disorders. (118) _____ personality disorder tends to run in families and may develop from some combination of genetic vulnerability (less gray matter in the prefrontal cortex of the brain, which may provide lower-than-normal levels of arousal), inconsistent discipline, and cynical processing of social information.

Reading for Understanding About "Eating Disorders"

What kinds of eating disorders are there? The (119) _____ disorders include anorexia nervosa and bulimia nervosa. (120) _____ is characterized by refusal to eat and extreme thinness. (121) _____ is characterized by recurrent cycles of binge eating and purging. (122) _____ are more likely than (123) _____ to develop these disorders.

What is known about the origins of eating disorders? The typical person with anorexia or bulimia is a (124) _____ European American (125) _____ of (126) _____ socioeconomic status. Theorists account for the gender gap in different ways. The major (127) _____ explanation of the eating disorders is that a conflicted female is attempting to remain prepubescent. (128) _____ approaches suggest that weight loss has strong reinforcement value because it provides feelings of personal perfectibility. However, most psychologists look to (129) _____ of the slender female-and the pressure that such idealization places on young women-as the major contributor.

Reflection Break 3

Compare and contrast the anxiety, dissociative, and somatoform disorders by completing the following chart.

	Characteristic Symptoms	Theoretical Origins
Mood Disorders		
Schizophrenic Disorders		
Personality Disorders		
Eating Disorders		

REVIEW: KEY TERMS AND CONCEPTS

FINAL CHAPTER REVIEW

Review

Visit the *Psychology in the New Millennium* Web site at www.harcourtcollege.com/psych/PNM/siteresources.html and take the Chapter Quizzes to test your knowledge.

Recite

Go to the Recite section for this chapter in your textbook. Use the tear-off card provided at the back of the book to cover the answers of the Recite section. Read the questions aloud, and recite the answers. This will help you cement your knowledge of key concepts.

Essay Questions

1. *How do we diagnose psychological disorders?* What is the DSM-IV? When was it published? What is its goal? Why does the DSM group disorders on the basis of observation features or symptoms? In a brief report, describe the five axes of the DSM-IV system. What do you see as the strengths and weaknesses of the current diagnostic system? In your report, suggest an alternative system or any changes to the current system that you feel would address its weaknesses and make diagnosis more effective. Be sure to explain your rationale.

2. *Is anxiety normal?* Do you ever find your self "in a panic" or know people who repeatedly check that the doors are locked or the gas jets are turned off before they leave home? Or people who refuse to step on the cracks in the sidewalk? What is the difference between "being in a panic" and having a panic disorder? Between being concerned and thorough and having an obsessive-compulsive disorder? How are anxiety disorders abnormal? Prepare a brief (one- to two-page) essay comparing normal anxiety to an anxiety disorder.

3. *Dissociative disorders on the screen.* Have you seen a film or a TV show in which a character was supposed to have dissociative identity disorder (perhaps it was called "multiple personality")? In brief essay, describe the behavior of a movie character portraying the characteristics of a dissociative identity disorder. In your essay, be sure to identify which movie and which character you are discussing. What kind of behavior did the character display? In the film or TV show, what were the supposed origins of the disorder? Does the behavior seem consistent with the description of the disorder in the text?

4. *Controversy in psychology: Are somatoform disorders the special province of women?* Somatoform disorders were once referred to as "hysterical neuroses" and were once considered the special disorder of women. Why? In a brief essay, characterize the history of somatoform disorders. What does the word hysterical mean when used to describe somatoform disorders? What are the social problems in labeling these disorders as hysterical? What kinds of problems do you think are involved in trying to determine whether someone has a true physical health problem or a conversion disorder? Are somatoform disorders a women's disease?

5. *How would you distinguish between "normal" depression or "normal" enthusiasm and a mood disorder?* Do you ever feel depressed? What kind of experiences lead you to feel depressed? Do you find it easy or difficult to admit to having feelings of sadness or depression? How are your feelings of depression differ from a major depressive disorder? Explain.

6. *Suicide and diversity: Who commits suicide?* Your textbook discusses sociocultural factors that are connected with suicide. In a two-page essay, summarize these age, gender, educational, and ethnic differences in suicide attempts. Why do you think the differences exist? Be sure to fully explain your ideas in your essay.

7. *How have advances in biological psychology and brain imaging advanced the study of schizophrenia?* In a brief report, discuss the evidence for a biological and genetic role in schizophrenia. What would you tell the son or daughter of a person with schizophrenia? What would you tell the son or daughter of a person with schizophrenia about the likelihood of his or her developing schizophrenia? Explain.

8. *What is the difference between people with "bad personalities" and people with personality disorders?* Do you know people whom you consider to have a "bad personality?" How does the term bad personality differ from the diagnosis of a personality disorder? In a three-paragraph essay, describe the different types of personality disorders and how they differ from people with "bad personalities."

9. *Why might there be cultural differences in the occurrence of eating disorders?* Consider your sociocultural background. Are women from this background traditionally expected to be well rounded or slender? Are you happy with your body shape? Do you feel social pressure to be thinner (or heavier) than you are? What attitudes are connected with weight and body shape within your cultural traditions? How do they differ from the dominant U.S. cultural views on body size? In a brief essay, compare the differing cultural traditions surrounding body shape and their relationship with the frequency of eating disorders in that culture.

RELATE/EXPAND/INTEGRATE

1. **Historic View of Psychological Disorders: "The Devil Made Me Do It"?**
How does insanity differ from abnormality? Conduct a Web search using your favorite search engine (Google, Dogpile, Ask Jeeves) to examine the insanity defense. What is insanity? Who determines whether someone is "insane"? How often does the insanity defense lead to an acquittal? Also, what happens to an individual after he or she is found "not guilty by reason of insanity"? Present your findings to your classmates in a format specified by your instructor.

2. **Classifying Psychological Disorders**
Controversy in psychology: Is a gay male or lesbian sexual orientation a psychological disorder? Your textbook discusses the position of the American Psychiatric Association and the controversy that remains. What do your friends think? Interview your classmates and friends as to their opinions. Do they consider the behavior of homosexual individuals indicative of a psychological disorder? Why or why not? Tally your results and share them with your study group.

3. **What are Psychological Disorders?**
Cultural differences in defining abnormality. Behavior that may be considered appropriate or "normal" in one culture may be considered as abnormal in another culture. After reading the information presented at http://www.stlcc.cc.mo.us/mc/users/vritts/psypath.htm, choose one culture and compare the perceptions and views of abnormality to those of the United States.

4. **Anxiety Disorders**
What are the characteristics of anxiety disorders? Pick one of the anxiety disorders and look up the major characteristics, using your favorite Internet search engine. How does the disorder differ from normal behavior? Compare what you find with the information found on the Mental Help Net at http://mentalhelp.net/. Share your findings with your classmates.

5. **Dissociative Disorders**
What are the characteristics of dissociative disorders? Pick one of the dissociative disorders and look up the major characteristics, using your favorite Internet search engine. How does the disorder differ from normal behavior? Compare what you find with the information found on the Mental Help Net at http://mentalhelp.net/.

6. Somatoform Disorders

Psychology and modern life: A (possible) hypochondriac goes online. Visit the online mental health resource discussed in your textbook: Diseaseworld.com at http://www.diseaseworld.com and the NIMH page at http://www.nimh.nih.gov/publicat/index.cfm, and take the quizzes. What disorders do you show symptoms of? Do the results of the two quizzes compare? What disorder do the quizzes indicate that you may show symptoms of? What differentiates your behavior from that of a mentally ill person?

7. Mood Disorders

Psychology and Modern Life: Alleviating Depression (Getting Out of the Dumps)

How do we cope with depression? Visit the American Psychiatric Association's public information page on depression at http://www.psych.org/public_info/depression.cfm. It contains numerous links for coping with depression. Prepare a brief promotional piece for your college's counseling department on methods of coping with depression. Use the format provided by your instructor to present your information.

8. Schizophrenia

What are schizophrenic disorders? Have you ever heard the expression "split personality"? Does the expression seem to apply more to dissociative identity disorder or schizophrenia? Look up the major characteristics of schizophrenic disorders on the Mental Help Net at http://mentalhelp.net/ or using your favorite Internet search engine (Google, Dogpile, Ask Jeeves). Compare the characteristics of schizophrenia to those of dissociative identity disorder on a posterboard. Share your poster with your study group and discuss why people often confuse these two disorders.

9. Personality Disorders

What kinds of personality disorders are there? Pick two different types of personality disorders and, using the advanced search on Mental Help Net at http://mentalhelp.net/, look up their major characteristics. How does each disorder differ from normal behavior? How do they compare with each other? Prepare a report for your class in a format specified by your instructor.

10. Eating Disorders

What is an eating disorder? Do you show any of the symptoms of an eating disorder? Visit the Something Fishy.org Web site on eating disorders, and take their eating disorder questionnaire at http://www.something-fishy.org/isf/questionnaire.php. After completing the questionnaire, visit some of the other links on the site, and report your findings to your classmates in a format specified by your instructor.

ANSWERS FOR CHAPTER 15

Reading for Understanding About "Historic Views of Psychological Disorders: 'The Devil Made Me Do It'?"

1. spiritual intervention
2. Greeks
3. devil

Reading for Understanding About "What Are Psychological Disorders" and "Classifying Psychological Disorders"

4. disability
5. disorders
6. classification
7. observable symptoms
8. multiaxial
9. I
10. II
11. III
12. IV
13. V
14. diagnoses

Reflection Break 1

1. II
2. V
3. I
4. III
5. IV

Reading for Understanding About "Anxiety Disorders"

15. Anxiety
16. phobias
17. fears
18. panic
19. persistent anxiety
20. obsessions
21. compuls ions
22. stress
23. Posttraumatic
24. acute
25. psychodynamic
26. repressing
27. unconscious impulses
28. learning
29. observational learning
30. Cognitive
31. Biological
32. genetically predisposed
33. Anxiety
34. biochemical
35. neurotransmitters

Reading for Understanding About "Dissociative Disorders"

36. Dissociative
37. Amnesia
38. fugue
39. identity
40. depersonalization
41. odder
42. skepticism
43. Psychodynamic
44. Learning
45. shame
46. sexual

Reading for Understanding About "Somatoform Disorders"

47. Somatoform
48. conversion
49. la belle indifférence

50. hypochondriasis
51. hysterical neuroses
52. physical

53. Psychodynamic

Reflection Break 2

Compare and contrast the anxiety, dissociative, and somatoform disorders by completing the following chart.

	Characteristic Symptoms	**Theoretical Origins**
Anxiety Disorders	Anxiety disorders are characterized by motor tension, feelings of dread, and overarousal of the sympathetic branch of the autonomic nervous system. These disorders include: • Irrational, excessive fears, or phobias, or persistent fears of specific objects; • Panic disorder, characterized by sudden attacks in which people typically fear that they may be losing control or going crazy; • Generalized or pervasive anxiety, in which the central feature is persistent anxiety; • Obsessive-compulsive disorder, in which people are troubled by intrusive thoughts (obsessions) or impulses to repeat some activity (compulsions); • Stress disorders, in which a stressful event is followed by persistent fears and intrusive thoughts about the event; • Posttraumatic stress disorder, which can occur 6 months or more after the event, whereas acute stress disorder occurs within a month.	• The psychodynamic perspective tends to view anxiety disorders as conflicts originating in childhood. Generalized anxiety disorder is explained as difficulty in repressing primitive impulses, and obsessions are explained as leakage of unconscious impulses. • Learning theorists view phobias as conditioned fears. • Social-cognitive learning theorists note that observational learning plays a role in acquisition of fears. • Cognitive theorists focus on ways in which people interpret threats. • Biological factors also play a role in anxiety disorders. Some people may be genetically predisposed to acquire certain kinds of fears. • Some psychologists suggest that biochemical factors—which could be inherited—may create a predisposition toward anxiety disorders. One such factor is faulty regulation of neurotransmitters.

Dissociative Disorders	Dissociative disorders are characterized by sudden, temporary changes in consciousness or self-identity. • Dissociative amnesia involves loss of memory or self-identity; • Dissociative fugue involves forgetting plus fleeing and adopting a new identity; • Dissociative identity disorder, otherwise known as multiple personality disorder, in which a person behaves as if more than one personality occupies his or her body; • Depersonalization, characterized by feelings that one is not real or that one is standing outside oneself.	Dissociative disorders are some of the odder psychological disorders, and there is some skepticism about their existence. • Psychodynamic theory proposes that people with dissociative disorders use massive repression to keep disturbing memories or ideas out of mind. • Learning theories propose that people with dissociative disorders have learned not to think about bad memories or disturbing impulses to avoid feelings of guilt and shame. Surveys find that the memories being avoided may involve episodes of childhood sexual or physical abuse.
Somatoform Disorders	People with somatoform disorders exhibit or complain of physical problems, although no medical evidence of such problems can be found. • In conversion disorder, stress is converted into a physical symptom, and the individual may show la belle indifférence (indifference to the symptom). • In hypochondriasis, people insist that they are suffering from a serious physical illness, even though no medical evidence of illness can be found.	• These disorders were once called "hysterical neuroses" and expected to be found more often among women. However, they are also found among men and may reflect the relative benefits of focusing on physical symptoms rather than fears and conflicts. • Psychodynamic theory proposes that symptoms of somatoform disorders protect the individual from feelings of shame and guilt, or another source of stress.

Reading for Understanding About " Mood Disorders"

54. Mood
55. Depression
56. Major
57. eating
58. delusional
59. Bipolar
60. manic
61. Women
62. men
63. gender
64. stresses
65. Women

66. earned helplessness
67. attributional
68. serotonin
69. psychodynamic
70. Learning
71. Cognitive
72. self-blaming
73. global
74. biological
75. Genetic
76. glutamate
77. serotonin

78. warning
79. suicide
80. hopelessness
81. genetic
82. environmental
83. more likely
84. attempt
85. succeed
86. European
87. African
88. Native
89. stressful

Reading for Understanding About "Schizophrenia"

90. delusions
91. hallucinations
92. stupor
93. mood
94. social interaction
95. schizophrenia

96. Paranoid
97. delusions
98. Disorganized
99. Catatonic
100. waxy flexibility
101. psychodynamic

102. Learning
103. Biologically
104. dopamine
105. multifactorial

Reading for Understanding About "Personality Disorders"

106. Personality
107. personality
108. paranoid
109. schizotypal
110. Social withdrawal

111. antisocial
112. shame
113. avoidant
114. Psychodynamic
115. Learning

116. Cognitive
117. Genetic
118. Antisocial

Reading for Understanding About "Eating Disorders"

119. eating
120. Anorexia
121. Bulimia
122. Women

123. men
124. young
125. female
126. higher

127. psychodynamic
128. Social-cognitive
129. cultural idealization

Reflection Break 3

Compare and contrast the anxiety, dissociative, and somatoform disorders by completing the following chart.

	Characteristic Symptoms	**Theoretical Origins**
Mood Disorders	Mood disorders involve disturbances in expressed emotions. • Depression is the most common of the psychological disorders. Major depression is characterized by persistent feelings of sadness, loss of interest, feelings of worthlessness or guilt, inability to concentrate, and physical symptoms that may include disturbances in regulation of eating and sleeping. Feelings of unworthiness and guilt may be so excessive that they are considered delusional. • Bipolar disorder, formerly known as manic-depressive disorder, is characterized by dramatic swings in mood between elation and depression; manic episodes include pressured speech and rapid flight of ideas.	• From the psychodynamic perspective, bipolar disorder may be seen as alternating states in which the personality is dominated by the superego and ego. • Leaning theorists, on the other hand, suggest that depressed people behave as though they cannot obtain reinforcement and point to links between depression and learned helplessness. • Cognitive theorists note that people who tend to ruminate about feelings of depression are more likely to prolong them. Seligman notes that people who are depressed are more likely than other people to make internal (self-blaming), stable, and global (large) attributions for failures; factors that they are relatively powerless to change. • Researchers are also searching for biological factors in mood disorders. Genetic factors involving regulation of neurotransmitters may also be involved in mood disorders. For example, bipolar disorder has been linked to inappropriate levels of the neurotransmitter glutamate. Moreover, people with severe depression often respond to drugs that heighten the action of serotonin.

| Schizophrenic Disorders | Schizophrenia is a most severe psychological disorder that is characterized by disturbances in thought and language, such as loosening of associations and delusions; in perception and attention, as found in hallucinations; in motor activity, as shown by a stupor or by excited behavior; in mood, as in flat or inappropriate emotional responses; and in social interaction, as in social withdrawal and absorption in daydreams or fantasy.

• Paranoid schizophrenia is characterized largely by systematized delusions and frequently related auditory hallucinations. Sufferers often have delusions of grandeur and persecution.
• Disorganized schizophrenia is characterized by incoherence, loosening of associations, disorganized behavior and delusions and flat or highly inappropriate emotional responses; extreme social impairment is common with disorganized schizophrenia.
• Catatonic schizophrenia is characterized by a striking motor impairment; often it is a slowing of activity into a stupor that may suddenly change into an agitated phase. Catatonic schizophrenics may also show a waxy flexibility in which they maintain positions into which they have been manipulated by others, and mutism. | • The pychodynamic view argues that schizophrenia occurs because the ego is overwhelmed by sexual or aggressive impulses form the id and the person regresses to an early phase of the oral stage.
• Learning theorists explain schizophrenia in terms of conditioning and observational learning.
• Biologically, schizophrenia is connected with smaller brains, especially fewer synapses in the prefrontal region, and larger ventricles in the brain.
• According to the dopamine theory of schizophrenia, people with schizophrenia use more dopamine than other people do, perhaps because they have more dopamine in the brain along with more dopamine receptors than other people.
• According to the multifactorial model, genetic vulnerability to schizophrenia may interact with other factors, such as stress, complications during pregnancy and childbirth, and quality of parenting, to cause the disorder to develop. |

| Personality Disorders | Personality disorders are inflexible, maladaptive behavior patterns that impair personal or social functioning and cause distress for the individual or others.
• The defining trait of paranoid personality disorder is suspiciousness.
• People with schizotypal personality disorders show oddities of thought, perception, and behavior but the bizarre behaviors of schizophrenia are absent.
• Social withdrawal, indifference to relationships, and flat emotional response are the major characteristic of schizoid personality disorder.
• People with antisocial personality disorders persistently violate the rights of others and are in conflict with the law. They show little or no guilt or shame over their misdeeds and are largely undeterred by punishment.
• People with avoidant personality disorder tend to avoid entering relationships for fear of rejection and criticism. | • Psychodynamic theory connected many personality disorders with hypothesized Oedipal problems.
• Learning theorists suggest that childhood experiences can contribute to maladaptive ways of relating to others.
• Cognitive psychologists find that antisocial adolescents encode social information in ways that bolster their misdeeds.
• Genetic factors may be involved in some personality disorders.
• Antisocial personality disorder tends to run in families and may develop from some combination of genetic vulnerability (less gray matter in the prefrontal cortex of the brain, which may provide lower-than-normal levels of arousal), inconsistent discipline, and cynical processing of social information. |
| **Eating Disorders** | • Anorexia is characterized by refusal to eat and extreme thinness.
• Bulimia is characterized by recurrent cycles of binge eating and purging.
• Women are more likely than men to develop these disorders. | • The major psychodynamic explanation of the eating disorders is that a conflicted female is attempting to remain prepubescent.
• Social cognitive approaches suggest that weight loss has strong reinforcement value because it provides feelings of personal perfectibility.
• However, most psychologists look to cultural idealization of the slender female—and the pressures that such idealization places on young women—as the major contributor. |

Chapter 16

Methods of Therapy

PREVIEW

Skim the major headings in this chapter in your textbook. Jot down anything that you are surprised or curious about. After this, write down four or five questions that you have about the material in this chapter.

Things that surprised me/I am curious about from Chapter 16:

Questions that I have about methods of therapy:

▲

▲

▲

▲

QUESTION

These are some questions that you should be able to answer after you finish studying this chapter.

What Is Therapy? The Search for a "Sweet Oblivious Antidote"

▲ *What is psychotherapy?*

▲ *How have people with psychological problems and disorders been treated throughout the ages?*

Psychodynamic Therapies: Digging Deep Within

▲ *How, then, do psychoanalysts conduct a traditional Freudian psychoanalysis?*

▲ *How do modern psychodynamic approaches differ from traditional psychoanalysis?*

Humanistic-Existential Therapies: Strengthening the Self

▲ *What is Carl Rogers's method of client-centered therapy?*

▲ *What is Fritz Perls method of Gestalt therapy?*

Behavior Therapy: Adjustment Is What You Do

▲ *What is behavior therapy?*

▲ *What are some behavior therapy methods for reducing fears?*

▲ *How do behavior therapists use aversive conditioning to help people break bad habits?*

▲ *How do behavior therapists apply principles of operant conditioning in behavior modification?*

▲ *How can you use behavior therapy to deal with temptation and enhance your self-control?*

Cognitive Therapies: Adjustment Is What Your Think (and Do)

▲ *What is cognitive therapy?*

▲ *What is Aaron Beck's method of cognitive therapy?*

▲ *What is Albert Ellis's method of rational emotive behavior therapy?*

Group Therapies

▲ *What are the advantages and disadvantages of group therapy?*

▲ *What are encounter groups? What are their effects?*

▲ *What is family therapy?*

▲ *What kinds of problems do researchers encounter when they conduct research on psychotherapy?*

▲ *What do we know about the effectiveness of psychotherapy?*

▲ *What kinds of issues develop when people from different ethnic groups, women, and gay males and lesbians could profit from psychotherapy?*

Biological Therapies

▲ *What kinds of drug therapy are available for psychological disorders?*

▲ *What is electroconvulsive therapy (ECT)?*

▲ *What is psychosurgery? How is it used to treat psychological disorders?*

▲ *What do we know about the effectiveness of biological therapies?*

READING FOR UNDERSTANDING/REFLECT

The following section provides you with the opportunity to perform 2 of the R's of the PQ4R study method. In this section, you are encouraged to check your understanding of your reading of the text by filling in the blanks in the brief paragraphs that relate to each of the Preview questions. You will also be prompted to rehearse your understanding of the material with periodic Reflection breaks. Remember, it is better to study in more frequent, short sessions than in one long "cram session." Be sure to reward yourself with short study breaks before each Reflection exercise.

Reading for Understanding About "What Is Therapy? The Search for a "Sweet Oblivious Antidote"

What is psychotherapy? (1) _____ is a systematic interaction between a therapist and a client that uses psychological principles to help the client overcome psychological disorders or adjust to problems in living.

How have people with psychological problems and disorders been treated throughout the ages? Mostly badly. It has been generally assumed that psychological disorders represented (2) _____ due to witchcraft or divine retribution, and cruel methods such as (3) _____ were used to try to rid the person of evil spirits. (4) _____ were the first institutions for people with psychological disorders, and eventually mental hospitals, whose function is (5) _____, not warehousing, and the community mental health movement came into being.

Reading for Understanding About "Psychodynamic Therapies: Digging Deep Within"

How, then, do psychoanalysts conduct a traditional Freudian psychoanalysis? The goals of psychoanalysis are to provide (6) _____ into the conflicts that are believed to be the roots of a person's problems; encourage the spilling forth, or (7) _____, of psychic energy; and replace (8) _____ behavior with coping behavior. The main method is (9) _____, in which the client is asked to talk about any topic that comes to mind; but (10) _____ and interpretations are used as well. Freud felt that although (11) _____ impulses clamor for release, the (12) _____ persists in trying to repress unacceptable urges and shows (13) _____, or the tendency to block the free expression of impulses and primitive ideas. The job of the therapist is to occasionally offer an (14) _____ of an utterance showing how it suggests (15) _____ or deep-seated feelings and conflicts. Additionally, the therapist must help the client work through any (16) _____, or the translating of one's feelings and attitudes toward another. For example, a (17) _____ may help clients gain insight into the ways in which they are transferring feelings toward their parents onto a spouse, or even onto the analyst. Psychoanalysis can extend for (18) _____ or even (19) _____.

How do modern psychodynamic approaches differ from traditional psychoanalysis? Modem approaches are (20) _____, less intense, and more (21) _____, and the therapist and client usually sit face to face. Additionally, the focus tends to be on the (22) _____ rather than the (23) _____.

Reading for Understanding About "Humanistic-Existential Therapies: Strengthening the Self"

What is Carl Rogers's method of client-centered therapy? Whereas (24) _____ therapies focus on internal conflicts and unconscious processes, humanistic-existential therapies focus on the quality of the clients' (25) _____ experience. Client-centered therapy uses (26) _____ methods to help clients overcome obstacles to (27) _____. Rogers's method is intended to help people get in touch with their (28) _____ feelings and pursue their own interests, regardless of other people's wishes. In (29) _____ therapy, the therapist shows a respect for clients as human beings with unique values and goals, or (30) _____; (31) _____ understanding, or a recognition of the client's experiences and feelings; and (32) _____, or an openness in responding to the client. Client-centered therapy is popular on college campuses. (33) _____ therapists do not tell others what to do; they help clients arrive at their own decisions.

What is Fritz Perls's method of Gestalt therapy? Like client-centered therapy, (34) _____ therapy assumes that people disown parts of themselves that might meet with social disapproval. Perls also argues that they put on (35) "_____" and pretend to be things they are not. Perls's highly (36) _____ method aims to help people (37) _____ these conflicting parts of their personality. He aimed to make clients aware of (38) _____, accept its (39) _____, and make (40) _____ despite fear.

Reflection Break 1

Compare and contrast psychodynamic, client-centered, and Gestalt therapy by completing the table below.

Type of Therapy	Characteristics
Psychodynamic Therapy	
Client-Centered Therapy	
Gestalt Therapy	

Reading for Understanding About "Behavior Therapy: Adjustment Is What You Do"

What is behavior therapy? Behavior therapists focus on what people (41) _____. Behavior therapy, also called (42) _____, relies on psychological (43) _____ principles (for example, conditioning and observational learning) to help clients develop adaptive behavior patterns and discontinue maladaptive ones.

What are some behavior-therapy methods for reducing fears? (44) _____ therapy methods include flooding, systematic desensitization, and modeling. (45) _____ exposes a person to fear-evoking stimuli without aversive consequences until fear is extinguished. (46) _____ counterconditions fears by gradually exposing clients to a hierarchy of fear-evoking stimuli while they remain relaxed. (47) _____ encourages clients to imitate another person (the model) in approaching fear-evoking stimuli.

How do behavior therapists use aversive conditioning to help people break bad habits? (48) _____ conditioning is a controversial form of behavior-therapy method used for discouraging undesirable behaviors by repeatedly pairing clients' (49) _____ goals (for example, alcohol, cigarette smoke, and deviant sex objects) with aversive stimuli so that the goals become aversive rather than tempting.

How do behavior therapists apply principles of operant conditioning in behavior modification? In the operant conditioning section of the chapter on learning, we learned that behavior that is not reinforced tends to become (50) _____. Behavior therapists also use the principles of (51) _____ conditioning to change behavior. Operant conditioning behavior methods are behavior therapy methods that foster adaptive behavior through principles of (52) _____. Examples include token economies, successive approximation, social skills training, and biofeedback training. In a (53) _____, a controlled environment is created in which people are reinforced for desired behaviors with tokens that may be exchanged for privileges. (54) _____ is often used to help people build good habits by successively reinforcing a series of behaviors that become progressively more similar to the target behavior. In (55) _____ training, behavior therapists attempt to decrease social anxiety and build social skills by encouraging the client to (56) _____, or keep a record of his or her own behavior and record successes, practice, and provide feedback. (57) _____ training helps clients become more aware of and gain control over various body functions by attaching devices that measure the body function and signal desired changes.

How can you use behavior therapy to deal with temptation and enhance your self-control? Behavior-therapy methods for adopting desirable behavior patterns and breaking bad habits begin with a (58) _____ to determine the antecedents and consequences of the problem behavior, along with the details of the behavior itself. They then focus on modifying the (59) _____ (stimuli that act as triggers) and (60) _____ (reinforcers) of behavior, and then on modifying the behavior itself.

Reading for Understanding About "Cognitive Therapies: Adjustment Is What You Think (and Do)"

What is cognitive therapy? Cognitive therapies aim to give clients insight into (61) _____ beliefs and cognitive (62) _____ and replace these cognitive (63) _____ with rational beliefs and accurate perceptions.

What is Aaron Beck's method of cognitive therapy? Aaron (64) _____'s therapy method focuses on the client's cognitive distortions and notes that clients develop emotional problems such as depression because of cognitive errors that lead them to (65) _____ accomplishments and (66) _____ failures. The cognitive errors that contribute to the client's misery include a selective (67) _____ of the world, (68) _____ and magnification of events, and (69) _____ thinking, or seeing the world in shades of black and white. He found that depressed people experience cognitive distortions such as (70) _____; that is, they expect the worst of themselves, the world at large, and the future. Beck teaches clients how to (71) _____ dispute cognitive errors.

What is Albert Ellis's method of rational-emotive behavior therapy? Albert Ellis originated (72) _____ therapy (REBT), which holds that people's beliefs about events, not only the events themselves, shape people's responses to them. Ellis points out how (73) _____ beliefs, such as the belief that we must have social approval, can worsen problems. Ellis's methods are active and (74) _____—he literally argues clients out of irrational beliefs.

Reflection Break 2

Compare and contrast behavior therapy, Beck's cognitive therapy, and Ellis's rational-emotive behavior therapy by completing the table below.

Type of Therapy	Description:
Behavior Therapy	
Beck's Cognitive Therapy	
Ellis's Rational Emotive Behavior Therapy	

Reading for Understanding About "Group Therapies"

What are the advantages and disadvantages of group therapy? The methods and characteristics of (75) _____ therapy reflect the needs of the members and the theoretical orientation of the group leader. Group therapy has advantages; first, it is more (76) _____ than individual therapy. Moreover, group members benefit from the (77) _____ and experiences of other members, and appropriate behavior receives support. Also, in individual therapy it is easy to imagine that we are (78) _____ from others, so affiliating with others with similar problems (79) _____ this. However, (80) _____ therapy is not for everyone; some clients cannot (81) _____ their problems in the group setting or risk group disapproval. They need individual attention.

What are encounter groups? What are their effects? (82) _____ attempt to foster personal growth by heightening awareness of people's needs and feelings through intense confrontations between strangers. Encounter groups can be harmful when they urge too (83) _____ disclosure of personal matters or when several members (84) _____ an individual.

What are couple and family therapies? (85) _____ therapy helps couples enhance their relationship by improving communication skills and helping them manage conflict. In (86)

_____ therapy, one or more families make up the group. Family therapy undertaken from the (87) "_____ approach" modifies family interactions to enhance the growth of individuals in the family and the family as a whole.

Reading for Understanding About "Controversy in Psychology: Does Psychotherapy Work?"

What kinds of problems do researchers encounter when they conduct research on psychotherapy? The ideal method for evaluating the effectiveness of treatment is the (88) _____. However, experiments are difficult to arrange and (89) _____. It is difficult and perhaps impossible to (90) _____ clients to therapy methods such as traditional psychoanalysis. Moreover, clients cannot be kept (91) _____ as to the treatment they are receiving. Further, it can be difficult to sort out the effects of nonspecific therapeutic factors such as instillation of (92) _____ from the effects of specific methods of therapy.

What do we know about the effectiveness of psychotherapy? Despite the problems in evaluating the effectiveness of therapy, research has been ongoing. Statistical analyses such as a (93) _____ show that people who obtain most forms of psychotherapy fare better than people who do not. Psychodynamic and client-centered approaches are particularly helpful with highly (94) _____ and (95) _____ individuals. Cognitive and behavior therapies are probably most effective. Cognitive therapy appears to be as effective as drug therapy in the treatment of (96) _____.

What kinds of issues develop when people from different ethnic groups, women, and gay males and lesbians could profit from psychotherapy? Ethnic minority groups are (97) _____ likely to seek therapy than European Americans. Reasons include: (98) _____ that therapy will help; lack of (99) _____ about the availability of professional services, or the inability to pay for them; and (100) _____ barriers. Additionally, people from ethnic minority groups are frequently (101) _____ of European American therapists, and therapy methods and goals may conflict with their (102) _____. (103) _____ therapy heightens awareness of sociocultural issues that contribute to women's problems and challenges the tradition of male dominance. Many professionals believe that psychotherapy should not attempt to change a gay male or lesbian's (104) _____ but should help that person adjust to social and cultural pressures to be heterosexual.

Reflection Break 3

1. Under what circumstances would you recommend that someone go for group therapy rather than individual therapy? Why?

2. Briefly summarize the difficulties that arise when psychologists try to assess the effectiveness of therapy.

Reading for Understanding About "Biological Therapies"

Psychotherapies apply (105) _____ principles to treatment, whereas (106) _____ therapies apply knowledge of biological structures and processes to the treatment of psychological disorders. Biological approaches to treating psychological disorders include drug therapy, (107) _____ therapy, and psychosurgery.

What kinds of drug therapy are available for psychological disorders? (108) _____ drugs belong to the chemical class known as the benzodiazepines and act by depressing the activity of the central nervous system, which in turn decreases sympathetic activity. (109) _____ is the most common side effect of antianxiety medication. The use of antianxiety drugs for (110) _____ tensions and anxieties is not recommended because people who use them rapidly build (111) _____ for the drugs, and withdrawal may lead to (112) _____ in which the patient's anxiety may become worse than it was initially. Also, these drugs do not (113) _____ personal or social problems, and people attribute their resultant calmness to the drug and not to (114) _____.

Antipsychotic drugs help many people with schizophrenia by blocking the action of (115) _____ receptors. (116) _____ drugs reduce agitation, delusions, and hallucinations.

Antidepressants often help people with severe depression, apparently by raising levels of (117) _____ available to the brain. There are several different types of (118) _____ drugs. (119) _____ inhibitors block the activity of an enzyme that breaks down noradrenaline and serotonin. (120) _____ antidepressants prevent the reuptake of noradrenaline and serotonin and selective serotonin-uptake inhibitors block the reuptake of serotonin. (121) _____ appear to be more effective than tricyclics. (122) _____ often helps people with bipolar disorder, apparently by regulating levels of glutamate, and can be used to strengthen the effects of antidepressant medication.

What is electroconvulsive therapy (ECT)? In ECT an electrical current is passed through the temples, inducing a seizure and frequently relieving severe (123) _____. ECT is controversial because of side effects such as loss of (124) _____ and because nobody knows why it works.

What is psychosurgery? How is it used to treat psychological disorders? (125) _____ is a controversial method for alleviating agitation by severing nerve pathways in the brain. The best-known psychosurgery technique, (126) _____, has been largely discontinued because of side effects.

What do we know about the effectiveness of biological therapies? There is (127) _____ as to whether psychotherapy or drug therapy should be used with people with anxiety disorders or depression. (128) _____ do not teach people how to solve problems and build relationships. Having said that, (129) _____ are apparently advisable when psychotherapy does not help people with depression; furthermore, (130) _____ appears to be helpful in some cases in which neither psychotherapy nor drug therapy (antidepressants) is of help. Psychosurgery is all but (131) _____because of questions about whether it is effective and because of side effects. Most health professionals agree that (132) _____ drugs are of benefit to large numbers of people with schizophrenia.

Reflection Break 4

Compare the different types of biological therapy by completing the following table.

Therapy Types	Description
Drug Therapy	
Electroconvulsive Shock Therapy	
Psychosurgery	

REVIEW: KEY TERMS AND CONCEPTS

FINAL CHAPTER REVIEW

Review

Visit the *Psychology in the New Millennium* Web site at www.harcourtcollege.com/psych/PNM/siteresources.html and take the Chapter Quizzes to test your knowledge.

Recite

Go to the Recite section for this chapter in your textbook. Use the tear-off card provided at the back of the book to cover the answers of the Recite section. Read the questions aloud, and recite the answers. This will help you cement your knowledge of key concepts.

Essay Questions

1. How has psychology's approach to therapy changed over the past millennium? In a three-page essay, trace the evolution of thinking about psychological disorders in western culture and the various approaches to treatment. What reforms have taken place in treatment? What changes do you foresee occurring in the next decade? Why?

2. What do the humanistic therapies of Carl Rogers and Fritz Perls have in common? How are they different? Compare and contrast the two approaches to therapy in a three-paragraph essay.

3. Imagine that you are a psychologist and that a woman comes into your office complaining that she washes her hands over 100 times a day. In a two-page report, describe how you would approach therapy with your patient if you were to use cognitive therapy. Explain how, as a cognitive therapist, you would explain this woman's problem and what methods you would use to help her overcome this problem. How would your approach to treatment be different if you used behavioral therapy? Why?

4. Approaches to psychotherapy differ in the degree to which the client is directed by the therapist. Compare and contrast the directiveness of the following therapies: psychoanalysis, client-centered, and behavior.

5. In what ways are the client's characteristics such as ethnicity, gender, and sexual orientation relevant to psychological treatment? In a three-page essay, discuss the part that factors such as ethnicity, gender, and sexual orientation play in the effectiveness of therapy. Also, in your conclusion to your essay be sure to answer the question "What do you think can be done to increase the willingness of ethnic minority groups to seek therapy, and why?" Format your paper as directed by your instructor.

6. Why do many health-care professionals prefer the use of psychotherapy to prescribing medicine? Prepare a one-page essay that provides your view in a format specified by your instructor.

RELATE/EXPAND/INTEGRATE

1. **What Is Therapy? The Search for a "Sweet Oblivious Antidote"**
What is psychotherapy, and who can provide therapy? Visit the APA's Web site on therapy at http://helping.apa.org/. Research the information there concerning what psychotherapy is and is not and the type of credentials that a therapist must have. What are the APA's licensing requirements? Are there any special requirements for licensing of psychotherapists in your state? (Hint: You should be able to find this information on the Internet by looking up your state professional regulations.) Prepare an informational pamphlet for aspiring therapists in a format specified by your instructor.

2. **Psychodynamic Therapies: Digging Deep Within**
With your study group, create a hypothetical transcript of a session of traditional Freudian psychoanalysis. Create a second transcript of an exchange between the same patient and a more current-day psychoanalyst. Present your "sessions" to your class, and lead a discussion on the differences between traditional Freudian psychoanalysis and modern psychoanalysis.

3. **Humanistic-Existential Therapies: Strengthening the Self**
Can an AI-based humanistic therapist help you solve your problems? Talk to Eliza at http://www-ai.ijs.si/eliza/eliza.htm about a problem you have been experiencing. Does the interaction seem real? Do you think that Eliza could help you solve a problem? Why or why not? Compare your experiences with those of your study partners.

4. **Psychology and Modern Life: Virtual Reality Finds a Real Place as an Aid in Therapy**
Can "online counseling" help? Visit the Web sites of any of the "cyberpsychologists" listed below, and examine the information provided. Using your critical thinking skills, evaluate these "online counseling" centers. Would you use an online counselor? Why or why not? What might be the advantages and disadvantages of an Internet-based counselor?
Cyberpsychologist at http://www.cyberpsych.com/. The site claims to belong to Dr. Rob Sarmiento, a "licensed psychologist in practice for 20 years in Houston, Texas."

> **Cyber-Psych** at http://www.cyber-psych.com/. This site claims that "Cyber-Psych is committed to bringing high-quality, professional psychological information to the online community."

> **Psychology.com's Advice Center** at http://www.psychology.com/Advice/. This site claims to provide someone to offer personal direction, plus personal online consultation with a licensed clinical therapist.

> **Metanoria by Martha Ainsworth** at http://www.metanoia.org/imhs/. Claims to be the original and only independent consumer guide to therapists and counselors who provide services over the Internet—compiled by consumers, for consumers.

5. **Controversy in Psychology: Does Psychotherapy Work? Psychotherapy and Human Diversity**
Are there cultural differences in acceptance of psychotherapy? Consider your part of the country and your sociocultural background. Do people in your area and from your background frequently go for "therapy"? Is psychotherapy considered a normal option for people having problems in your area, or is it stigmatized? What about people in other countries and cultures? Visit the Infusing Culture into Psychopathology Web site at http://www.stlcc.cc.mo.us/mc/users/vritts/psypath.htm, and research the cultural views on psychopathology and therapy in two different countries. Prepare a brief oral report comparing the differences in cultural traditions pertaining to therapy. Present your report to your classmates at a time specified by your instructor.

6. **Biological Therapies**
Research the use of antidepressant medication. How prevalent is it? Conduct a survey of 25 college students as to their usage of antidepressant medication. What percentage of your sample is currently taking antidepressants? How many have ever taken them? Which type of antidepressant seems to be the most frequently prescribed? Report your findings to your classmates, and lead a discussion as to the benefits that have been demonstrated by antidepressant drugs. What concerns are being raised regarding the widespread use of Prozac and other antidepressants?

ANSWERS FOR CHAPTER 16

Reading for Understanding About "What Is Therapy? The Search for a "Sweet Oblivious Antidote"

1. Psychotherapy
2. possession
3. exorcism
4. Asylums
5. treatment
6. self-insight
7. catharsis
8. defensive
9. free association
10. dream analysis
11. repressed
12. ego
13. resistance
14. interpretation
15. resistance
16. transference
17. psychoanalyst
18. months
19. years
20. briefer
21. directive
22. ego
23. id

Reading for Understanding About "Humanistic-Existential Therapies: Strengthening the Self"

24. psychodynamic
25. subjective, conscious
26. nondirective
27. self-actualization
28. genuine
29. client-centered
30. unconditional positive regard
31. empathic
32. genuineness
33. Client-centered
34. Gestalt
35. social masks
36. directive
37. integrate
38. conflict
39. reality
40. choices

Reflection Break 1

Compare and contrast psychodynamic, client-centered, and Gestalt therapy by completing the table below.

Type of Therapy	Characteristics
Psychodynamic Therapy	The goals of psychoanalysis are to provide self-insight in to the conflicts that are believed to be the roots of a person's problems; encourage the spilling forth, or catharsis, of psychic energy; and replace defensive behavior with coping behavior. The main method is free association, in which the client is asked to talk about any topic that comes to mind; but dream analysis and interpretations are used as well. Freud felt that although repressed impulses clamor for release, the ego persists in trying to repress unacceptable urges and shows resistance, or the tendency to block the free expression of impulses and primitive ideas. Modem approaches are briefer, less intense, and more directive, and the therapist and client usually sit face to face. Additionally, the focus tends to be on the ego rather than the id.

Client-Centered Therapy	Whereas psychodynamic therapies focus on internal conflicts and unconscious processes, humanistic-existential therapies focus on the quality of the clients' subjective, conscious experience. Client-centered therapy uses nondirective methods to help clients overcome obstacles to self-actualization. Rogers's method is intended to help people get in touch with their genuine feelings and pursue their own interests, regardless of other people's wishes. In client-centered therapy, the therapist shows a respect for clients as human beings with unique values and goals, or unconditional positive regard; empathic understanding, or a recognition of the client's experiences and feelings; and genuineness, or an openness in responding to the client. Client-centered therapists do not tell others what to do; they help clients arrive at their own decisions.
Gestalt Therapy	Like client-centered therapy, Gestalt therapy assumes that people disown parts of themselves that might meet with social disapproval. Perls also argues that they put on "social masks" and pretend to be things they are not. Perls's highly directive method aims to help people integrate these conflicting parts of their personality. He aimed to make clients aware of conflict, accept its reality, and make choices despite fear. Perls's ideas about the conflicting personality elements are similar to psychodynamic therapy; however, in Gestalt therapy the emphasis is on the here and now.

Reading for Understanding About "Behavior Therapy: Adjustment Is What You Do"

41. do
42. behavior modification
43. learning
44. Behavior
45. Flooding
46. Systematic desensitization
47. Modeling
48. Aversive
49. self-defeating
50. extinguished
51. operant
52. reinforcement
53. token economy
54. Successive approximation
55. social skills
56. self-monitor
57. Biofeedback
58. functional analysis
59. antecedents
60. consequences

Reading for Understanding About "Cognitive Therapies: Adjustment Is What You Think (and Do)"

61. irrational
62. distortions
63. errors
64. Beck
65. minimize
66. catastrophize
67. perception
68. overgeneralization
69. absolutist
70. the cognitive triad
71. scientifically
72. rational emotive behavior
73. irrational
74. directive

© 2002 Thomson Learning, Inc.

Reflection Break 2

Compare and contrast behavior therapy, Beck's cognitive therapy, and Ellis's rational-emotive behavior therapy by completing the table below.

Type of Therapy	Description:
Behavior Therapy	In contrast to the focus of psychodynamic and humanistic-existential forms of therapy on what people think and feel, behavior therapy tends to focus on what people do. Behavior therapy, also called behavior modification, relies on psychological learning principles (for example, conditioning and observational learning) to help clients develop adaptive behavior patterns and discontinue maladaptive ones. Behavior therapy methods include flooding, systematic desensitization, and modeling. Aversive conditioning is a controversial form of behavior therapy used for discouraging undesirable behaviors by repeatedly pairing clients' self-defeating goals (for example, alcohol, cigarette smoke, deviant sex objects) with aversive stimuli so that the goals become aversive rather than tempting. Behavior therapists also use the principles of operant conditioning to change behavior. Operant conditioning behavior methods are behavior therapy methods that foster adaptive behavior through principles of reinforcement. Examples include token economies, successive approximation, social skills training, and biofeedback training.
Beck's Cognitive Therapy	Cognitive therapies aim to give clients insight into irrational beliefs and cognitive distortions and replace these cognitive errors with rational beliefs and accurate perceptions. Aaron Beck's therapy method focuses on the client's cognitive distortions and notes that clients develop emotional problems such as depression because of cognitive errors that lead them to minimize accomplishments and catastrophize failures. The cognitive errors that contribute to the client's misery include a selective perception of the world, overgeneralization and magnification of events, and absolutist thinking, or seeing the world in shades of black and white. He found that depressed people experience cognitive distortions such as the cognitive triad; that is, they expect the worst of themselves, the world at large, and the future. Beck teaches clients how to scientifically dispute cognitive errors.
Ellis's Rational Emotive Behavior Therapy	Cognitive therapies aim to give clients insight into irrational beliefs and cognitive distortions and replace these cognitive errors with rational beliefs and accurate perceptions. Originally Ellis called his approach rational-emotive therapy because his focus was cognitive. However, he has always promoted behavioral changes to cement cognitive changes; in keeping with this, he changed the name of the therapy to rational-emotive behavior therapy. Albert Ellis originated rational-emotive behavior therapy (REBT), which holds that people's beliefs about events, not only the events themselves, shape people's responses to them. Ellis points out how irrational beliefs, such as the belief that we must have social approval, canworsen problems. Ellis's methods are active and directive-he literally argues clients out of irrational beliefs.

Reading for Understanding About "Group Therapies"

75. Group
76. economical
77. social support
78. different
79. minimizes

80. group
81. disclose
82. Encounter groups
83. rapid
84. attack

85. cognitive behavioral
86. family
87. systems

Reading for Understanding About "Controversy in Psychology: Does Psychotherapy Work?"

88. experiment
89. control
90. randomly assign
91. blind
92. hope
93. meta-analysis

94. verbal
95. motivated
96. depression
97. less
98. unawareness
99. information

100. language
101. mistrustful
102. cultural values
103. Feminist
104. sexual orientation

Reflection Break 3

1. Under what circumstances would you recommend that someone go for group therapy rather than individual therapy? Why?

   The methods and characteristics of group therapy reflect the needs of the members and the theoretical orientation of the group leader. Group therapy can be advantageous since it is more economical than individual therapy. Group therapy might be recommended if the problem is one in which the social support and experiences of other members would be beneficial to the individual. If the person is imagining that he or she is different from others; group therapy can help by allowing the person to affiliate with others who have similar problems. However, group therapy is not for someone who cannot disclose his or her problems in the group setting or risk group disapproval.

2. Briefly summarize the difficulties that arise when psychologists try to access the effectiveness of therapy.

   The ideal method for evaluating the effectiveness of treatment is the experiment. However, experiments are difficult to arrange and control. It is difficult, and perhaps impossible, to randomly assign clients to therapy methods such as traditional psychoanalysis. Moreover, clients cannot be kept blind as to the treatment they are receiving. Further, it can be difficult to sort out the effects of nonspecific therapeutic factors, such as instillation of hope, from the effects of specific methods of therapy.

Reading for Understanding About "Biological Therapies"

105. psychological
106. biological
107. electroconvulsive
108. Antianxiety
109. Sedation
110. daily
111. tolerance
112. rebound anxiety
113. solve
114. self-efficacy

115. dopamine
116. Antipsychotic
117. serotonin
118. antidepressant
119. Monoamine oxidase
120. Tricyclic
121. Serotonin-uptake inhibitors
122. Lithium
123. depression

124. memory
125. Psychosurgery
126. prefrontal lobotomy
127. controversy
128. Drugs
129. antidepressants
130. ECT
131. discontinued
132. antipsychotic

Reflection Break 4

Compare the different types of biological therapy by completing the following table

Type of Therapy	Description
Drug Therapy	• Antianxiety drugs belong to the chemical class known as the benzodiazepines and act by depressing the activity of the central nervous system, which in turn decreases sympathetic activity. Sedation is the most common side effect of antianxiety medication. • Antipsychotic drugs help many people with schizophrenia by blocking the action of dopamine receptors. Antipsychotic drugs reduce agitation, delusions, and hallucinations. • Antidepressants often help people with severe depression, apparently by raising levels of serotonin available to the brain. There are several different types of antidepressant drugs. • Monoamine oxidase inhibitors block the activity of an enzyme that breaks down noradrenaline and serotonin. • Tricyclic antidepressants prevent the reuptake of noradrenaline and serotonin and selective serotonin-uptake inhibitors block the reuptake of serotonin. • Serotonin-uptake inhibitors appear to be more effective than tricyclics. • Lithium often helps people with bipolar disorder, apparently by regulating levels of glutamate, and can be used to strengthen the effects of antidepressant medication.

Electroconvulsive Shock Therapy	In ECT, an electrical current is passed through the temples, inducing a seizure and frequently relieving severe depression. ECT is controversial because of side effects such as loss of memory and because nobody knows why it works.
Psychosurgery	Psychosurgery is a controversial method for alleviating agitation by severing nerve pathways in the brain. The best-known psychosurgery technique, prefrontal lobotomy, has been largely discontinued because of side effects.

Chapter 17

Social Psychology

PREVIEW

Skim the major headings in this chapter in your textbook. Jot down anything that you are surprised or curious about. After this, write down four or five questions that you have about the material in this chapter.

Things that surprised me/I am curious about from Chapter 17:

Questions that I have about social psychology:

▲

▲

▲

▲

QUESTION

These are some questions that you should be able to answer after you finish studying this chapter.

Social Psychology

▲ *What is social psychology?*

Attitudes—"The Good, the Bad, and the Ugly"

▲ *What are attitudes?*

▲ *Do people do as they think? (For example, do people really vote their consciences?)*

▲ *Where do attitudes come from?*

▲ *Can you really change people-their attitudes and behavior, that is?*

▲ *What is prejudice? Why are people prejudiced?*

Social Perception: Looking Out, Looking Within

▲ *Do first impressions really matter? What are the primacy and recency effects?*

▲ *What is attribution theory? Why do we assume that other people intend the mischief that they do?*

▲ *What is body language?*

Social Influence: Are You an Individual or One of the Crowd?

▲ *Why will so many people commit crimes against humanity if they are ordered to do so? (Why don't they refuse?)*

▲ *Why do so many people tend to follow the crowd?*

Group Behavior

▲ *Do we run faster when we are in a group?*

▲ *How do groups make decisions?*

▲ *Are group decisions more risky or more conservative than those of the individual members of the group? Why?*

▲ *What is groupthink?*

▲ *Do mobs bring out the beast in us? How is it that mild-mannered people commit mayhem when they are part of a mob?*

▲ *Why do people sometimes sacrifice themselves for others and, at other times, ignore people who are in trouble?*

Environmental Psychology: The Big Picture

▲ *What is environmental psychology?*

▲ *What are the effects of noise on behavior and mental processes?*

▲ *What are the effects of temperature on our bodies and on our behavior and mental processes?*

▲ *What are the effects of air pollution on behavior and mental processes?*

▲ *When are we too close for comfort? What are the effects of crowding on behavior and mental processes?*

READING FOR UNDERSTANDING/REFLECT

The following section provides you with the opportunity to perform 2 of the R's of the PQ4R study method. In this section, you are encouraged to check your understanding of your reading of the text by filling in the blanks in the brief paragraphs that relate to each of the Preview questions. You will also be prompted to rehearse your understanding of the material with periodic Reflection breaks. Remember, it is better to study in more frequent, short sessions than in one long "cram session." Be sure to reward yourself with short study breaks before each Reflection exercise.

Reading for Understanding About "Social Psychology"

What is social psychology? (1) _____ psychology is the field of psychology that studies the factors that influence people's thoughts, feelings, and behaviors in social situations. Areas of interest include: attitudes, social (2) _____, social (3) _____, group behavior, and (4) _____ psychology.

Reading for Understanding About "Attitudes—The Good, the Bad, and the Ugly"

What are attitudes? (5) _____ are behavioral and cognitive tendencies expressed by evaluating particular people, places, or things with favor or disfavor. Attitudes are (6) _____, and they affect behavior. Attitudes can be (7) _____, but not easily.

Do people do as they think? (For example, do people really vote their consciences?) When we are free to act as we wish, our behavior is often (8) _____ with our beliefs and feelings. But as indicated by the term A-B problem, the links between (9) _____ (A) and (10) _____ (B) are often weak to moderate. The following factors strengthen the (11) _____ connection: specificity of attitudes, strength of attitudes, whether people have a vested interest in the outcome of their behavior, and the accessibility of the attitudes. People are more likely to behave in accordance with their attitudes when the attitude is (12) _____, strong, (13) _____, and when they have a (14) _____ in the outcome.

Where do attitudes come from? Attitudes are (15) _____ (not inborn). They can be learned somewhat mechanically by means of (16) _____ or learning by (17) _____. Attitudes formed through (18) _____ may be stronger and easier to recall. However, people also appraise and evaluate situations and often form their own judgments.

Can you really change people—their attitudes and behavior, that is? People attempt to change other people's attitudes and behavior by means of (19) _____. According to the (20) _____ model, persuasion occurs through both central and peripheral routes. Change occurs through the (21) _____ route by means of consideration of arguments and evidence. (22) _____ routes involve associating the objects of attitudes with positive or negative cues, such as attractive or unattractive communicators. (23) _____ messages generally "sell" better than messages delivered only (24) _____. People tend to show greater response to (25) _____ than to purely factual presentations. This is especially so when the appeals offer (26) _____ advice for avoiding negative outcomes. Persuasive communicators tend to show (27) _____, trustworthiness, (28) _____, or similarity to the audience. People, however, (29) _____ always just absorb what information is fed to them. If the information discredits their own (30) _____ and prejudices, they often show selective (31) _____ and selective (32) _____. That is, they will seek out communicators whose outlook (33) _____ with their own and (34) _____ those whose outlook does not. Research shows that people who have lower (35) _____ are less likely to resist social pressure. Additionally, the (36) _____ technique suggests that people are more likely to comply with larger requests if they already have complied with smaller ones.

What is prejudice? Why are people prejudiced? (37) _____ is an attitude toward a group that leads people to evaluate members of that group negatively. (38) _____ is a form of negative behavior that results from prejudice; discrimination takes forms such as (39) _____ of access to jobs, housing, and the voting booth. Prejudices are typically based on (40) _____, which are fixed, conventional ideas about groups of people. Sources of prejudice include dissimilarity, social (41) _____, social learning, the relative ease of processing information according to stereotypes, social categorization, and (42) _____ by prejudice. Prejudice can be combated by: encouraging (43) _____ contact and cooperation; attacking (44) _____ behavior; holding discussion forums; and examining your own beliefs.

Reflection Break 1

Match the term with its proper description.

a. central route
b. attitudes
c. selective exposure
d. stereotypes
e. fear appeal
f. elaboration likelihood model

g. peripheral route
h. selective avoidance
i. prejudice
j. discrimination
k. foot-in-the-door technique

_____ 1. The diversion of one's attention from information that is inconsistent with one's attitudes.

_____ 2. Behavioral and cognitive tendencies that are expressed by evaluating people, places, or things positively or negatively.

_____ 3. An attitude toward a group that leads people to evaluate members of that group negatively.

_____ 4. Describes the ways in which people respond to persuasive messages.

_____ 5. The deliberate attention to information that is consistent with your attitudes.

_____ 6. The denial of privileges to a person or a group on the basis of prejudice.

_____ 7. Route of persuasion that inspires thoughtful consideration of arguments and evidence.

_____ 8. A type of persuasive communication that influences behavior on the basis of arousing fear instead of a rational analysis of the issues.

_____ 9. A method for inducing compliance in which a small request is followed by a larger request.

_____ 10. Route of persuasion that relies on the association of the product with appealing images or attractive communicators.

_____ 11. Prejudices about certain groups that lead people to view members of those groups in a biased fashion.

Reading for Understanding About "Social Perception: Looking Out, Looking Within"

Do first impressions really matter? What are the primacy and recency effects? First impressions can last (45) _____ because we tend to label or describe people in terms of the behavior we see initially. The (46) _____ appears to be based on the fact that, other things being equal, recently learned information is easier to remember. (47) _____ can be managed in a number of ways, including: being aware of the impression you make on others, smiling, dressing neatly, and making eye contact.

What is attribution theory? Why do we assume that other people intend the mischief that they do? An (48) _____ is an assumption about why people do things. The tendency to infer the motives and traits of others through observation of their behavior is referred to as the (49) _____. (50) _____ psychologists describe two types of attributions: dispositional and situational attributions. In (51) _____ attributions, we attribute people's behavior to internal factors such as their personality traits and decisions. In (52) _____ attributions, we attribute people's behavior to their circumstances or external forces. In cultures that view the self as (53) _____, people tend to attribute other people's behavior to internal factors; this error, or bias in the attribution process, is known as the (54) _____ error. According to the (55) _____ effect, we tend to attribute the behavior of others to internal, dispositional factors and our own behavior to external, situational factors. The (56) _____ bias refers to the finding that we tend to attribute our successes to internal, stable factors and our failures to external, unstable factors. The attribution of behavior to internal or external causes is influenced by three factors: (57) _____, or the number of people responding in a certain way; (58) _____, or the degree to which the person responds the same in other situations; and (59) _____, or the extent to which the person responds differently in different situations. For example, when few people act in a certain way, that is, when the consensus is low, we are likely to attribute behavior to (60) _____ factors.

What is body language? (61) _____ refers to the tendency to infer people's thoughts and feelings from their postures and gestures. For example, people who feel positively toward one another position themselves (62) _____ together and are more likely to touch. Touching results in a (63) _____ reaction when it suggests more intimacy than is desired. (64) _____ into another's eyes can be a sign of love, but a hard stare is an aversive challenge. (65) _____ are more likely than (66) _____ to touch people with whom they are interacting.

Reading for Understanding About "Social Influence: Are You an Individual or One of the Crowd?"

Why will so many people commit crimes against humanity if they are ordered to do so? Why don't they refuse? (67) _____ is the area of social psychology that studies the ways in which people alter the thoughts, feelings, and behavior of others. Classic studies by Stanley (68) _____ examined one aspect of social influence, obedience to an authority. The majority of the subjects in the Milgram studies (69) _____ with the demands of authority figures, even when the demands required that they (70) _____ innocent people by means of electric shock. Factors contributing to (71) _____ include socialization, lack of social comparison, perception of legitimate authority figures, the foot-in-the-door technique, inaccessibility of values, and buffers between the perpetrator and the victim.

Why do so many people tend to follow the crowd? Another area of interest in the study of social influence is (72) _____, or the changing of our behavior in order to adhere to social (73) _____, or widely accepted expectations concerning social behavior. Social norms can be (74) _____, as in rules and laws that are directly spoken to us; and (75) _____, or unspoken rules. Solomon (76) _____'s research, in which subjects judged the lengths of lines, suggests that the majority of people will follow the crowd, or (77) _____, even when the crowd is wrong. Personal factors such as desire to be (78) _____ by group members, low (79) _____, high (80) _____, and shyness contribute to conformity. Belonging to a (81) _____ society and group size also contribute to conformity.

Reflection Break 2

1. Why do we tend to hold others accountable for their misbehavior and excuse ourselves for the same behavior?

2. What is conformity, how is it different from obedience, and what makes us conform to group norms?

Reading for Understanding About "Group Behavior"

Do we run faster when we are in a group? The concept of social (82) _____ refers to the effects on performance that result from the presence of other people. The presence of others may (83) _____ performance for reasons such as increased arousal and (84) _____, or the concern that others are evaluating our performance. However, the presence of others can also (85) _____ performance. When we are anonymous group members, we may experience (86) _____, in which each person feels less obligation to help because others are present, and task performance may fall off. This phenomenon is termed social (87) _____.

How do groups make decisions? Social psychologists have identified several rules, or social (88) _____, that govern group decision making. These include the majority-wins scheme, the truth-wins scheme, the two-thirds majority scheme, and the (89) _____ rule, in which the group tends to adopt the decision that reflects the first shift in opinion expressed by any group member.

Are group decisions more risky or more conservative than those of the individual members of the group? Why? Group decisions tend to be more (90) _____ and (91) _____ than individual decisions, largely because groups diffuse responsibility. Group (92) _____ refers to the tendency of groups to take a more extreme position than the individuals in the group would individually. This tends to lead groups make riskier decisions, or show a (93) "_____". Group decisions may be highly productive when group members are (94) _____, there is an explicit procedure for arriving at decisions, and there is a process of give and take.

What is groupthink? (95) _____ is an unrealistic kind of decision making that is fueled by group cohesiveness and the perception of external threats to the group or to those whom the group wishes to protect. It is facilitated by a dynamic group (96) _____, feelings of invulnerability, the group's belief in its rightness, the discrediting of information that contradicts the group's decision, conformity, and the stereotyping of members of the (97) _____. In groupthink, group members tend to be more influenced by the group (98) _____ and a dynamic leader than by the realities of the situation. (99) _____ decisions are frequently made as a result of groupthink. Groupthink can, however, be avoided if the leaders encourage members to remain (100) _____ about options and feel free to ask questions and disagree with one another.

Do mobs bring out the beast in us? How is it that mild-mannered people commit mayhem when they are part of a mob? Highly emotional crowds may induce attitude-discrepant behavior through the process of (101) _____, which is a state of reduced self-awareness and lowered concern for social evaluation. The high emotions are connected with (102) _____ that makes it more difficult to access one's own values. Many factors lead to deindividuation; these include (103) _____, diffusion of (104) _____, and arousal due to noise and (105) _____. (106) _____ behavior can be averted by dispersing small groups that could gather into a large crowd and having individuals remind themselves to stop and think whenever they begin to feel aroused in a group.

Why do people sometimes sacrifice themselves for others and, at other times, ignore people who are in trouble? (107) _____, or the selfless concern for the welfare of others, is connected with heroic behavior. A number of factors contribute to altruism. Among them are (108) _____, being in a good mood, feelings of (109) _____, knowledge of how to help, and acquaintance with-and similarity to-the person in need of help. According to the (110) _____ effect, or the failure to come to the aid of someone in need, we are unlikely to aid people in distress when we are members of crowds. (111) _____ tend to diffuse responsibility.

Reflection Break 3

1. Why does group membership sometimes enhance performance and sometimes lessen performance?

2. What factors affect decisions to help (or not to help) other people?

Reading for Understanding About "Environmental Psychology: The Big Picture"

What is environmental psychology? As people, we have needs that must be met if we are to remain physically and psychologically (112) _____. Environmental conditions such as (113) _____ and (114) _____ affect our capacities to meet these needs. (115) _____ psychology is the field of psychology that studies the ways in which humans and the physical environment influence each other. Environmental psychologists apply knowledge of (116) _____ to design environments that produce positive emotional responses and contribute to human performance.

What are the effects of noise on behavior and mental processes? High (117) _____ levels, such as those imposed by traffic or low-flying planes, are stressful and can lead to health problems such as hearing loss, hypertension, and neurological and intestinal disorders. High noise levels impair (118) _____ and memory. Loud noise also dampens (119) _____ behavior and heightens (120) _____.

What are the effects of temperature on our bodies and on our behavior and mental processes? Moderate shifts in (121) _____ are mildly arousing and usually have positive effects such as facilitating learning and performance and increasing feelings of (122) _____. But extremes of temperature tax the body, are a source of (123) _____, and impair performance. High temperatures are also connected with (124) _____.

What are the effects of air pollution on behavior and mental processes? The (125) _____ in auto fumes may impair learning and memory. Carbon monoxide (126) _____ the capacity of the blood to carry oxygen and thus impairs learning ability and perception and contributes to accidents. Unpleasant odors decrease feelings of (127) _____ and heighten aggression.

When are we too close for comfort? What are the effects of crowding on behavior and mental processes? (128) _____ refers to the number of people in an area. (129) _____ suggests aversive high density. A sense of (130) _____ or choice, as in choosing to attend a concert or athletic contest, helps us cope with the stress of high density. Perhaps because of crowding, noise, and so on, city dwellers are (131) _____ likely than people who live in small towns to interact with or help strangers. One aversive effect of crowding is the invasion of one's (132) _____, or the invisible boundary that surrounds a person. You are likely to become (133) _____ and angry when others invade your personal space. There appear to be (134) _____ differences in personal space requirements. North Americans and European Americans appear to maintain a (135) _____ distance between themselves, and those who dwell in high (136) _____ areas tend to interact at closer spaces than those reared in (137) _____ dense areas.

Reflection Break 4

1. Prepare a brief paragraph that describes the need for and role of an environmental psychologist.

2. Briefly summarize the major areas of interest for environmental psychologists.

REVIEW: KEY TERMS AND CONCEPTS

social psychology	579	discrimination	583	social facilitation	597
attitude	579	social perception	587	evaluation apprehension	597
A-B problem	579	primacy effect	587	diffusion of responsibility	597
stereotype	580	recency effect	587	social decision schemes	598
elaboration likelihood	581	fundamental attribution	589	polarization	598
model		error		risky shift	598
fear appeal	581	actor-observer effect	589	groupthink	599
selective avoidance	583	self-serving bias	590	deindividuation	600
selective exposure	583	consensus	590	altruism	600
foot-in-the-door	583	social influence	592	environmental	603
technique		conform	592	psychology	
prejudice	583	social norms	594	personal space	606

FINAL CHAPTER REVIEW

Review

Visit the *Psychology in the New Millennium* Web site at www.harcourtcollege.com/psych/PNM/
siteresources.html and take the Chapter Quizzes to test your knowledge.

Recite

Go to the Recite section for this chapter in your textbook. Use the tear-off card provided at the
back of the book to cover the answers of the Recite section. Read the questions aloud, and recite
the answers. This will help you cement your knowledge of key concepts.

Essay Questions

1. *What is social psychology?* Prepare a one-page essay that briefly describes the field of
social psychology. What type of topics are social psychologists interested in? What career
opportunities are available for social psychologists?

2. *Where do attitudes come from? How well do they predict behavior?* Is what you say and do
always consistent with your attitudes? How did you develop these attitudes? (Are you
sure?) Have you ever encountered information that disconfirmed an attitude, stereotype, or
prejudice that you held? Did you change you attitude? Why or why not? In a two-page
essay, explain how attitudes are formed and maintained and the relationship between
attitudes and behavior.

3. *Stereotypes, prejudice and discrimination.* Do people hold any stereotypes of your
sociocultural group? Are these stereotypes positive or negative? How do you treat people of
different religions or races? Do you treat them as individuals, or are your expectations based
on stereotypes? What are the effects of the stereotypes? In a brief essay, explain the
difference between prejudice, discrimination, and stereotypes using examples from your
own behavior.

4. *Do you make the fundamental attribution error of attributing too much of other people's
behavior to choice and not your own behavior?* Do you ever do anything that is wrong? (Be
honest!) How do you explain your misdeeds to yourself? Do you try to excuse your
behavior by making a situational or dispositional attribution? Describe an example of a time
when you tried to excuse your behavior and the type of attribution that you used. Now think
about a friend's behavior. What type of attribution do you usually make about their
behavior? Why? Using the key concepts of attribution theory, explain the differences in
your attribution process in the two situations.

5. *Why do we sometimes go along with others—even when we don't want to?* You are eating at
a restaurant with a group of people. All the others in your party have ordered, and now it is
your turn to order. Using the research on conformity, what factors will influence whether
you are likely to conform? In a brief essay, describe the conditions that will influence the
likelihood of conformity and how.

6. *Does being in a group change our behavior? How?* In a brief essay, explain the effect that groups have on individual behavior. Why do we sometimes go along with others—even when we don't want to? What factors encourage/hinder bystanders in helping during emergencies? Why does group membership sometimes enhance performance and sometimes lessen performance?

RELATE/EXPAND/INTEGRATE

1. **Social Psychology**
Social Psychology Research on the Web. Go to The Social Psychology Network at http://www.socialpsychology.org/expts.htm and participate in one of the social psychology studies taking place online. Report your experience to your classmates in a format specified by your instructor.

2. **Attitudes—"The Good, the Bad, and the Ugly"**
Using the information about persuasion, attitude formation, and prejudice, create a persuasive advertisement for a product or event. Share your advertisement with your study group and discuss the effectiveness of the various principles used. What could you change to make the ad more persuasive?

3. **Psychology and Modern Life: Combating Prejudice**
What to tell your children about prejudice and discrimination from the Anti-defamation League. The Internet article at: http://www.adl.org/what_to_tell/whattotell_intro.html introduces the concepts of prejudice and discrimination with the goal of preparing all children to live and work harmoniously and productively alongside others who represent various and many racial and cultural groups, backgrounds, and abilities in our society. After reading this article and discussing it with your study group, create a children's game that would apply the principles discussed to teach children ages 4–10 years of age about prejudice and discrimination. Share your game with your class.

4. **Social Perception: Looking Out, Looking Within**
Psychology and Modern Life: Making a Good First Impression. Participate in an impression-formation study on the Internet at either http://tornado.wcp.muohio.edu/kretschmar/intro.html or http://cogweb.iig.uni-freiburg.de/IF/new-index.html. Report your experience to your classmates in a format specified by your instructor.

5. **Group Behavior**
How does being a member of a group influence your behavior? Have you ever done something as a member of a group that you would not have done as an individual? What motivated you? How do you feel about it? What psychological factors were at work that affected the behavior of the individuals in the group? Interview 15 individuals by asking them the above questions. Prepare a brief report that describes and summarizes the answers you obtained. In your report, be sure to also address the various kinds of behaviors that you found were mostly prone to group influences. In the conclusion to your report, be sure to

discuss the importance of understanding group behavior and group dynamics and the benefits this knowledge provides.

6. **Environmental Psychology: The Big Picture**
Which environmental issue do you think is the most pressing issue for environmental psychologists in this millennium? Why? Using the brief introduction to environmental psychology at http://www-personal.umich.edu/~rdeyoung/envtpsych.html and your favorite search engine (Dogpile, Yahoo, Google), research the field of environmental psychology. What type of topics are environmental psychologists interested in? What career opportunities are available for environmental psychologists? How can understanding and studying environmental psychology help you become better informed about environmental issues and problems?

ANSWERS FOR CHAPTER 17

Reading for Understanding About "Social Psychology"

1. Social
2. perception
3. influence
4. environmental

Reading for Understanding About "Attitudes—The Good, the Bad, and the Ugly"

5. Attitudes
6. learned
7. changed
8. consistent
9. attitudes
10. behaviors
11. A-B
12. specific
13. accessible
14. vested interest
15. acquired
16. conditioning
17. observation
18. direct experience
19. persuasion
20. elaboration likelihood
21. central
22. Peripheral
23. Repeated
24. once
25. fear appeals
26. concrete
27. expertise
28. attractiveness
29. will not
30. stereotypes
31. avoidance
32. exposure
33. coincides
34. avoid
35. self-esteem
36. foot-in-the-door
37. Prejudice
38. Discrimination
39. denial
40. stereotypes
41. conflict
42. victimization
43. intergroup
44. discriminatory

Reflection Break 1

Matching:

1. h
2. b
3. I
4. f

5. c
6. j
7. a
8. e

9. k
10. g
11. d

Reading for Understanding About "Social Perception: Looking Out, Looking Within"

45. the primacy effect
46. recency effect
47. First impression
48. attribution
49. attribution process
50. Social
51. dispositional
52. situational

53. independent
54. fundamental attribution
55. actor-observer
56. self-serving
57. consensus
58. consistency
59. distinctiveness
60. internal

61. Body language
62. closer
63. negative
64. Gazing
65. Women
66. men

Reading for Understanding About "Social Influence: Are You an Individual or One of the Crowd?"

67. Social Influence
68. Milgram
69. complied
70. hurt
71. obedience

72. conformity
73. norms
74. explicit
75. implicit
76. Asch

77. conform
78. liked
79. self-esteem
80. self-consciousness
81. collectivist

Reflection Break 2

1. Why do we tend to hold others accountable for their misbehavior and excuse ourselves for the same behavior?

The tendency to infer the motives and traits of others through observation of their behavior is referred to as the attribution process. Social psychologists describe two types of attributions: dispositional and situational attributions. In dispositional attributions, we attribute people's behavior to internal factors such as their personality traits and decisions. In situational attributions, we attribute people's behavior to their circumstances or external forces. In North American culture, we view the self as independent and tend to attribute other people's behavior to internal factors. This error, or bias in the attribution process, is known as the fundamental attribution error and occurs because we tend to infer traits from external behavior rather than from social roles and obligations. According to the actor-observer effect, we tend to attribute the behavior of others to internal, dispositional factors and our own behavior to external, situational factors since we see them as willing participants. The self-serving bias refers to the finding that we tend to attribute our successes to internal, stable factors and our failures to external, unstable factors. In other words, we take credit for our successes but blame our failures on someone or something else. This attribution of behavior to internal or external causes is influenced by three factors: consensus, or the number of people responding in a certain way; consistency, or the degree to which the person responds the same on other situations; and distinctiveness, or the extent to which the person responds differently in different situations.

2. What is conformity, how is it different from obedience, and what makes us conform to group norms?

Obedience occurs when people obey the commands of others, even when they are required to perform immoral tasks. Conformity, on the other hand, involves the changing of our behavior in order to adhere to social norms, or widely accepted expectations concerning social behavior.

Factors contributing to obedience include socialization, lack of social comparison, perception of legitimate authority figures, the foot-in-the-door technique, inaccessibility of values, and buffers between the perpetrator and the victim. Personal factors such as desire to be liked by group members, low self-esteem, high self-consciousness, and shyness contribute to conformity. Belonging to a collectivist society and group size also contribute to conformity.

Reading for Understanding About "Group Behavior"

82. facilitation
83. facilitate
84. evaluation
    apprehension
85. impair
86. diffusion of
    responsibility
87. loafing
88. decision-making
    schemes
89. first-shift

90. polarized
91. riskier
92. polarization
93. risky shift
94. knowledgeable
95. Groupthink
96. leader
97. out-group
98. cohesiveness
99. Flawed
100. skeptical

101. deindividuation
102. arousal
103. anonymity
104. responsibility
105. crowding
106. Mob
107. Altruism
108. empathy
109. responsibility
110. bystander
111. Crowds

Reflection Break 3

1. Why does group membership sometimes enhance performance and sometimes lessen performance?

Social facilitation refers to the effects on performance that result from the presence of other people. The presence of others may facilitate performance for reasons such as increased arousal and evaluation apprehension, or the concern that others are evaluating our performance. However, the presence of others can also impair performance. When we are anonymous group members, we may experience diffusion of responsibility, in which each person feels less obligation to help because others are present, and task performance may fall off. This phenomenon is termed *social loafing*. Group decisions tend to be more polarized and riskier than individual decisions, largely because groups diffuse responsibility. Group polarization refers to the tendency of groups to take a more extreme position than the individuals in the group would individually. This tends to lead groups make riskier decisions, or show a "risky shift."

Groupthink can also occur in group decision making. Groupthink is an unrealistic kind of decision making that is fueled by group cohesiveness and the perception of external threats to the group or to those whom the group wishes to protect. It is facilitated by a dynamic group leader, feelings of invulnerability, the group's belief in its rightness, the discrediting of information that contradicts the group's decision, conformity, and the stereotyping of members of the out-group. In groupthink, group members tend to be more influenced by the group cohesiveness and a dynamic leader than by the realities of the situation. Flawed decisions are frequently made as a result of groupthink. Groupthink can, however, be avoided if the leaders encourage members to remain skeptical about options and feel free to ask questions and disagree with one another.

2. What factors affect decisions to help (or not to help) other people?

Altruism, or the selfless concern for the welfare of others, is connected with heroic behavior. A number of factors contribute to altruism. Among them are empathy, being in a good mood, feelings of responsibility, knowledge of how to help, and acquaintance with—and similarity to—the person in need of help. According to the bystander effect, or the failure to come to the aid of someone in need, we are unlikely to aid people in distress when we are members of crowds. Crowds tend to diffuse responsibility.

Reading for Understanding About "Environmental Psychology: The Big Picture"

112. healthy
113. temperature
114. population density
115. Environmental
116. sensation and
         perception
117. noise
118. learning
119. helping
120. aggressiveness
121. temperature
122. attraction
123. stress
124. aggression
125. lead
126. decreases
127. attraction
128. Density
129. Crowding
130. control
131. less
132. personal space
133. anxious
134. cultural
135. greater
136. density
137. less

Reflection Break 4

1. Prepare a brief paragraph that describes the need for and role of an environmental psychologist.

   People have needs that must be met if they are to remain physically and psychologically healthy. Environmental conditions such as temperature and population density affect our capacities to meet these needs. Environmental psychology is the field of psychology that studies the ways in which humans and the physical environment influence each other. Environmental psychologists apply knowledge of sensation and perception to design environments at produce positive emotional responses and contribute to human performance.

2. Briefly summarize the major areas of interest for environmental psychologists.

   Noise: High noise levels, such as those imposed by traffic or low-flying planes, are stressful and can lead to health problems such as hearing loss, hypertension, and neurological and intestinal disorders. High noise levels impair learning and memory. Loud noise also dampens helping behavior and heightens aggressiveness.

   Temperature: Moderate shifts in temperature are mildly arousing and usually have positive effects such as facilitating learning and performance and increasing feelings of attraction. But extremes of temperature tax the body, are a source of stress, and impair performance. High temperatures are also connected with aggression.

   Air Quality: The lead in auto fumes may impair learning and memory. Carbon monoxide decreases the capacity of the blood to carry oxygen and thus impairs learning ability and perception and contributes to accidents. Unpleasant odors decrease feelings of attraction and heighten aggression.

   Crowding: Density refers to the number of people in an area. Crowding suggests aversive high density. A sense of control or choice, as in choosing to attend a concert or athletic contest, helps us cope with the stress of high density. Perhaps because of crowding, noise, and so on, city dwellers are less likely than people who live in small towns to interact with or help strangers. One aversive effect of crowding is the invasion of one's personal space, or the invisible boundary that surrounds a person. You are likely to become anxious and angry when others invade your personal space. There appear to be cultural differences in personal space requirements. North Americans and European Americans appear to maintain a greater distance between themselves, and those who dwell in high density areas tend to interact at closer spaces than those reared in less dense areas.

Appendix A

Statistics

PREVIEW

Skim the major headings in this appendix in your textbook. Jot down anything that you are surprised or curious about. After this, write down four or five questions that you have about the material in this appendix.

Things that surprised me/I am curious about from Appendix A:

Questions that I have about statistics:

▲

▲

▲

▲

QUESTION

These are some questions that you should be able to answer after you finish studying Appendix A.

Statistics

▲ *What is statistics?*

▲ *What are samples and populations?*

Descriptive Statistics

▲ *What is descriptive statistics? (Why isn't it always good to be a "10"?*

▲ *What is a frequency distribution?*

▲ *What are measures of central tendency?*

▲ *What are measures of variability?*

The Normal Curve

▲ *What is a normal distribution?*

The Correlation Coefficient

▲ *What is the correlation coefficient?*

Inferential Statistics

▲ *What are inferential statistics?*

▲ *What are "statistically significant" differences?*

READING FOR UNDERSTANDING/REFLECT

The following section provides you with the opportunity to perform 2 of the R's of the PQ4R study method. In this section, you are encouraged to check your understanding of your reading of the text by filling in the blanks in the brief paragraphs that relate to each of the Preview questions. You will also be prompted to rehearse your understanding of the material with periodic Reflection breaks. Remember, it is better to study in more frequent, short sessions than in one long "cram session." Be sure to reward yourself with short study breaks before each Reflection exercise.

Reading for Understanding About "Statistics"

What is statistics? (1) _____ is the science concerned with obtaining and organizing numerical information or measurements. Statistics assembles (2) _____ in such a way that they provide useful information about measures or scores. Such measures or scores include people's height, weight, and scores on (3) _____ such as IQ tests.

What are samples and populations? A (4) _____ is part of a population. A (5) _____ is a complete group from which a sample is drawn. The example with basketball players shows that a sample must (6) _____ its population if it is to provide accurate information about the population. Psychologists are careful in their attempts to select a (7) _____ that accurately represents the entire (8) _____.

Reading for Understanding About "Descriptive Statistics"

What is descriptive statistics? (Why isn't it always good to be a "10"?) (9) _____ statistics is the branch of statistics that provides information about distribution of scores. Descriptive statistics can be used to clarify our understanding of a (10) _____ of scores such as heights, test grades, IQs, or anything else.

What is a frequency distribution? A (11) _____ organizes a set of data, usually from low scores to high scores, and indicates how frequently a score appears. (12) _____ may be used on large sets of data to provide a quick impression of how the data tends to cluster. The histogram and frequency polygon are two ways of (13) _____ data to help people visualize the way in which the data are distributed. In both these types of graphs, the class intervals are drawn on the (14) _____ line, or x-axis, and the frequency is drawn on the (15) _____ line, or Y-axis.

What are measures of central tendency? Measures of (16) _____ are "averages" that show the center or balancing points of a frequency distribution. There are (17) _____ commonly used types of measures of central tendency: mean, median, and mode. The (18) _____— which is what most people consider the average—is obtained by adding up the scores in a distribution and dividing by the number of scores. The (19) _____ is the score in the middle, or the central case in a distribution. The (20) _____ is the most common score in a distribution. Distributions can be (21) _____ (having two modes) or multimodal. When there are a few extreme scores in a distribution, the (22) _____ is a better indicator of central tendency.

What are measures of variability? Measures of (23) _____ provide information about the spread of scores in a distribution. Two commonly used measures of variability are the range and the (24) _____. The (25) _____ is defined as the difference between the highest and lowest scores. The range is an imperfect measure of variability because it is highly influenced by (26) _____ scores. The standard deviation is a statistic that shows how scores cluster around the (27) _____. The (28) _____ does a better job of showing how the scores in a distribution are spread about the mean because it considers every score in the distribution, not just the extreme scores. The standard deviation is calculated by taking the sum of the squared deviations from the mean, dividing this sum by the number of scores, and then taking the (29) _____. Distributions with higher standard deviations are (30) _____ spread out.

Reading for Understanding About "The Normal Curve"

What is a normal distribution? Many human characteristics examined by psychologists appear to be distributed in a pattern known as a (31) _____ distribution. The normal, or (32) _____, curve is hypothesized to occur when the scores in a distribution occur by chance. The normal curve has one (33) _____, its mean, median, and mode fall at the (34) _____, and approximately two of the three scores (68%) are found within one (35) _____ of the mean. Fewer than 5 % of cases are found beyond (36) _____ standard deviations from the mean.

Reflection Break 1

Match the term with its proper description.

a. mode
b. statistics
c. sample
d. range
e. descriptive statistics
f. frequency distribution
g. median

h. frequency polygon
i. mean
j. population
k. bimodal
l. standard deviation
m. frequency histogram
n. normal curve

_____ 1. Numerical facts assembled so that they provide useful information scores.

_____ 2. A graphic representation of the frequency of occurrence of scores that connects points to represent the frequency with which scores occur.

_____ 3. A complete group that is of interest.

_____ 4. In a frequency distribution, the most frequently occurring score.

_____ 5. The central score in a frequency distribution, beneath which 50% of the cases fall.

_____ 6. A portion of the group of interest; the group that is actually tested.

_____ 7. A measure of variability found by summing the squared deviations from the mean, dividing by the number of scores, and taking the square root.

_____ 8. Graphic representation of a symmetrical distribution that is assumed to reflect chance fluctuations.

_____ 9. A measure of variability calculated by subtracting the lowest score from the highest score.

_____ 10. A type of average calculated by adding all scores and then dividing by the number of scores.

_____ 11. Branch of statistics concerned with providing description information about a distribution of scores.

_____ 12. Refers to a distribution that has two modes.

_____ 13. A graphic representation of the frequency of occurrence of scores that uses bars to represent the frequency with which scores occur.

_____ 14. A set of data that indicates how often the scores appears.

Reading for Understanding About "The Correlation Coefficient"

What is the correlation coefficient? The (37) _____ is a statistic that describes how variables such as IQ and grade point average are related. Correlational research is used to examine (38) _____ between variables that cannot be manipulated. Correlation research shows that variables are related but cannot reveal information about (39) _____. Correlation coefficients vary from +1.00 to (40) _____. When correlations between two variables are (41) _____, it means that one (such as school grades) tends to rise as the other (such as IQ) rises. (42) _____ correlations indicate that as one variable tends to rise, the other tends to fall. A numerical value of 1.00 (whether it is positive or negative) indicates a (43) _____ correlation, and a correlation of (44) _____ reveals no relationship between the variables.

Reading for Understanding About "Inferential Statistics"

What are inferential statistics? (45) _____ statistics is the branch of statistics that indicates whether researchers can extend their findings with samples to the populations from which they were drawn. In other words, inferential statistics help researchers (46) _____ , or determine whether their results are "real" or "chance" occurrences.

What are "statistically significant" differences? Instead of speaking of "real" or "actual differences," researchers use the term (47) "_____." Statistically significant differences are believed to represent (48) _____ differences between groups, and not (49) _____ fluctuation.

Reflection Break 2

1. Briefly explain the limitations of correlational methods.

2. What does it mean when a researcher says that the differences in scores between the two groups is statistically significant?

REVIEW: KEY TERMS AND CONCEPTS

statistics	614	frequency histogram	615	normal distribution	619
sample	614	frequency polygon	615	normal curve	619
population	614	mean	616	correlation coefficient	620
range	614	median	616	inferential statistics	622
average	614	mode	617	infer	622
descriptive statistics	615	bimodal	617		
frequency distribution	615	standard deviation	618		

FINAL CHAPTER REVIEW

Review

Visit the *Psychology in the New Millennium* Web site at www.harcourtcollege.com/psych/PNM/siteresources.html and take the Chapter Quizzes to test your knowledge.

Recite

Go to the Recite section for this chapter in your textbook. Use the tear-off card provided at the back of the book to cover the answers of the Recite section. Read the questions aloud, and recite the answers. This will help you cement your knowledge of key concepts.

Essay Questions

1. *Frequency Distributions.* The following scores represent the amount of weight loss that each member of a weight loss class had over the previous month. Draw a frequency histogram and frequency polygon for the distribution using two different class intervals. Which class interval presents the data best?

Dieter	Weight Loss (in lbs.)
1	10
2	12
3	25
4	31
5	22
6	8
7	6
8	17
9	9
10	28
11	7
12	16
13	8
14	2
15	1
16	20
17	11
18	9
19	10
20	13

2. *Descriptive Statistics*. Calculate the three measures of central tendency (mean, median, mode) and the range and standard deviation for the data in question 1.

3. *Correlation Coefficients*. A research study indicated a negative correlation between the amount of Lucky Charms eaten as a child and cancer rate. (In other words, Lucky Charms eaters were less likely to develop cancer.) Another study found a positive correlation between eating oatmeal as a child and the development of cancer. Can the authors of these **correlational** studies conclude that Lucky Charms prevents cancer while oatmeal **causes** it? Why or why not? (Hint: What kind of conclusions can be drawn from correlations?)

RELATE/EXPAND/INTEGRATE

1. **Statistics.** Visit David Stockburger's Online Statistics textbook at http://www.psychstat.smsu.edu/introbook/sbk02.htm and read his introduction to descriptive statistics entitled A Mayoral Fantasy to gain a better understanding of the need for statistics.

2. **Descriptive Statistics.** Visit Descriptive Statistics Online at http://www.mste.uiuc.edu/hill/dstat/dstat.html for further insights into and practice calculating the mean, median, mode, standard deviation, and range. Once you have a firm grasp of these concepts, with the help of your study group take a survey of your classmates. Ask them to tell you how many siblings they have, the age at which they first got their drivers license, the age at which they graduated from high school, and how many cups of coffee they drink per day. Draw a frequency histogram and frequency polygon for each frequency distribution. Calculate each of the measures of descriptive statistics for each measurement. Report your findings to your classmates in a format specified by your instructor.

3. **The Correlation Coefficient.** Read the section on correlation in David Stockburger's Online Statistics text at http://www.psychstat.smsu.edu/introbook/sbk17.htm and then complete the Correlation Estimation for Scatterplots exercises at http://www.psychstat.smsu.edu/introbook/exercises/scattermain.htm.
   In the *Learning Mode,* these exercises will allow you to view many different scatterplots and the corresponding correlation coefficients. Clicking the "Generate" button will cause the program to generate a new set of paired data values. The data pairs are displayed in a scatterplot, and the correlation coefficient is given in a text box. The "Exit" button will return to the main selection screen. In the *Test Mode* you are required to click on an estimated correlation before the actual correlation is presented. The selected button will turn yellow and the correct button will turn red if the estimated correlation coefficient is incorrect. The selected button will turn green if it is correct. The program will keep track of the number of correct estimates in a row you have made without making an error.

ANSWERS FOR APPENDIX A: STATISTICS

Reading for Understanding About "Statistics"

1. Statistics
2. data
3. psychological tests
4. sample
5. population
6. represent
7. sample
8. population

Reading for Understanding About "Descriptive Statistics"

9. Descriptive
10. distribution
11. frequency distribution
12. Class intervals
13. graphing
14. horizontal
15. vertical
16. central tendency
17. three
18. mean
19. median
20. mode
21. bimodal
22. median
23. variability
24. standard deviation
25. range
26. extreme
27. mean
28. standard deviation
29. square root
30. more

Reading for Understanding About "The Normal Curve"

31. normal
32. bell-shaped
33. mode
34. same point
35. standard deviation
36. two

Reflection Break 1

1. b
2. h
3. j
4. a
5. g
6. c
7. l
8. n
9. d
10. i
11. e
12. k
13. m
14. f

Reading for Understanding About "The Correlation Coefficient"

37. correlation coefficient
38. relationships
39. cause and effect
40. −1.00
41. positive
42. Negative
43. perfect
44. zero

Reading for Understanding About "Inferential Statistics"

45. Inferential
46. infer
47. statistically significant
48. real
49. chance

Reflection Break 2

1. Briefly explain the limitations of correlational methods.

   The correlation coefficient is a statistic that describes how variables such as IQ and grade point average are related. Correlational research is used to examine relationships between variables that cannot be manipulated. Correlational research show that variables are related but cannot reveal information about cause and effect.

2. What does it mean when a reseacher says that the differences in scores between two groups is statisitically significant?

   Statistically significant differences are believed to represent real differences between groups, not chance fluctuation. The researcher would then conclude that differences between the two groups were the result of the manipulation and were real differences.